COMPARATIVE CIVIL RIGHTS AND LIBERTIES

Daniel C. Kramer
College of Staten Island,
City University of New York

UNIVERSITY
PRESS OF
AMERICA

LANHAM • NEW YORK • LONDON

Library of Congress Cataloging in Publication Data
Kramer, Daniel C., 1934–
    Comparative civil rights and liberties.

    Includes bibliographical references and index.
    1. Civil rights. I. Title.
K3240.4.K72   342'.085   81–40040
ISBN 0–8191–2255–6   342.285   AACR2
ISBN 0–8191–2256–4 (pbk.)

All University Press of America books are produced on acid-free
paper which exceeds the minimum standards set by the National
Historical Publications and Records Commission.

TO RICHENDA, TAMSYN, BRUCE AND ELSPETH KRAMER:
MY TEACHERS IN THE MEANING OF LIFE.

ACKNOWLEDGMENTS

I wish to warmly thank the following publishers for permission to quote from books to which they hold the copyright: Oxford University Press, for permission to quote from page 146 of Philip Mason, Patterns of Dominance, copyright 1970; Simon and Schuster, for American rights to quote from pages 278 and 296 of Sybille Bedford, The Faces of Justice, copyright 1961; the Macmillan Company, for American rights to use the first stanza of William Butler Yeats's poem The Second Coming, included in Yeats's Collected Poems, published by them in 1951; and A.P. Watt, Ltd., for all other rights to use the first stanza of that poem.

In addition, I would like to express my appreciation to the following journals for permission to use in this book sections of earlier articles of mine:

1. The Board of Editors of the Emory Law Journal (formerly Journal of Public Law) of the Emory University School of Law for permission to use portions of The Right to Denounce Public Officials in England and the United States: A Comparative Analysis, appearing in 17 Emory L.J. 78 (1969).

2. The Johns Hopkins University Press for permission to use portions of The Courts as Guardians of Fundamental Freedoms in Times of Crisis, appearing in Universal Human Rights (now Human Rights Quarterly), Vol. 2, No. 4, p. 1 (October-December, 1980).

3. The Editors of Social Research, published by the New School for Social Research, for permission to use portions of White Versus Colored in Britain: An Explosive Confrontation?, appearing in Social Research, 36:585 (Winter, 1969).

TABLE OF CONTENTS

PREFACE

A book on civil rights and liberties is likely to irk many. Among the small segment of the public that pays attention to issues such as freedom of speech and press, freedom of religion, race relations, and the rights of the criminal defendant, emotions run high; and any deviation from one's own views is apt to be viewed as original sin. Moreover, one of the countries I deal with is the U.S.S.R.; and there are those on both the right and the left who cannot tolerate any attempt to be objective about Soviet policy. All I can ask the reader to do is to place his/her intensely-felt views about civil rights and liberties and Soviet Communism into a state of suspended animation while reading this work and judge it solely on criteria such as the accuracy and comprehensiveness of my data and the extent to which the facts I present justify my conclusions.

Of course, this book and the other works on comparative civil rights and liberties it cites amount, even when taken together, to just the first footsteps onto a satellite discipline of law and political science that deserves systematic exploration. I myself cover but five countries: the United States, the United Kingdom, India, the Soviet Union and France, my selection having been dictated by the importance of these nations in today's world, by the frequent emulation of their civil rights and liberties policies, and by the considerable information about these policies available in English or French, the only languages I read with facility. Conspicuously absent from this list are any Far Eastern or Middle Eastern state, any country whose culture is Iberian, and any African land. I had space to concentrate only on selected rights and liberties issues; and had to ignore numerous topics. Omitted, for example, are the rights of women, the free-press-versus-fair-trial controversy, the rights of gay people, dis-crimination against Hispanics in the United States, double jeopardy, the right to health care and employment, and freedom to contract. I focus entirely upon governmental policies; and ignore the treatment religious and political dissenters and racial minorities receive at the hands of private citizens. On the whole, I spend less time with the United States than with the other four countries, mainly because most of my readers will be relatively familiar with it. I had no room to append a Bibliography or to explore the relationship between a country's history, on the one hand, and its current civil rights policies, on the other.

The civil rights and liberties approaches of any country are in continuous flux; and so some of the policies described in this book will have been modified or reversed by the time it appears in print. Also, President Ronald Reagan might be able to appoint enough Justices to the United States Supreme Court to insure that it will overturn some of the decisions described on the following pages that are highly tolerant of speech or that make it more difficult for the prosecution in a criminal case to introduce evidence. Unless otherwise indi-cated, the American, British, Soviet and French policies discussed were in force in mid-1981 while their Indian counterparts were operative at the end of 1980. Information about India does not arrive in U.S. libraries on the wings of Mercury!

A word about the classificatory schemes used in this book is desirable. I eschewed as misleading the simple dichotomy "liberal versus conservative" simply because there are many concrete situations to which it is not applicable. For example, is a court decision overturning a law that city employees must live in the city "liberal" because it safeguards personal mobility or "conservative" because many people who style themselves liberal favor the enact-ment of such a law? I would have preferred a typology that covered all the areas dealt with in

x

the volume but was unable to develop one. Consequently, I employ one applicable to freedom of speech, press, religion and race relations and a second applicable to criminal procedure. In the latter area, I eschewed as too simplistic the familiar "pro-prosecution vs. pro-defendant" framework. This conceals, for example, the reality that different approaches benefitting the defendant may have significantly different impacts upon him and/or the public. Thus decisions requiring speedy trial and decisions excluding illegally seized evidence are both "pro-defendant." However, only the latter makes it more likely that he ultimately will be acquitted.

Many people helped substantially in the preparation of this volume. Mary Geisler, Catherine O'Callaghan Codd, Loretta Seidenfaden and Ann Cosgrove did outstanding jobs of typing the several drafts of the manuscript. The College of Staten Island, when it was known as Richmond College, financed some of the typing. My sister, Mrs. Judith Kramer Greene, went beyond the call of duty in performing the laborious task of proofreading. Prof. Stuart Nagel of the University of Illinois stimulated my interest in comparative civil rights and liberties when he urged me to teach the Comparative Rights course he had developed. My colleague at the College of Staten Island, Prof. Oleh Fedyshyn, enlightened me about ethnic tensions in the U.S.S.R., though I'm afraid he would disagree with some of the conclusions I have drawn. The faculty of Harvard Law School taught me how to do legal research; while Prof. Henry Abraham, under whom I did graduate work at the University of Pennsylvania, is a model for those whose research seeks to combine the disciplines of law and political science. Special thanks are due Professor Richard Claude of the University of Maryland, who went out of his way to suggest many changes in an earlier version of the manuscript. These alterations enabled me to transform a rambling potpourri into what I hope is an organized, coherent whole. All the aforesaid institutions and individuals should be given credit for the strengths of this volume: the blame for the errors of fact, style or interpretation that may have crept into it must rest squarely on my shoulders.

Last but not least, I would like to declare my gratitude to the following libraries for allowing me to use their collections: The Law Library of the Richmond County Bar Association; New York University Law Library; and the Law and Lehman International Relations Libraries of Columbia University. And it would be unforgivable to fail to mention Jerome Mardison and the other librarians and staff of the College of Staten Island Library, as all these men and women were of great help to me on numerous occasions and in numerous ways.

CHAPTER I

INTRODUCTION

A. Definitions

Jimmy Carter was no sooner inaugurated
President of the United States in January, 1977
than he began criticizing the Soviet Union,
Ethiopia, and various Latin American nations for
denying their citizens fundamental human freedoms.
"Human rights abroad" suddenly became Page One and
prime-time news; and America's syndicated column-
ists and telecasters began musing about the plight
of abstract artists in Moscow or the condition of
political prisoners in Chile. True, the administration of President Ronald Reagan refrains from
castigating non-communist dictatorships; but the
responsive chord aroused by his predecessor's
crusade will not be extinguished by Washington's
adoption of a "see no evil, hear no evil, speak
no evil" attitude.

There have always been a few social scientists and lawyers interested in how foreign
countries deal with civil rights and liberties
problems, but all in all the scholarly literature
is rather sparse.[1] This book, which will compare
the state of civil rights and liberties in the
United Kingdom, the Republic of India, the Union
of Soviet Socialist Republics, France, and the
United States, will therefore be a venture into
seas that are far from fully charted. Before it
weighs anchor, however, it must dispose of some
preliminary questions and give an overview of the
judicial systems of the five countries.[2]

First, civil rights and liberties policy is
ONE FORM OF PUBLIC POLICY. As some political

1

scientists would put it, it is an aspect of the "output" of the political system. In other words, this book is, in a sense, closer to a comparative study of fiscal and tax policies rather to one of political parties or judicial systems.

Next, various terms must be defined. Throughout history, but more self-consciously during the past two or three hundred years, groups and individuals have explicitly or implicitly claimed that they are entitled to this or that liberty. Governments have to respond in one way or another to these claims; and the approach that they adopt when doing so will fall into one of the following broad categories. (Omitted until Chapter V is the question of how to classify the steps they take respecting a hearing for persons brought into contact with the police, courts or other agencies of social control.)

1. <u>Toleration</u> - Approaches falling into this category involve the state's refraining from imposing disabilities upon religious, racial, political, ideological, ethnic or sexually defined groups.

2. <u>Encouragement of Diversity</u> - Approaches here not only tolerate (as defined above) but also encourage the growth or prevent the disappearance of ethnic, racial, political, ideological or religious groups. A public subsidy to anti-government newspapers is one example; enhancing the prestige (and thus potential growth) of a small political party by bringing it into the governing coalition is another.

3. <u>Stimulating Intergroup Contact</u> - Approaches here not only tolerate (as defined above) but also encourage, or make it newly feasible for, members of different groups to interact with one another. Examples include laws banning racial discrimination in the sale of housing; giving financial aid to interdenominational religious services; sponsoring "encounter

sessions" at which persons of differing political
viewpoints can begin a dialogue; subsidizing persons who adopt across racial lines; and requiring
that all school children learn a common language
(if they are permitted to learn that of their
parents as well).

4. Repression - Approaches here (a) impose
disabilities upon an individual or an ethnic,
political, religious, racial, ideological or
sexually-defined group or (b) create non-penal
obstacles to a group's attempt to retain its
language or identity. "(a)" includes fining, firing, jailing or executing those who disagree with
the government, who incite others to violence, who
belong to a particular race, or who study their
ancestral tongue. It also includes compelling the
members of racial, ethnic, religious, ideological,
etc., groups to serve as a source of inexpensive
labor for the government or another group. "(b)"
includes signalling that a group's tongue or
culture is "inferior" or refusing to let a state-
owned meeting hall be used by a dissenting political group or religious sect.

5. Massive Repression - Approaches here not
only repress, as just defined, but impose severe
penalties upon a large number of persons. The
best-known twentieth-century example is the Nazi
murder of 6 million Jews.

Into whichever of these five categories a
step taken by the government to respond to a civil
rights or liberties claim falls, public policy is
made. When the polity's response falls into the
category of encouragement of diversity or toleration, one predictable albeit perhaps latent consequence is compliance with the prescriptions of
James Madison's Federalist Essay #10. That is,
the chances are at least fair that encouragement
of diversity or toleration will make the society
more "pluralistic," harboring and nurturing a
myriad of political, ethnic, and religious groups;
that it will, to employ the oft-quoted Madisonian

3

phraseology, have the society "take in a greater variety of parties and interests."[3] (Following Robert Merton,[4] a "latent" effect of an action is one neither intended nor recognized. Thus, among the latent consequences of the development of corrupt urban political machines were the centralization of legally dispersed power and the dispensing of aid in a humane rather than an impersonal, bureaucratic way.[5] Note that for stylistic purposes these pages will often simply say "encouraging diversity," "toleration," "repression," etc., even though what is referred to is a concrete policy falling into the category.)

Repression or massive repression is normally unlikely to give birth to Madisonian pluralism, though, as will be discussed later, repression of an anti-pluralistic group may sometimes be necessary to preserve the heterogeneity of a nation and toleration of such a group may thwart the realization of the Madisonian vision. Stimulation of intergroup contact, a category that includes but goes beyond toleration, is as essential to pluralism as are toleration and encouragement of diversity. Though the encounters between the groups at times may be antagonistic, without any interaction the trust and cooperation that lubricate the gears of a pluralist nation and permit it to function smoothly cannot exist. Admittedly, whether the contact itself will increase, decrease or hold constant the number of groups dotting the society depends on events that are hard to predict. For example, contact between two religious groups could produce a realization that their creeds are identical and thus hasten merger. On the other hand, the dialogue could father a desire for unity on the part of some believers but leave others with the feeling that the sects' dogmas vary significantly. In this event, the two churches would continue in being and side-by-side with them would spring up a third, whose communicants would be the "unifiers."

This book will assume, partly because

4

Madison seems correct in saying that the more groups in a society the less likely one will be to play the tyrant over others,[6] that the development of a society characterized by diversity is an admirable aim. Yet measures that tolerate, encourage diversity, or stimulate intergroup contact and thus on their face contribute to pluralism could have other, initially latent consequences. They could, first, "polarize" the nation. A polarized society is one where at least one group that has or shares political power or that is strategically placed for conquering this goal wants to:

1. Illegally overthrow the political system or bring about the secession of a geographical region, or

2. Suppress dissent or exterminate, evict or exploit another cultural, ethnic, racial or religious group.

There are, of course, degrees of polarization as there are of, e.g., poverty, ugliness, stupidity and their opposites. A nation is the more polarized the more polarizing groups within its borders, the stronger these groups, and the greater their nearness to political power. (A politically polarizing group is one whose ideology and propinquity to, or control of, political power makes the country a polarized one.) For example, from its start in 1919 to its collapse in 1933, the Weimar government in Germany presided over a polarized nation. The army, the large landholders, the wealthy industrialists, and many judges never accepted the legitimacy of the republican regime.[7] Between 1919 and 1924 the degree of polarization was high. Armed bands attempted uprisings, the most famous of which was Hitler's Munich Beer Hall Putsch in 1923. In 1924, with the return of economic prosperity, polarization diminished, the Nazis and other anti-democratic right-wing parties losing popular votes and seats in Parliament in the half decade that began with that year.[8] Then came the Great Depression of 1929 and a

5

reintensification of polarization. In the 1928
elections, the Nazis had pulled only 810,000 votes
and had obtained only 12 seats in Parliament. The
1930 elections saw these figures grow to over 6
million and 107 respectively; and the Party became
the second largest in the almost 500 member legislature. The same year, the Communists on the far
left increased their representation from 54 to 77.
Then the Nazis obtained and consolidated their
political power in 1933; and unfortunate Germany,
dominated by a gang of madmen eager to suppress
all dissent and eradicate or enslave most non-
German minorities, became perhaps the most polarized nation in history.

From the government's point of view, polarization is intolerable. (This is not to say it is
always an evil. Many would agree that it was
better that Russian Tsarism be confronted by a
myriad of groups hating it than that it rule un-
checked over millions of cowering nobles, peasants,
and bureaucrats.) Almost as unsatisfactory to
those who fill its highest offices is another
possible by-product of toleration, etc., "incumbency instability." This occurs when high-ranking
public officials are likely to be removed from
office by a body with a legal right to remove
them. This group is usually the nation's voters
casting their ballots in an election; but in a
state with no free elections a smaller group could
have this right. Thus in 1964 the Presidium of
the Supreme Soviet of the USSR exercised its legal
prerogative to oust Nikita S. Khrushchev as the
nation's Prime Minister.

Polarization and incumbency instability are
confessedly different states of affairs. United
Kingdom voters replaced Laborite James Callaghan
with Tory Margaret Thatcher in 1979: their selection of a new Prime Minister did not take place in
an environment in which the Callaghan administration was threatened by armed mobs surrounding 10
Downing Street or by a coup plotted by disaffected
British admirals. Likewise, the Tsar of all the

6

Russias ruled over a polarized nation even though there was no legal way this Emperor who claimed his rule was ordained by God Himself could be unseated. Yet when a policy maker becomes aware that toleration, encouragement of diversity, or stimulation of intergroup contact may well produce either polarization or incumbency instability, he may opt instead for a measure that represses. That is, when the consequences of toleration, etc., are no longer latent and he sees them as leading to one of the situations that define a polarized society or, simply, as threatening to convince the electorate to return him to private life, he will be tempted to follow the path of repression. This, in turn, may produce a less pluralistic society.

It is important, therefore, to acquire the following information about encouraging diversity, toleration and stimulation of intergroup contact. (1) Under what circumstances is it plausible that policies falling into these categories (and analogous criminal procedure approaches) will reduce, or at least not increase, polarization or incumbency instability? A demonstration that these circumstances prevail should make it easier to convince policy makers to follow these types of course of action. (2) Under what circumstances will policies falling into these categories be likely to breed or exacerbate polarization or incumbency instability? When these circumstances exist it will be impossible to persuade policy makers to adopt policies of this nature unless one has at his beck and call appealing and well-reasoned arguments demonstrating that in the long run these projects will further other values they cherish.

The next four chapters will describe steps taken by the governments of the five countries in various areas of civil rights and liberties, including freedom of speech, press and religion, separation of church and state, race and ethnic relations, and criminal procedure. All these fields feature issues that raise strong emotions

among that minority of the people that pays close
attention to public affairs. Official policies of
tolerance, repression, etc., adopted in these
spheres thus are specially apt to create, increase
or lessen polarization or incumbency instability.
Accordingly, the data obtained from a study of
toleration, etc., undertaken there will be helpful
--and will be used in the concluding Chapter--for
answering the questions posed in the above paragraph. These responses will lead into a case study
showing that when confronted with a polarizing
group that unmistakably threatens to take the reins
of power, it may be extremely difficult for a
democratic polity to reconcile effectively the con-
flicting demands of promoting political and
ideological diversity and of preventing thoroughgoing polarization, a situation that often may
aptly be described in the words of the Irish poet
William Butler Yeats:

Turning and turning in the widening gyre
The falcon cannot hear the falconer;
Things fall apart; the centre cannot hold;
Mere anarchy is loosed upon the world,
The blood-dimmed tide is loosed, and everywhere
The ceremony of innocence is drowned;
The best lack all conviction, while the worst
Are full of passionate intensity.[9]

Moreover, comparison of the civil rights and
liberties policies of various nations can have
immediate practical applications. It can show
that an unsatisfactory situation deemed incurable
can in fact be eliminated. Thus a discovery that
racially integrated neighborhoods are common in
one country should make it clear to those living
in a nation dotted by black ghettos that these do
not exist by God's command. A comparative
approach can spot civil liberties problems in
other lands that may develop in one's own in the
future. A glance overseas can suggest ideas for
use at home and give some idea what would happen
were a particular civil liberties policy to be
adopted here. In the United States, many poor

8

people who are arrested have to remain in jail pending trial because they cannot pay a bondsman the premium for a bail bond. Some writers contend, therefore, that an accused normally ought to be freed when taken before a magistrate on his promise to appear in court when his case is called for trial. To get some indication whether a change such as this would significantly increase the percentage of "vanishing" criminal defendants, one can, at least as a start, look to the experiences of countries where it is easy for indigents to be released prior to trial. Similarly, lawyers and sociologists who argue that the death penalty ought to be totally abolished in America usually rely on statistics from countries and states where it has already been repudiated. The first sections of the final Chapter will, therefore, discuss some ideas for change (primarily for the United States) suggested by the information from the other countries. They also will note, in the light of this data, some problems with one or two reforms frequently proposed for implementation on this side of the Atlantic; and will indicate a few trouble spots facing the other nations that the United States may have to deal with soon.

B. Overview of the Five Countries' Judicial Systems

The broad outlines of the political systems of the United States, Great Britain, India, the Soviet Union and France are probably well known to most readers of this book and thus there is no need to summarize them here. However, the structure of their courts is less familiar even though these institutions often play more of a role in the civil rights and liberties arena than they do in others.

With the exception of such specialized courts as the Court of Customs and Patent Appeal and the Court of Military Appeals, the American federal judiciary is a three-tiered structure. At the lowest level are the district courts, over ninety in all. Right above these are the twelve circuit courts of appeal and above these is the United States Supreme Court, consisting at present of nine members who, like district and circuit court judges, are appointed by the President with the consent of the Senate and serve during "good behavior." So federal judges can keep their jobs for life if they wish, though pension plans now make it possible for them to retire at 70. Also helping to preserve the independence of the American federal judiciary is that clause of Article III, Section I of the Constitution providing that judges' salaries may not be reduced while they are in office.

Notwithstanding its considerable independence of the executive and legislative branches of government and of the electorate, the American federal judiciary cannot continuously buck the prevailing political winds in the country. There are aspects of the political system that can be used to overturn unpopular decisions of the courts or make these institutions unable to completely frustrate the popular will. If they construe a federal law differently from the way Congress thinks it should be interpreted, all Congress has to do is reenact the law in a way that nullifies the judicial interpretation (and get the President to sign the act). If they declare a federal or state law, administrative practice or administrative regulation unconstitutional, the decision can be overturned by constitutional amendment or by the passage of a bill that meets their objections. If Congress becomes highly disturbed by the way the Supreme Court is moving, it can do one of several things to change its direction (assuming that it can get Presidential approval). It can "pack" it by increasing its seats from nine to ten, eleven or any number so that the President can fill the vacancies with persons who are likely to decide cases in accordance with the ideology of the majority of the people at that moment. By virtue of Article III, Section 2, clause 2 of the United States Constitution, it can deprive it of the power to hear appeals in one or several types of cases, for instance, cases involving the rights of Communists. And, finally, it can oust any member of the federal judiciary by "impeaching" him --the House impeaches him and the Senate then decides whether or not he is guilty of the action for which the House has impeached him: for conviction a vote of two-thirds of the Senators present is necessary. (Only one Supreme Court judge has ever been impeached--and he was not convicted by the Senate.)

The United States federal judiciary has the power of "judicial review": i.e., it can overturn federal and state statutes that are contrary to the Constitution of the United States. The words of the Constitution are, however, very vague. As a result, the federal judiciary, especially the Supreme Court, has a great deal of discretion in determining whether to annul a statute (or executive or administrative ruling). It is not so much the wording of the Constitution but the sanctions mentioned above and the Justices' view of their proper role, including a respect for the Court's decisions in prior cases ("precedents"), that prevent it from striking down right and left popular statutes that meet with the personal disapproval of a majority of its members. The Court is not, however, constitutionally obliged to follow its own precedents; and has overturned or emasculated quite a few. The lower federal courts, plus all state courts, are bound by the decisions of the Supreme Court. This fact does not really make it impossible for other courts to evade its decisions, for it is usually open to them to say that the case before them is essentially different from the Supreme Court case supposedly applicable and, therefore, that that holding need not be followed in the instant situation.

11

The part of the Constitution most important
for the purposes of a book on rights and liberties
is the first nine Amendments, popularly known as
the Bill of Rights, plus the Fourteenth. These
amendments will be described in the chapters of
this book to which they are most relevant; but
suffice it to say here that, taken together, and as
interpreted by the Supreme Court, they guarantee
freedom of speech, press and religion, separate
church and state, secure certain privileges to an
individual accused of crime, and provide that no
individual shall be discriminated against by public agencies on account of his race.[10] The Court
also holds that most of the Bill of Rights is
binding on state and local governments by virtue
of that clause of the Fourteenth Amendment providing that no state shall deprive any person of life,
liberty or property without due process of law.
For constitutional purposes, the word "state" includes cities, counties and other political
subdivisions of the state and any institution
operated by the state or by its political subdivisions.

The name of the next country to be studied
presents a terminological difficulty. Technically,
it is called the United Kingdom of Great Britain
and Northern Ireland; while Great Britain consists
of England, Wales and Scotland. However, except
when dealing with Northern Ireland, the phrase
"United Kingdom" will rarely be used. When these
pages refer to law enacted by Parliament, they
will, for stylistic purposes, use "(Great) Britain"
("British") and "England" ("English") interchangeably. However, as Scotland's judiciary and judge-
made law differ from the English-Welsh, English-
Welsh courts and court cases will be labelled
English, not British.

Great Britain, unlike the United States, has
no one document known as "the Constitution."
There is a British constitution, but it consists
of customs, conventions, and several documents.
Among the documents are Magna Carta, the Petition

of Right of 1628, the Bill of Rights of 1689 and the Act of Settlement of 1701. Among the conventions is that English courts have no power of judicial review. This means that no law passed by Parliament may be invalidated by a court on the ground that it contravenes one of the provisions, written or unwritten, of the British constitution. Even a statute repealing one of the instruments that help make up this constitution may not be judicially annulled. Though Parliament may thus enact any law whatsoever, no matter how tyrannical, in practice it rarely violates fundamental freedoms. It can overrule any decision of any English court, and often will pass a statute overturning or modifying a judicially-fabricated rule.

The judicial system of England and Wales is a rather complex one. Only its criminal half will be described here, since most civil liberties decisions come from this sector. Ninety-seven percent of the criminal cases arising in England are handled by (usually) unsalaried and part-time justices of the peace, most of whom have had no legal training. Arrested defendants must be brought before them to determine whether there is any evidence to warrant their being held for trial and, if there is, to set bail. When trying cases, they usually sit in groups of at least two--and when they do so, they have jurisdiction over a considerable number of misdemeanors. Above the magistrates is a Crown Court, which in 1972 replaced the old Quarter Session, Assize, and various other courts.[11]

On the Crown Court sit two "tiers" of judges --High Court and Circuit judges. The High Court of Justice is the main English court for civil matters; but its judges sit in the Crown Court for the trial of the most serious criminal offenses to be brought before that body. Both High Court and Circuit judges hold full time appointments. Appeals from the Crown Court are taken to the Criminal Division of the Court of Appeal, composed of the Lord Chief Justice, who is the head of the

13

Queen's Bench Division of the High Court of
Justice, and two or four other Queen's Bench justices. From an adverse judgment in the Court of
Appeal an appeal can be taken to the House of
Lords--if the former Court certifies that an issue
of public importance is involved and if the House
of Lords decides to hear the appeal. It is not the
entire House of Lords but just the nine "law lords"
who resolve the case.[12]

In England judges are appointed, not elected.
There are about a thousand vacancies in the ranks
of the justices of the peace each year: these are
filled by the Lord Chancellor, who is usually of
the Prime Minister's party. However, he is not
supposed to stack the vacant magistracies with his
own political supporters but, rather, to accept the
recommendations of local advisory committees that
represent all segments of the community and the
Labour, Tory and Liberal parties. In practice, the
choices of the advisory committees are divided
among the political parties so that no one party
will totally dominate the magistracy in its area.[13]
As for the rest of the judiciary that has a role in
the criminal justice process:

> The Prime Minister, guided by the Lord Chan-
> cellor, nominates judicial members of the
> House of Lords, the Court of Appeal, and the
> heads of divisions of the High Court (of
> Justice, which furnishes many of the Crown
> Court judges): the Lord Chancellor himself
> nominates the other judges of the High Court
> as well as the lesser judiciary. . . . It is
> only by a fairly recently developed tradition
> (still lacking in the U.S.) that party poli-
> tics plays no part in this process, but this
> tradition is very strong today.[14]

Some feel, though, that both Labour and Conservative Lord Chancellors select ideologically
conservative judges.[15] Judges sit until they retire or (usually) age seventy-five, whichever
comes sooner. Parliament has not removed a judge

since 1700, though it theoretically has the power to do so.[16]

India has an American-type Constitution--one written document which is binding on the entire political system. Part III of the Constitution (Articles 14 through 35) is the Indian Bill of Rights, and owes an obvious debt to its American predecessor. The major provisions of the Indian Bill will be sketched in the appropriate passages of this book. It is easier to amend the Indian Constitution than the American: all that is generally needed is approval in each House of Parliament by a majority of the total membership of the House which is at the same time a two-thirds majority of those present and voting--plus the assent of the President (Article 368). The Indian Supreme Court said in 1967 that from then on it would be impossible to amend the Bill of Rights in this way: however, the case, Golak Nath v. Punjab, has itself been overturned by a constitutional amendment.[17]

Under the Constitution, the federal government has exclusive jurisdiction over certain matters; the states have exclusive jurisdiction over others; while both states and federal government can legislate on forty-seven subjects, including preventive detention. There is a Penal Code and a Code of Criminal Procedure enacted by the central government; but these codes can be and are supplemented by the state legislatures. The Bill of Rights is, thanks to Article 12 of the Constitution, binding on national, state and local polities.

Indian courts possess the power of judicial review and thus can invalidate laws of the national or state governments that in their opinion run counter to the Constitution. At the apex of the Indian judicial system is the Indian Supreme Court. This consists of a Chief Justice and of at least seven other judges--the number, whether seven or more, is to be determined by Parliament (Article

15

124(1)) and has varied. Judges of the Supreme Court are appointed by the President after consultation with current judges of the Supreme Court and the High Courts (Article 124(2)). To insure judicial independence, Article 124(2) provides that judges shall hold office until they reach sixty-five except (Article 124(4)) when ousted by a two-thirds vote in each house of Parliament; and Article 125(2) holds that the various prerogatives (e.g., pension plans) that become theirs upon appointment may not be varied to their disadvantage after they take office. Most of the justices were not active in politics prior to their appointment, which indicates that party politics did not play much of a role in their selection.[18] However, in 1973, Prime Minister Indira Gandhi named a relatively junior Supreme Court justice as the Chief Justice of the Court. This step was politically controversial, for she passed over three more senior justices who had delivered minority opinions asserting as invalid certain amendments to the Constitution that give the Government greater power to modify property rights. Likewise in 1977 she ignored seniority in picking a Chief Justice: the senior Associate Justice, Mr. H. R. Khamma, had been the only dissenter from the Court's ruling of April, 1976 that a political prisoner could not challenge his detention during the duration of the State of Emergency proclaimed by her in 1975. (The informal rule prior to these political refusals to appoint, one adhered to by the administration of Morarji Desai that succeeded Mrs. Gandhi's, was that the place of the outgoing Chief Justice was to be taken by the most senior Associate.) Also, about 20 lower court judges who issued anti-government rulings during the emergency were transferred or demoted.

Though there is a High Court in each state, it is not a "state court" but, rather, part of the one system of courts in the country. (The Union Territory of Delhi also has a High Court.) The High Courts have the power to supervise the functioning of the subordinate courts in their

16

state (Article 227). Each state is divided into districts, most of which have district courts with jurisdiction over major crimes. Minor crimes are triable by various classes of magistrates or by the village courts known as Nyaya Panchayats.

The Soviet Union in 1977 adopted a new Constitution, the "Brezhnev" Constitution. (Leonid Brezhnev was the nation's most powerful political figure at that time.) References here will be to both this and the 1936 Stalin Constitution, since many of the events to be described took place when the latter was in force.

The country, like the United States and India, is constitutionally a federal state whose major subdivisions are fifteen "equal" and "voluntarily united" (Article 13, Stalin Constitution; Article 69, Brezhnev Constitution) Soviet Socialist Republics (henceforth often referred to as "SSR's" or "Union Republics"). By far the largest and most important Soviet Socialist Republic is the Russian Soviet Federated Socialist Republic (RSFSR). The RSFSR and a few other SSR's contain within their borders Autonomous Soviet Socialist Republics (ASSR's) and autonomous regions.

Articles 33-68 of the Brezhnev Constitution (analogous to Articles 118-133 of the Stalin Constitution) constitute the Soviet Bill of Rights. Sections of both Constitutions grant Soviet citizens freedom of speech, press, assembly, etc., but in some cases only "in conformity with the interests of the working people and for the purposes of strengthening the socialist system." Various Articles of both documents accord "economic" rights such as those to rest, leisure and education. Others impose upon the people certain duties, such as obeying the laws, maintaining labor discipline, and defending the country. Other rights guaranteed by the Soviet Bill of Rights will be described in the relevant chapters.

17

The judiciary of the Soviet Union has no power of judicial review. However, one of the many prerogatives of the officials known as "procurators" is to "protest" an allegedly unconstitutional law or illegal regulation to the executive body that is the immediate superior of the body that issued it.[19] They have no authority, however, to protest plans and decrees of the national, Union Republic or autonomous republic Councils of Ministers or Soviets (legislatures). The most important court of the nation is the U.S.S.R. Supreme Court. Primarily an appelate court, it can overturn decisions of lower courts and issue general decrees for their guidance. Its members are elected by the Supreme Soviet for a term of five years (Stalin Constitution, Article 105; Brezhnev Constitution, Article 150). The law prescribes no definite number of judges; but the figure is set by the Supreme Soviet (the national legislature) at every Supreme Court election. In 1967, for example, there were twenty elected judges on the Court, of whom fifteen had been re-elected.[20]

In each Union Republic there are elective Supreme Courts that have appellate power. Below the Union Republic Supreme Courts are the Supreme Courts of the Autonomous Regions and Autonomous Republics and the "oblast" (regional) Courts. The lowest "regular" courts are the "People's" Courts, at least one in each city and one in each of the units of local government called districts. Most civil and criminal cases are heard by these, which are almost wholly courts of original jurisdiction. Trials in the People's Courts must be conducted by one judge and two laymen known as "people's assessors." (Even on the USSR Supreme Court people's assessors, who outnumber the judges,[21] sit when it functions as a trial court.) The People's Court judges are elected by the citizens of the appropriate city or district for five-year terms: the people's assessors who sit in People's Court are members of panels elected for two and one-half years (Brezhnev Constitution, Article 151)

18

from their place of work or residence. Each member of a panel usually serves as an assessor not more than a fortnight during the year. Finally, below the regular judicial system are "comrades courts" set up in factories, offices and apartment buildings to hear the most minor crimes and civil cases.

Actually, it is somewhat misleading to speak of Soviet judges on the People's Court and higher tribunals as "elected." After one has completed his legal education at university or law institute, he can opt for a judicial career before spending much if any time as a practicing lawyer-- though a few courtroom lawyers do become judges. At judicial "elections" only one candidate stands and thus is guaranteed victory. If a judge shows professional ability and has the proper political qualifications, i.e., is a loyal Communist, he will be "promoted" to a higher court, i.e., be picked as the one candidate for the seat on the superior tribunal. Formerly, persons with little or no legal training made up a significant proportion of the Soviet judiciary; but this is not true now.[22]

In France, minor cases are heard by the Police Tribunals (Tribunaux de Police). More important misdemeanors and lesser felonies are dealt with by the Correctional Court (Tribunal Correctionel); while the Assize Courts (Cours d'Assises) receive appeals from the Correctional Courts and, using a jury, hear major felony cases. The highest court of the ordinary judicial system is the Court of Cassation (Cour de Cassation), divided into civil and criminal sections. It cannot issue a final decision in a case appealed to it, but must remand to a lower court for this purpose. As in the Soviet Union, a hopefully - impartial government official called in France the juge d'instruction (examining magistrate) carries out a thorough investigation of certain crimes before the trial.

19

Unlike Great Britain, the United States and India, but not too differently from the Soviet Union, the ordinary judiciary is not recruited from the corps of practicing lawyers. The "sitting" magistracy, which is the name given to the ordinary judiciary as a whole, is made up of career civil servants. A young person with a law degree who wishes to be a judge takes a competitive examination to enter a school known as the National Center for Judicial Studies. Upon graduation, he is posted to the court for which he has received special training while at the Center. A High Council of the Judiciary, headed by the President of the Republic, picks judges for the Court of Cassation and the First Presidents of the various Courts of Appeal (a civil court, which provides much of the personnel for the Assize Court). The Minister of Justice selects other judges for appointments and promotion, though the High Council may give advice on these matters. The President, whose Constitution Article 16 power to take severe measures in a national emergency is a threat to civil liberties, has the final say on all these nominations. In theory, these powers of the President and Minister of Justice give the executive considerable control over the judiciary. In practice, however, the Fifth Republic has not witnessed grave abuses in judicial selection and promotion, though under the Third Republic the Minister of Justice did often refuse to advance troublesome magistrates. Since 1833, a judge cannot be removed without his consent unless he has been subject to disciplinary action. However, in 1945 the statute was ignored and some judges suspected of having been too enthusiastic for the quasi-fascistic Vichy regime (1940-45) of Marshal Henri Pétain were discharged.[23]

French judges do not have the power of judicial review: they cannot invalidate unconstitutional statutes. The Constitution does recognize an organ known as the Constitutional Council, which can review a Parliamentary measure before promulgation for unconstitutionality. All ex-Presidents of the Republic are ex-officio members of the Council for life; and it has nine other members with nine year, non-renewable terms.

Side by side with the "ordinary" system of civil and criminal courts exists an administrative court system, headed by the Council of State (Conseil d'État), a body which has had a considerable impact upon the development of civil liberties policy in France. The Council and the lower administrative tribunals are the major forums for disputes between citizens and the government or its agents, including suits by individuals or civil servants arising from breach of contract, negligence, or arbitrary or illegal action by the officials or employees of the national and local governments.[24] In cases of doubt, a Tribunal of Conflicts (Tribunal des Conflits) determines whether one involved in a legal quarrel with a government agency should bring his case before the administrative or ordinary courts. When an administrator's action is far outside the scope of his authority, the ordinary courts may give damages.[25]

Like the ordinary sitting judiciary, the Council of State is part of the career civil service. It is in fact one of the elite branches of that service: most of its members are recruited directly from the brightest graduates of the prestigious École Nationale d'Administration. Some of its members later became important political figures, e.g., Léon Blum, Socialist Prime Minister of the country in 1936 and Michel Debré, the first Prime Minister of the Fifth Republic and one of the major authors of the 1958 Constitution currently in force. In practice, the appointment and promotion process is free from partisan political influence and the members of the Council may be discharged only under the same conditions as other civil servants.[26] However, its Jewish members were removed by the Vichy government in 1941 and, after Liberation, the 20 percent of the Council that was thought to have been too

21

pro-Vichy was itself purged.[27]

When one wishes to bring an action against the French government or one of its agents in the Council or another administrative court, he will sue for damages or request that an official action be annulled as ultra vires. A step by the government will be quashed on this ground where it is in violation of a law; where there was a failure to observe the procedures required by law; where the bureaucrat had no authority to act; and/or where there was an abuse of power (détournement de pouvoir). Under its power to nullify actions of the state for abuse of power, the administrative court "considers very thoroughly the motives behind a decision, whether stated or not, and it has to be convinced that these motives were genuinely in the public interest. It is particularly exacting when faced with regulations restricting public liberties. It considers whether the restrictions are genuinely necessary in the circumstances and are not out of proportion to the seriousness of the situation."[28] Also, it has assumed for itself the power of overturning executive actions violating "general principles of law" though no specific statute. Among such "general principles" are the non-retroactivity of administrative decisions, freedom of conscience, and the equality of all citizens.[29]

The administrative courts are also denied the power of judicial review. That is, they cannot invalidate statutes passed by Parliament after they have been put into effect. Nonetheless, they still have a major say in framing civil liberties rules. Much of the French policy relevant to civil liberties is promulgated in the form of executive decree-laws, ordinances or circulars; and these are cognizable by the administrative court system. Moreover, this system can review the decisions of officials of regional and local government such as prefects and mayors; and, as in other countries, decisions emanating from sources such as this (for example, refusals to permit

22

political meetings) pose real civil liberties problems.

To discover what the French Bill of Rights provides on a particular topic, the lawyer or citizen may have to prowl among several documents. The Preamble to the Constitution of 1958 commences by declaring that "The French People hereby solemnly proclaims its attachment to the Rights of Man. . . . as defined by the Declaration of 1789, confirmed and complemented by the Preamble of the Constitution of 1946"--the basic document of the defunct Fourth French Republic. That Preamble proclaims, in turn, that "every human being, without distinction of race, religion, or belief, possesses inalienable and sacred rights." It then "solemnly reaffirms the rights and freedoms of man and of the citizen consecrated by the Declaration of Rights of 1789. . . ." That 1789 Declaration contains much familiar phraseology. It defines liberty as the ability to do that which does not hurt others and proclaims that the law alone can fix the boundaries of liberty. Private property is "inviolable and sacred" (Article 17). Article 10 asserts that "no one may be disturbed for his opinions, even religious." Article 11 declares that "the free communication of thoughts and opinions is one of the most precious rights of man." Moreover, "no man may be accused, arrested, or detained other than in the case determined by the law and according to the forms which it has prescribed." Article 6 maintains that "all citizens being equal in its (the law's) eyes are equally admissible to all dignities, places and public employment, according to their capacities and without any distinction beyond that of their virtues and their talents."

Thus, placing the 1958 Preamble alongside the 1946 Preamble and the 1789 Declaration, both of which it incorporates, the French Constitution has a Bill of Rights guaranteeing, among other things, equality before the law, freedom of speech, press and religion, and fair criminal procedure.

23

Also among the rights mentioned in the 1946 Preamble are "the fundamental principles recognized
by the laws of the Republic." These tenets include the liberty of the press safeguarded by the
Press Law of July 29, 1881; the freedom of association protected by the law of July 1, 1901;
religious freedom and church-state separation
proclaimed by the law on Separation of Church and
State of December 9, 1905; and certain rights
allowed criminal defendants by the Code of Criminal Procedure. (These statutes will be considered
in detail in subsequent chapters.)

Some commentators believe that the Bill of
Rights of the Constitution of the Fourth Republic
(the Preamble plus the 1789 Declaration incorporated therein) had no legal status but was simply
a collection of maxims to which the Framers hoped
the French legislature and executive would adhere.
However, laws antagonistic to the current Bill of
Rights (i.e., the 1958 and 1946 Preambles and the
1789 Declaration) are legally invalid and thus
voidable by the Constitutional Council before
promulgation. The Council in 1971 first voided a
statute on the ground that it was an invasion of
a fundamental constitutional freedom. The freedom
infringed was that of association, which is part
of the Bill of Rights by virtue of the fact that
it is a fundamental principle recognized by a law
of the Republic and is therefore enshrined by the
Preamble to the 1946 Constitution which in turn is
incorporated by the Preamble to the 1958 Constitution. In the summer of 1975 it overturned as contrary to the 1789 Declaration's principle of
equality before the law a court reform measure
giving the president of a tribunal the option to
decide whether a defendant should be tried by a
three-person or one-person court. And in January,
1977, it struck down a law giving certain police
the right to search any moving vehicle on the
grounds that the law violated the "individual
liberty constituting one of the fundamental principles guaranteed by the laws of the Republic and
proclaimed by the preamble to the 1946

24

Constitution, confirmed by the Preamble to the 1958 Constitution."[30]

There is a set of transnational civil liberties institutions that must be sketched briefly here, as their decisions are now slowly being incorporated into the domestic law of Great Britain and France. The members of the Council of Europe, including these two nations, signed in 1950 a treaty known as the Convention for the Protection of Human Rights and Fundamental Freedoms, henceforth referred to as the Convention. It entered into force in 1953, though it did not become binding on France until that country's tardy ratification in 1974. The first twenty clauses of the Convention protect freedoms regarded as fundamental in most of non-communist Europe. For example, the pact bans slavery and ex-post-facto laws; protects freedom of expression and association; requires the parties to respect political liberty and to hold free elections at reasonable intervals; safeguards religious freedom; and forbids discrimination against racial and national minorities.

The first tier of the system created by the Convention is the European Commission on Human Rights. Alleged violations of Convention-safeguarded liberties by one party to the treaty may be brought before the Commission by another party or, in certain cases, by the victims themselves, but only after they have exhausted all the domestic remedies made available to them by the government that is the accused malefactor. The Commission will try to bring about a friendly settlement. If it fails, it may indicate whether the defendant nation is in breach of the Convention; but its decision is not binding. To obtain a binding judgment, an appeal must be taken either to the Committee of Ministers (a body made up of certain representatives of the parties to the treaty) or to the judicial tribunal known as the European Court of Human Rights.

25

The Commission has already declared in-
fringements of the Convention the Isle of Man's
practice of birching criminals and the British
military's mistreatment of Irish Republican Army
internees in Northern Ireland. The I.R.A. decision has been upheld by the Court, which earlier
refused to proclaim a British obscenity conviction
contrary to the Convention's Article 10; but which
in Golder[31] held that the refusal of the British
government to let a prisoner consult a lawyer to
help him bring a libel suit infringed the fair
trial guarantee of Article 6(1) and Article 8's
assertion that everyone's "right to correspondence"
must be respected. In 1979, the Court held it
wrongful for Britain to have prevented the publication of an article on the drug thalidomide during litigation initiated by families whose children
were born deformed because of the drug.[32] Having
ratified the Convention only a few years ago,
France has not yet felt its stings. However, during the next decade the human rights practices of
that nation could provide the Commission and Court
with a significantly increased workload.[33]

26

FOOTNOTES TO CHAPTER I

[1]Kurt Glaser and Stefan Possony's Victims of Politics (New York: Columbia, 1979) discusses ethnic and religious conflict in numerous nations. Richard Claude (ed.), Comparative Human Rights (Baltimore: Johns Hopkins University Press, 1976) contains, inter alia, articles comparing freedom of expression in Japan and the United States; the right to privacy in Great Britain, Canada and the United States; and militancy on the part of European linguistic minorities. Willem Veenhoven (ed.), Human Rights Case Studies (5 vols.; The Hague: M. Nijhoff, 1975-76); Ben Whitaker (ed.), The Fourth World: Victims of Group Oppression (London: Sigdwick and Jackson, 1972); and Ronald Bunn and William Andrews (eds.), Politics and Civil Liberties in Europe: Four Case Studies (Princeton: D. Van Nostrand, 1967) all contain excellent case studies, but no systematic attempt is made in any of these works to relate the studies to each other. Frede Castberg's Freedom of Speech in the West (Dobbs Ferry, N.Y.: Oceana, 1960) is a fine discussion, albeit another eschewing systematic comparison, of certain freedom of speech and press issues in France, West Germany and the United States. Jerome B. King's Law v. Order (Hamden: Shoe String Press, 1975) discusses aspects of freedom of the press in France. Zelman Cowen's Individual Liberty and the Law (Dobbs Ferry, N.Y.: Oceana, 1977) is a superbly written comparison of libel, obscenity, wiretap and free press-fair trial law in Britain, the United States, and Australia. The discussion of obscenity also brings in Indian cases. David H. Bayley's Public Liberties in the New States (Chicago: Rand McNally, 1964) and Ivo Duchacek's Rights and Liberties in the World Today (Santa Barbara, Cal.: ABC Clio Press, 1973) are also "must" reading for persons interested in seeing how countries other than their own try to

solve civil liberties problems. However, neither consistently employs a set of general categories as a framework for making comparisons among the countries discussed. Additionally, some important comparative analyses of race and ethnic relations are Michael Banton, Race Relations (New York: Basic Books, 1967); Philip Mason, Patterns of Dominance (New York: Oxford U. Press, 1970); Alvin Rabushka and Kenneth Shepsle, Politics in Plural Societies (Columbus: Merrill, 1972); and Pierre Van den Berghe, Race and Racism (New York: Wiley, 1967). Finally, Mauro Cappelletti and William Cohen, Comparative Constitutional Law (Indianapolis: Bobbs Merrill, 1979); Walter Murphy and Joseph Tanenhaus, Comparative Constitutional Law (New York: St. Martins, 1977); and Harry Groves, Comparative Constitutional Law (Dobbs Ferry: Oceana, 1963) all contain cases from abroad on civil rights and liberties matters.

[2]For stylistic reasons only, in this book the masculine includes the feminine unless the contrary is clear from the context.

[3]Roy Fairfield (ed.), The Federalist Papers (New York: Doubleday Anchor, 1961), p. 22.

[4]Social Theory and Social Structure, rev. and enlarged ed. (New York: Free Press, 1957), p. 51.

[5]Ibid., pp. 71-82.

[6]Fairfield (ed.), op. cit., pp. 19, 22.

[7]William Shirer, The Rise and Fall of The Third Reich (New York: Simon and Schuster, 1960), pp. 59-60.

[8]Ibid., pp. 112, 118.

[9]The Second Coming, appearing in Charles M. Coffin (ed.), The Major Poets: English and American (New York: Harcourt Brace, 1954), p. 477.

[10]Some civil liberties guarantees are to be found in the main body of the Constitution. Thus Article VI, Sec. 3 provides that "no religious Test shall ever be required as a Qualification to any office or public Trust under the United States."

[11]The Quarter Session and Assize Courts are described in Delmar Karlen, Anglo-American Criminal Justice (New York: Oxford U. Press, 1967), pp. 51-52; the Crown Court in Henry J. Abraham, The Judicial Process, 3rd ed. (New York: Oxford U. Press, 1975), p. 246.

[12]The preceding paragraphs are based on Karlen, op. cit., pp. 48-53, 57-60; and David Fellman, The Defendant's Rights Under English Law (Madison: Wisconsin U. Press, 1966), Ch. 1.

[13]Karlen, op. cit., pp. 61-62.

[14]Ibid., p. 67.

[15]New Statesman, January 13, 1978, p. 36.

[16]Henry Cecil, The English Judge (London: Stevens and Sons, 1970), p. 12.

[17]Golak Nath is cited (1967) All India Rep. S. Ct. 1643. In 1973, the Supreme Court declared constitutional the Amendment overruling Golak Nath, subject to the reservation that no constitutional amendment could alter the basic structure and framework of the Constitution. The case is Kesavananda Bharati v. Kerala, (1973) All India Rep. St. Ct. 1461.

[18]George Gadbois, Jr., Indian Supreme Court Justices: A Portrait, Law and Society Review, 3: 317, 330 (1968-69); The Times (London), January 29, 1977, p. 4.

[19]Harold Berman, Justice in the U.S.S.R., rev. ed. (New York: Random House Vintage, 1963), p. 238.

[20]Donald Barry, The U.S.S.R. Supreme Court: Recent Developments, Soviet Studies, Vol. 20, pp. 511-512 (1969).

[21]Ibid., p. 512.

[22]Donald Barry and Harold Berman, The Soviet Legal Profession, Harv. L. Rev., 82:1, 9-21 (1968).

[23]F. Ridley and J. Blondel, Public Administration in France (New York: Barnes and Noble, 1965), pp. 130-35.

[24]Charles Freedeman, The Conseil D'Etat in Modern France (New York: Columbia U. Press, 1961), pp. 1-6.

[25]Ridley and Blondel, op. cit., pp. 154-56; Frede Castberg, Freedom of Speech in the West, pp. 65-66.

[26]Ridley and Blondel, op. cit., pp. 151-52.

[27]Freedeman, op. cit., pp. 45-48.

[28]Ridley and Blondel, op. cit., pp. 157-58.

[29]M. Long, P. Weil, and G. Braibant, Les Grands Arrêts de la Jurisprudence Administrative, 5th ed. (Paris: Sirey, 1969), pp. 346-49.

[30]The Constitutional Council's decision on freedom of association has no name but may be found in L'Actualité Juridique, 24:537 (1971). The three-judge decision, likewise nameless, can be found at p. 1352 of Revue du Droit Publique et de la Science Politique, 1975. Le Monde, Jan. 14, 1977, p. 12, reprints the vehicle search decision. The decisions are discussed in Barry Nicholas, Fundamental Rights and Judicial Review in France, (1978) Public Law 82-101, 155-77.

[31](1975) 18 Eur. Court Human Rights.

[32]New York Times, April 27, 1979, p. A2.

[33]The above discussion of the Convention is based mainly on Sigmund Cohn, International Adjudication of Human Rights and the European Court of Human Rights, Ga. Journal of International and Comparative Law 7:315ff (1977). See also New York Times, August 26, 1950, p. 7; The Times (London), April 25, 1977, p. 5; August 22, 1977, p. 1.

CHAPTER II

FREEDOM OF SPEECH, PRESS AND ASSOCIATION
IN THE FIVE COUNTRIES

The comparison of freedom of speech, press, and assembly problems will cover the following areas:

A. Speech that may lead to rioting, i.e., localized violence.

B. The advocacy of doctrines that the government perceives as subversive, i.e., demanding change in the political status quo through illegal means.

C. Criticism of the government and of public officials.

D. Oral or written matter primarily concerned with sex.

A. Speech That May Lead to Localized Violence

Speech that may lead to localized violence is speech that threatens the use of physical force against persons and property but is not directed toward the violent overthrow of the political system. It ranges from language that may result in an attack on one person to words that produce large-scale rioting over several days, such as occurred in Newark, New Jersey and Detroit in the summer of 1967; but does not include, for example, a directive from a modern-day British Lenin to his followers to seize Parliament and proclaim a dictatorship of the proletariat. (However, an

33

Indian case that must be mentioned here does feature defendants who urged revolution.)

The state's actions against those whose remarks might lead to localized violence may come at any one of three stages. It

(a) may ban in advance the meeting at which, or document in which, the words will be uttered. ("Speaker" will refer to "writer" as well except when the contrary is clear from the context.);

(b) through the police or other security officials, it may interrupt the speaker in the midst of his words; or

(c) it may allow the speaker to finish but then, whether or not violence actually ensues, prosecute him for disorderly conduct or some other offense. Logically, there is a difference between these types of repression but, except for the United States, the courts make little distinction between them.

In the United States one illustrative case is Edwards v. South Carolina.[1] Here a group of 187 blacks gathered in 1961 in front of the South Carolina State House in Columbia, South Carolina, to protest the racial discrimination which then prevailed in the state. The area where they congregated, known as the State House grounds, was open to the general public. To get to the State House grounds, they passed through a driveway and parking area called the "horseshoe." They carried placards condemning segregation and saying, "I am proud to be a Negro." A crowd of 300 whites gathered on the horseshoe. Though no white actually threatened violence, many were hostile to blacks. Moreover, white-black tensions in the south had risen as a result of civil rights demonstrations such as the one taking place. Fearing trouble, the police told the blacks to disperse. Instead of doing so, they sang patriotic and religious songs while stamping their feet and

34

clapping their hands. In consequence, they were
arrested and convicted of breach of the peace. The
Supreme Court in reversing their conviction made
several points, one of which is particularly relevant here. Quoting the 1949 decision of Terminiello
v. Chicago it said that

> a function of free speech under our system of
> government is to invite dispute. It may indeed
> best serve its high purpose when it induces a
> condition of unrest, creates dissatisfaction
> with conditions as they are, or even stirs
> people to anger. Speech is often provocative
> and challenging. It may strike at prejudices
> and preconceptions and have profound unsettling
> effects as it presses for acceptance of an idea.
> That is why freedom of speech . . . is . . .
> protected against censorship or punishment, un-
> less shown likely to produce a clear and present
> danger of a serious substantive evil that rises
> far above public inconvenience, annoyance, or
> unrest.[2] (emphasis mine)

In other words, speech threatening localized violence which merely annoys or angers the listeners is
constitutionally protected by the First Amendment's
guarantee of freedom of speech and press: to be
punishable it must create a clear and present danger
of such violence, which the Court felt that the
demonstration here did not do. It emphasized two
matters: No one in the audience had actually
threatened or engaged in violence, and there were
over thirty policemen in the area to prevent a
physical clash between the protestors and the
whites. Note the logical demands of the clear and
danger test as applied to situations where speech
creates a chance of violence. If it is uncertain
that the words will produce violence or if the
violence threatened by the words will erupt in
the future rather than soon after they are
spoken, the speaker cannot be penalized for
uttering them. It is, of course, irrelevant
whether the actual crime for which he is charged
is labelled "disorderly conduct," "breach of the

peace," "sedition," or something else. It is also logically irrelevant whether the speaker was urging the audience to attack an innocent party or whether (as in Edwards) the speaker, because of the unpopularity of his ideas, was himself the potential target of its fury.

The English rules dealing with speech that has the potential to stir a crowd to tumult have been developed by the courts and by laws of Parliament and of local governments. In connection with the relevant judge-made rules, one leading case can be noted.

The defendant in Wise v. Dunning[3] was a Protestant fundamentalist who used to go through Roman Catholic neighborhoods in Liverpool and insult the Catholic faith. Riots and near-riots occurred several times as a result of these self-styled "crusades," and a Liverpool magistrate ordered that he file a bond and get sureties to keep the peace for the next twelve months and, in default, go to prison for three months. The appeals court here held against the defendant, though his intent was to insult Catholicism and convert Catholics, not to bring about the mob violence that was being aimed at him. Lord Alverstone, C.J., asserted that the action of the magistrate was proper because the defendant's language and behavior was "likely to occasion a breach of the peace." Darling J. concurring, reached the same result because "The natural consequence of this 'crusader's' eloquence has been to produce illegal acts," a point with which Channell, J., also concurring essentially agreed. Thus English judges have declared that anyone who utters something which is likely to lead to violence can be punished, assuming the absence of any statute setting forth the conditions under which the words are illegal.[4]

There exist Acts of Parliament governing words threatening violence uttered in certain situations. The tense days of the 1930's saw in

36

Britain frequent street clashes between fascists and communists and other left-wing groups. In response to this situation, the Government passed the Public Order Act of 1936, still in effect. Section 5, the part of most interest here, reads that "any person who in any public place or at any public meeting uses threatening, abusive or insulting words or behavior with intent to provoke a breach of the peace or whereby a breach of the peace is likely to be occasioned, shall be guilty of an offense." This Act does not supersede the other devices to eliminate the utterance of words threatening violence, such as binding speakers over to keep the peace. It is, rather, yet another weapon that can be used against many of them.

One of the most famous prosecutions under this Act occurred in the early 1960's. Colin Jordan, a British "Neo-Nazi," wanted to speak in London's Trafalgar Square. Many in the Square were young radicals and liberals, including some Jews, associated with the left-wing Campaign for Nuclear Disarmament. Jordan told this audience that "more and more people every day . . . are opening their eyes and coming to say with us Hitler was right. They are coming to say that our real enemies, the people we should have fought, were not Hitler and the National Socialists of Germany but world Jewry and its associates in this country." At that the crowd pressed forward and the police stopped the meeting. The Bow Street Magistrates' Court convicted him under Section 5 of the Public Order Act. London Quarter Sessions reversed the conviction on the ground that Jordan's words, though highly insulting, were not likely to lead reasonable people attending the meeting to commit breaches of the peace. The Divisional Court of Kings Bench, in Jordan v. Burgoyne,[5] reversed Quarter Sessions and agreed with the Magistrates' Court that Jordan was guilty of a violation of Section 5. Lord Parker, C.J., writing the opinion, took the words of this section literally. He assumed for the sake of argument that

37

the people who wanted to pummel Jordan were hooligans. Nonetheless, if one uses insulting words at a public meeting or in a public place, he "take(s) his audience as he finds them," and if these words when addressed to this audience are likely to lead to a breach of the peace, then the speaker is guilty. When Mr. Jordan uttered the anti-Semitic, pro-Hitler remarks quoted above to this particular group, he clearly violated the Act. According to Justice Parker, this law leaves an individual free to criticize his opponents and their policies as strongly as he likes, but it does prevent him from abusing, threatening or insulting them.

Parliament incorporated in the 1965 Race Relations Act a Section 6, forbidding people with wrongful intent to publish or distribute written matter or to use in any public place words which are threatening, abusive or insulting, "being matter or words likely to stir up hatred against (a group) on grounds of color, race or ethnic or national origins." One major difference between this and the original version of the Public Order Act is that this applied to some speech which is not likely to promote a breach of peace. It could have covered, for example, a talk by a candidate for public office to some of his electors in which he told them to vote for him "because he plans to get the dirty, criminal niggers out of Britain" even though there was no colored man in the audience and even though his listeners were not likely to engage in physical violence. Ironically, one of the first men convicted under this law designed to protect Jamaicans and Indians against white racists was a black militant, Michael Abdul Malik, who said at a public meeting: "I want to tell you about soul. . . . The black man has soul, the white man has no soul. He is a soul-less person. . . . Don't let the thought of prison terrify you. . . . You get to know a lot in prison, a lot that can terrify the white man."[6] In 1976 Section 6 was repealed. To replace it, the Public Order Act was amended to punish the publication or distribution of written matter, or the use in any public place, of language that is threatening, abusive or insulting and likely to foment hatred against any racial group. This section does not even require intent to stir up racial hatred: all that the prosecution need prove is the use of threatening, abusive or insulting language in circumstances that are likely to witness racial hatred. Under Section 6, 10 of 25 defendants were acquitted; under its successor, as of 1980, only 4 of 15 were found not guilty.[7]

Turning to India, Article 19 (1) (a) of the Constitution holds that "All citizens shall have the right to freedom of speech and expression." Article 19 (2) is a limit on Article 19 (1) (a) and reads that nothing there shall "prevent the State from making any law, insofar as such law imposes reasonable restrictions on the exercise of the right (conferred by Article 19 (1) (a)) in the interests of the sovereignty and integrity of India, the security of the State, friendly relations with foreign States, public order, decency or morality, or in relation to contempt of court. . . ." The original version of Article 19 (2) did not include "public order" as one of the "interests" for which freedom of speech and press could reasonably be limited; and therefore agitation which threatened localized rioting was immune from repression as long as it did not jeopardize the security of the state, as strange cases such as In Re Bharati Press[8] attest. Here a 1931 law allowed the state to demand security from the keeper of a printing press if it were used for publishing any matter which incites or tends to incite the commission of murder or any other offense involving violence. The state of Bihar tried to compel the keeper of the Bharati Press to post a bond of 2,000 rupees because it had printed a leaflet in Bengali which contained the following language in its call for revolution: "let all oppressors perish"; "death is my darling"; "I am blood-thirsty goddess Kali who lives and moves in the cremation ground"; "I am thirsty, I want blood, I want revolution--break, break the proud head of the aggressor."

39

The Patna High Court held that though this leaflet was covered by the appropriate section of the law, that section itself was invalid because it proscribed pamphlets inciting to ordinary murder and mayhem as well as pamphlets threatening the security of the state; and, it will be remembered, there was at that time nothing in Article 19 (2) of the Constitution that permitted the abridgment of free speech in the interest of public order alone. (What the High Court employed here is a device frequently used by the U.S. Supreme Court, too, declaring a statute invalid because it is on its face "overbroad," prohibiting acts which cannot constitutionally be outlawed as well as acts which can. The Patna court said the impugned act was aimed at all incitements to violence, not only at incitements of political killings.)

Hardly surprisingly, the Parliament of India was not too happy with the situation. So it modified Article 19 (2) to permit reasonable restrictions of freedom of speech in the interests of public order and the prevention of incitement to offenses. The present Indian rules determining when a speaker whose words threaten violence can constitutionally be punished can most clearly be seen in the case of Kedar Nath v. State of Bihar.[9] The defendants here were Communists who had been found guilty of violating Section 124A of the Indian Penal Code making it illegal by words spoken or written to bring into hatred or contempt, or excite disaffection toward, the government of India. They had made comments such as the following at various public meetings.

The people of India drove the Britishers out from this country and elected these Congress goondas (thugs) to the gaddi and seated them on it. Today these Congress goondas are sitting on the gaddi due to mistakes of the people. When we drove out the Britishers, we shall strike and turn out these Congress goondas as well. Official dogs will also be liquidated along with these Congress goondas.

40

The Congress goondas are banking upon the American dollars and imposing various kinds of taxes on the people today. The blood of our brothers . . . is being sucked. The capitalists . . . of this country help these Congress goondas. These . . . capitalists will also have to be brought before the people's court along with these Congress goondas. . . . The Forward Communist Party . . . had always been believing in revolution and does so even at present. We believe in that revolution, which will come and in the flames of which the capitalists . . . and the Congress leaders of India, who have made it their profession to loot the country, will be reduced to ashes and on their ashes will be established a Government of the poor and down-trodden people of India.

There was no doubt that the defendants' words brought them under the terms of the law: the question the Court had to consider seriously was the constitutionality of the measure. The defendants contended, obviously, that it ran afoul of the guarantee of freedom of speech. To this the Court answered that Article 19 (2), as amended in 1951, allows the Government of India to limit freedom of speech in the interests of public order; that this statute does not prohibit strongly worded criticisms of public measures or governmental action but merely words having a tendency, or intended to, disturb the public peace; and that it is thus perfectly valid. "It is only when the words, written or spoken . . . have the pernicious tendency or intention of creating public disorder or disturbance of law and order that the law steps in to prevent such activities in the interest of public order. So construed, the section, in our opinion, strikes the correct balance between individual fundamental rights and the interest of public order."[10]

Article 10 of the 1789 French Declaration of Rights provides that "no one ought to be molested

41

for his opinions, even religious" while Article 11
claims that "the free communication of thoughts
and opinions is one of the most precious rights of
man." The words of Article 2 that liberty consists
of the power to do all that which does not hurt
others emphasizes, however, that speech that
threatens others does not enjoy absolute immunity
in France any more than anywhere else. French
jurisprudence regarding the protection of speech
threatening riots is somewhat complicated. The
most cited case is that of the Council of State in
Benjamin.[11] Rene Benjamin was a member of the
monarchist, anti-Semitic, anti-Republican Action
Française of Charles Maurras, certainly the most
intellectually and politically significant of the
groups on the extreme right that appeared on the
French political scene during the first four decades of the twentieth century. He wanted to
sponsor a literary conference in the city of
Nevers on "Two Comic Authors: Courteline and
Sacha Guitry," a relatively non-political subject.
Benjamin had during the course of his career as a
right-wing speaker delivered attacks against the
public schools and their teachers--both firm supporters of the Third Republic and maintaining its
"laicity." The teachers made known to the mayor
of Nevers that they would oppose by all means a
conference headed by a man "who had dirtied in his
writings the personnel of laic instruction." By
using the press, tracts and posters they obtained
the support of the trade unions, of the groups of
the left, and of other defenders of the public
schools. The mayor, upon whom it is incumbent
under an 1884 law to maintain public order, thereupon banned the meeting in order to avoid violence.
The Council of State found the mayor's ban ultra
vires (entachée d'excès de pouvoir) and annulled
it. Though the mayor does have the duty to maintain public order, laws of the 30th of June, 1881
and of the 20th of March, 1907 guarantee freedom
of assembly ("liberté de réunion"). Although the
Council thought that the presence of M. Benjamin at
Nevers threatened public tranquillity, the threat
was not grave enough to make it impossible for the

42

police to keep order. In other words, to reconcile the laws of 1884 on the one hand and those of 1881 and 1907 on freedom of assembly on the other, the Council of State developed a test that indoor meetings not open to the public (and by implication, speeches uttered and literature distributed at such meetings) are protected even though they clearly threaten disorder unless the police at the government's disposal will not be able to nip the violence in the bud.

Several other decisions, some also involving the Action Française or its ideological allies, followed the reasoning of Benjamin. For example, a medical banquet was scheduled to be held in Lyons in February, 1936. Shortly before, the Action Française and other right-wing "leagues" had been dissolved under a law of January 10, 1936. The prefect of the Department of the Rhône (in which Lyons is located) banned this banquet on the grounds that it was sponsored by members of the dissolved leagues, that the meeting was really a meeting of the Action Française, that Charles Maurras, the head of the Action Française, was to preside, and that the banquet would thus threaten public order. The Council of State annulled the prefectorial decree in Bujadoux et autres.[12] The Council insisted that the fact that the gathering had been organized by members of groups legally dissolved did not of itself justify the ban. There was no indication in the record that grave troubles would break out if the dinner were held; nor was there any allegation that the prefect and the police at his disposal could not repress any rioting that did ensue.

The Council will not strike down all decrees preventing a conference or a meeting. In Bucard[13] the Council of State sustained a ban on meetings scheduled by an extreme right-wing organization called "Le Francism" in the tense Alsatian frontier town of Strasbourg. The Council did not describe the nature of the organization but elliptically noted that freedom of association could not prevent

43

public authorities from taking measures which are
needed to insure security and public tranquillity
and that the meetings of this group were of a
nature to bring about great troubles under the
(not spelled out) circumstances. It continued that
the prefect did not have enough police at his disposal to keep order, especially taking into account
the number and dispersion of the group's meetings.
And in Houphouët-Boigny[14] the Council sustained a
ban on a projected congress of the Rassemblement
Démocratique Africain scheduled to be held in a
"commune" (a unit of local government) of Upper
Volta, then a French colony. The Rassemblement
was an African independence movement that was gain-
ing strength in then-French West Africa, and
Houphouët-Boigny, now the President of the Ivory
Coast, was one of its leaders. The Council thought
that the congress might well provoke trouble that
the police could not control, given the extent of
the territory over which the security forces would
have to be deployed.

    The cases analyzed so far have mostly in-
volved "private" indoor meetings. Less tolerant
rules govern indoor meetings open to the public and
meetings on the public way (streets or sidewalks),
and one factor the Council took into account in
Houphouët-Boigny was that the congress would have
been held in part outdoors. Crucial is the decree-
law of October 23, 1935, which requires that all
organizers of corteges, parades, rallies and demonstrations "on the public way" submit a prior
declaration (déclaration préalable) to the relevant
local authorities between three and fifteen days
before the demonstration. The declaration is to
make known the names and domiciles of the organizers and the purpose, the place, the date, the
time and the itinerary of the cortege, etc. The
decree-law itself says nothing about the possibility of prohibiting the meeting, but a circular
of the Minister of the Interior (La circulaire
Paganon) handed down in November of 1935 allows
the mayors and prefects to prohibit every demonstration, of whatever nature, which is "susceptible

44

of provoking excitement of a nature such as to compromise public order." The prohibition can be general, even if the likelihood of trouble is not great. Bans can be issued when the circumstances threaten to create a situation necessitating the intervention of the police. It is a crime to hold a rally on the public way that has been forbidden or notice of which has not been given in advance.[15] The great majority of the decisions interpreting this decree-law and circular involve religious processions, and thus will be treated later. The leading decision in a secular context is Union des Syndicat Ouvriers de la Région Parisienne CGT.[16] The Council of State upheld a decree of the Paris prefect of police forbidding a demonstration scheduled by certain trade unionists. It made it clear that the 1935 decree-law and the supplementary circular mean what they say. Under these rules the local authorities can forbid a demonstration that is susceptible of troubling the public order, and it appeared from the record that the planned demonstration presented a menace to the public order of a nature such as to legally justify banning it. Moreover, the prefect's motives were simply to insure good order and public tranquillity. To this day, the French authorities do not hesitate to use their power to ban demonstrations on the public way when these might lead to rioting. In 1978, for example, they barred a leftist rally against French intervention in Zaire and an international neo-Nazi gathering; and in 1980 they forbade demonstrations before various embassies.

The French cases cited involve advance restrictions on speech (i.e., the problem of "prior restraint"): the British, Indian and American decisions treat attempts to punish speakers after they have made their points or, at least, while they are in the midst of their orations. As witnessed by Duncan v. Jones,[17] the English courts make no distinction between prior and subsequent restraint. Here a court declared justified a police refusal to allow a protest meeting of the unemployed to be held on the ground that the

constables "reasonably apprehended" a breach of
the peace. Similarly, the 1936 Public Order Act
allows the district or borough council (in London,
the Commissioner of the Metropolitan Police) to
ban marches when there are reasonable grounds to
believe that they may occasion serious disorder
that the police on hand will be unable to avert.
The ban must be approved by the Home Secretary.

In the United States attempts such as those
in Duncan to ban in advance a specific inflammatory speech would probably run afoul of Near v.
Minnesota[18] and New York Times Co. v. U.S.,[19] both
of which proclaimed that "prior restraints" on
speech and press are constitutionally highly suspect. New York Times Co. held, for example, that
two newspapers could not be enjoined by the courts
from publishing the classified Pentagon Papers
showing how the United States became involved in
the Vietnam War. Among the ideas that found favor
with a majority of the justices is that the
government carries a heavy burden of showing justification for the imposition of prior restraints
(including injunctions) against expression, a
burden that it had not met in the instant case.
The burden is a bit less when what is barred is an
outdoor demonstration or parade, and it is clear
that the state can require these to be scheduled
so as not to disrupt traffic or prevent hard-
working citizens from getting a good night's
sleep.[20] Nonetheless, processions with a potential for violence are more likely to be halted in
Britain than in the U.S. In 1977, 1978 and 1980
the racist National Front was kept from marching
in Manchester, London, and various Midlands
cities; while in 1978 the courts said Nazis could
parade in heavily Jewish Skokie, Illinois.[21]

In India, magistrates use Section 144 of the
Indian Code of Criminal Procedure to forbid more
than a certain number of persons from congregating
in a particular place where there is a risk of ob-
struction, injury or danger to human life. These
bans may stand for two months and be used not only

46

to prevent meetings and the gathering of crowds but, also, the carrying of weapons, the exhibition of provocative symbols, and the utterance of inflammatory words. In the U.S., many of these orders would be invalid under the anti-prior-restraint doctrine of New York Times Co. v. United States. The same is true of decrees prohibiting the publication of articles that might cause rioting, decrees upheld in India in Virendra v. Punjab.[22]

As has been seen, French law is not reluctant, under certain circumstances, to permit prior bans of speech that might provoke violence. The distribution of publications that threaten public order can also be forbidden, though the ban cannot be more extensive than is necessary to keep the peace. On February 7, 1934 the prefect of police seized all the copies of the newspaper l'Action Française at Paris and in the Department of the Seine. This seizure took place the day after bitter street fighting between right-wing groups and police that led to the downfall of the French government. The Tribunal of Conflicts said in Action Française[23] that to seize all copies of the newspaper on sale in the Paris region was tortious. However, the Tribunal, as well as the Council of State member known as the commissaire du gouvernement upon whose reasoning it based its conclusions, indicated that the prefect could have proscribed the sale of the paper in those areas where its distribution would have aggravated disorder, for example, the major streets. Actually, as will be seen in subsequent sections, it is not uncommon in France for written matter to be seized or subjected to other forms of prior restraint. The vast majority of these seizures and bans, however, are made for reasons having nothing to do with the prevention of localized street fighting and are based upon legal rules other than those giving prefects and mayors the duty to preserve public order.

To sum up the rules of the four nations about speech threatening riots, the United States'

approach is probably the most tolerant. Its clear
and present danger test permits more speech than do
the (also tolerant) English "likely to occasion a
breach of the peace" or "violence as the natural
consequences of one's statements" doctrines. Words
that are likely to produce riots not immediately
but in the future are punishable under the English
tests but not under the American. American courts,
unlike the English, will tolerate "prior restraint"
only in extreme circumstances; while the French
tolerance of rallies that could lead to brawls applies mainly where the meeting is indoors and
closed to the general public. The Indian ap--
proaches to inflammatory speech are repressive.
Bans on public demonstrations are not uncommon.
Furthermore, the leading constitutional decision
allows the government to outlaw words that have a
tendency or are intended to lead to violence. If
one takes this "bad tendency" rule literally, it,
unlike the clear and present danger doctrine, can
be used to penalize almost all political comment.
The Soviet Union, finally, has not enunciated
rules about the rights of the streetcorner orator
whose words may produce violence. That he usually
would be treated repressively is clear from the way
Soviet police break up purely peaceful, silent, and
small demonstrations to protest governmental curbs
on freedom (see the Pushkin Square episode, _infra_)
and to commemorate events such as Human Rights Day
that are suspect in the eyes of the authorities.[24]

B. Speech and Groups
Considered as Subversive

        This section will discuss the fate in the
five countries of groups that advocate, have in the
past advocated, or are perceived as advocating, the
violent overthrow of the government or the breakup
of the nation or that are considered to be under
the domination of a foreign power. These groups
and their utterance will be labelled "subversive."
Nonetheless, these organizations are of many
different sorts--in communist states, they would

include anti-communist groups, in non-communist states, they would include communist parties, and in every nation they would include unpopular associations about which the rulers of the country are paranoid but which are in fact loyal. The focus here is upon the approach taken by government to speech, anticipated conduct, and non-revolutionary activity undertaken by these groups and by "subversive" individuals acting alone--not upon the punishment meted out to those who actually commit acts of violence.

The United States between 1945 and 1957 adopted repressive approaches to the group it considered most subversive: the U.S. Communist Party (henceforth CPUSA). The weapons it used against the CPUSA were numerous; the best known is the Smith Act of 1940. Section 2 of this measure makes it unlawful for any persons to knowingly teach or advocate the overthrow of any government in the United States by force and violence; Section 3 makes it unlawful to conspire to commit the acts prohibited by Section 2 and other sections of the bill; while Section 7 makes it illegal to hold knowing membership in any organization which advocates the overthrow of the U.S. government by force and violence. Though the Act covers all subversive groups, and was in fact originally intended to deal with fascists as well as communists, since the end of World War II it has been used solely against the latter.

The states and cities joined in the attack on the CPUSA. State laws made it a crime to advocate the overthrow of the state or United States government by force or violence. Communists were barred from state, etc., jobs; they were prevented from becoming lawyers, jurors, or accountants and (in Indiana) from obtaining licenses as professional boxers. One path often taken to keep party members out of these positions was to require them to file loyalty oaths. These are pledges that one does not belong to a subversive organization or advocate the violent overthrow of the government

of the United States or of the state; that he will
promote respect for the flag and statutes of the
United States and of the state and reverence for
law and order; and/or that he will uphold the
constitution and laws of the state and the United
States. Both state legislatures and committees of
the United States Congress ordered suspected communists to appear before them and testify about
their party activities and friendships.

It would take a book in itself to discuss
all the major court cases which have dealt with
the above anti-communist activity; and so only a
few major opinions and trends can be analyzed. In
1948 the twelve leaders of the CPUSA were indicted
for violating Sections 2 and 3 of the Smith Act by
advocating the overthrow of the United States
Government by force and violence and by conspiring
to engage in such advocacy. The defendants argued
that since Sections 2 and 3 of the Smith Act prohibit words, not action, they are violative of the
First Amendment's guarantee of freedom of speech.
The government's evidence boiled down to the fact
that the defendants had taught as truth several of
the leading works of Marxism-Leninism such as The
Communist Manifesto and State and Revolution. Unfortunately for the defendants, there are
sentences in these works where their authors do
call for the violent overthrow of the bourgeois
state. The Supreme Court thus sustained their
conviction in Dennis v. United States.[25] Chief
Justice Vinson wrote an opinion in which he was
joined by three other justices; this "plurality
opinion" was later approved by a majority of the
full Court in Yates v. United States.[26] Accordingly, this plurality opinion can be taken as
"law," as setting forth doctrine which is binding
in future cases. Vinson stated that speech by
communists could be punished if the evil it produced was grave and not improbable, i.e., by looking to the "gravity" of such evil discounted by
its improbability. This "communist free-speech
test" of "grave and not improbable" is not the
same as a "clear and present danger" standard,

despite Vinson's intimations that they are equivalent. Events whose occurrence is not improbable still may be unlikely to take place soon: it is not improbable that poverty will be eliminated in the U.S., but one cannot say that its end is in sight.

So the Supreme Court in Dennis gave the United States executive and legislative branches the green light to eliminate the American Communist Party, though the test propounded in the case can be considered as moderately tolerant since on its face it safeguarded some subversive groups: i.e., those whose activities would be unlikely ever to result in revolution, attempted or successful. By 1957, eighty-nine United States Communist leaders had been convicted of violating Sections 2 and/or 3 of the Smith Act. By that year, too, Stalin was dead and the Soviet Union was under the control of less belligerent-looking dictators. Moreover, the spectre of McCarthyism no longer plagued the country, a spectre which had made many liberals vote for anti-communist legislation in order to prove to the voters that they were not "reds."[27] Also, three of the four members of the four-man Vinson plurality were no longer on the Court, Vinson himself having been succeeded by the more libertarian Earl Warren. Thus in Yates, decided that year, it was held that the Smith Act bans only advocacy of action, present or future, aimed at violent overthrow, and not advocacy of mere belief in such overthrow. Because the trial court in Yates had failed to include this rather technical distinction in its charge to the jury, the conviction of the fourteen was reversed. In practice, Yates emasculated Sections 2 and 3 of the Smith Act. Since the United States government does not believe that it can prove in court that American communists advocate action aimed at violent overthrow (as opposed to belief therein), it has not prosecuted anyone under these clauses since the date the Yates decision was announced.

In fact, serious doubt that the view of

51

Dennis (i.e., that the advocacy of violent revolution by members of a tightly knit, well-organized group dominated by a foreign power can be punished in certain cases, even though it creates no clear and present danger of a successful or attempted coup) is still the law of the land was created by the 1969 case of Brandenburg v. Ohio.[28] Brandenburg, a member of the Ku Klux Klan, was found to have violated an Ohio statute similar to the Smith Act. The Court, in reversing his conviction, not only said that speech advocating any sort of violence could not be abridged unless it was likely and intended to produce imminent lawless action (emphasis mine); but added that Dennis stood for this very proposition! Other aspects of the federal and state anti-communist program also have been attacked by the Supreme Court and lower courts. For example, numerous loyalty oaths have been invalidated as "too vague"[29] or as keeping people (including inactive members of subversive organizations) out of government employment who constitutionally cannot be denied such.[30]

Thus the American judiciary is now adopting a tolerant approach to the CPUSA. However, though the Smith Act's days are numbered, it would be incorrect to say that the conduct of other segments of the American polity toward that Party in particular and to subversive groups generally has definitively switched from policies of repression to ones of tolerance. It is in practice still difficult for an avowed communist to get a government job and the Party (and other subversive groups) are heavily infiltrated by the Federal Bureau of Investigation and local police forces. The members of radical associations are sometimes harassed by being arrested for violations of non-political criminal statutes, such as laws involving narcotics. In the 1960's, the FBI waged a "Cointelpro" campaign against individuals and organizations it deemed extremist. As part of that campaign, it wrote unfavorable letters to his College about an anti-Vietnam War professor; encouraged the New Jersey State Police to raid a vacation retreat maintained by the Trotskyist Socialist Workers' Party on the ground that it did not have a liquor license; and tried to get an individual discharged as a scoutmaster because his wife was a member of that party. Also, a meeting sponsored by a far-left group may well be subject to surveillance by law enforcement officials.

Early in the century, Britain's treatment of those who urged the use of force and violence to overthrow the government was repressive. In 1909 an Indian who had printed a magazine that defended the technique of political assassination to free India from British rule was convicted in the case of R. v. Aldred[31] and sent to jail for a year for the crime of "seditious libel." Judge Coleridge, in his summation to the jury, at one point went so far as to say that any incitement to the use of force against the state is a seditious libel; but then told the jurors to take into account the nature of the audience, distinguishing between "professors or divines" on the one hand and "an excited audience of young and uneducated men" on the other. He concluded that the defendant was guilty if the language used was "calculated" to produce the violence called for.

In 1924 J. R. Campbell, a member of the British Communist Party, was prosecuted for urging British soldiers to avoid war, to stop shooting strikers and to form committees that would be the nucleus of an organization making it possible to smash capitalism forever. Campbell was charged in 1924 under a 1797 Incitement to Mutiny Act but the accusation was then dropped. Britain's first Labour government (under J. Ramsey MacDonald) was in office at the time, and had to resign because of the criticism directed against it for deciding not to press the case. The Tories emerged victorious at the new elections, and in 1925 Campbell and 11 other communist leaders were arrested for conspiracy to publish seditious libels and to urge others to violate the 1797 Act: all the defendants were found guilty.[32]

53

Since World War II, the British government's policies towards domestic communists have on the whole been ones of toleration; though the police infiltrate meetings of radical groups, tap their wires, open their mail, and keep file cards on their members.[33] Presumably, any British communist or member of another subversive group who under certain circumstances urged violent overthrow could, under the doctrine of R. v. Aldred, supra, be prosecuted for publishing a seditious libel even though his words created no clear and present danger. But no such action has been brought against a communist or fascist and, in fact, the only such prosecution brought since World War II involved an editor who had published an anti-Semitic article as a reaction against Jewish terrorist attacks on British soldiers stationed in Palestine.[34] The editor was acquitted, the judge in his charge to the jury setting forth a "natural consequence" test but emphasizing the need for a free press.

The British government does not require its civil servants to take a loyalty oath. However, the defection of several high-ranking government employees to the Soviet Union induced it to set up a scheme for determining whether or not an employee engaged in work which involves the security of the state is a security risk. Not only homosexuals and drunkards, but also members and recent members of the British Communist or Fascist Parties or communists or fascist sympathizers or persons associated with communists or fascists or their sympathizers who are engaged in such work may be deemed security risks, and thus transferred to a non-sensitive position or dismissed from government service entirely. The Minister who heads the suspect's department first decides whether there is a "prima facie" case supporting the charge that he is a security risk. The suspect then has the right to a hearing conducted by three Advisers. At this hearing he is not allowed to have a lawyer, not informed of the evidence against him, and not permitted to cross-examine witnesses, since the government wants the identity of its witnesses to remain secret so that they will be available for informing in the future. He can ask people to testify about his character; but they cannot be used to rebut what he thinks to be the evidence against him. After hearing his case, the Advisers reach a decision, which the Minister does not have to follow. Actually, only a handful of British government employees have been transferred to new jobs as a result of these procedures and only a much smaller number have been discharged from government service as security risks.[35]

In America 14 million individuals, one-sixth of the nation's work force, are covered by federal or state loyalty-security procedures, including President Eisenhower's Executive Order 10450 for federal employees requiring that their hiring or retention by the government be "clearly consistent with national security"; while the analogous British procedures reach far fewer than one million people.[36] This Order as it was originally drafted contained, as one of the criteria which the Civil Service Commission was to apply in determining whether one's employment by the federal government would be so consistent, his membership in any one of the three hundred groups on the Attorney General's subversive list. This list was abolished in 1974 by order of President Nixon and so it can no longer be used in any way to determine fitness for federal employment. Standards still appropriate under Order 10450 include whether one advocates the violent overthrow of the government and whether he is an alcoholic or drug addict. For practical purposes, the Commission now concentrates on investigating the loyalty of applicants for "sensitive" jobs, and of the incumbents of these positions, which include those with defense and nuclear agencies. Since 1976, the standard federal job application form has ceased asking whether the applicant is a member of the Communist Party or of another group that advocates the overthrow of the government by violent means.[37]

55

The Communist Party of India (CPI) renounced violence in 1950 and in a democratic election won control of the government of Kerala state in 1957. It regularly puts up candidates for seats in both state and national parliaments; and has at times done rather well in national elections. However, it has been beset by the same factionalism that characterizes international communism as a whole. When the Sino-Soviet split became public, some Indian communists left the CPI and formed a pro-Maoist group called the CP (M) (Communist Party, Marxist). As a result of the 1977 West Bengal state elections, the CP (M) became the dominant party in a five-party Marxist coalition taking control of the state and is today probably the most important of India's Marxist groupings. An even more radical splinter group is the Communist Party of India, Marxist-Leninist (CPI-ML). The anti-police and landlord "Naxalite" violence inspired by this group in West Bengal caused the federal and state governments to jail thousands of its members and kill many more. It contested the 1977 state elections, however, and won one seat.

The Indian Government's treatment of communists has with the above-noted exception and a few others been closer to the British tolerant than to the American repressive approaches to domestic communism. As was just indicated, the Communist Party and its offshoots extensively participate in the electoral process. In fact, Indian policy vis-à-vis the CPI and CP (M) is in some respects one of encouragement of diversity, for they often enter into electoral alliances with other parties and thus are actually strengthened by the political leadership of these parties.

The central government did take over Kerala twice when in communist hands and West Bengal while that state was first under the control of the CP (M)-led United Front; in said instances, the reason given was that communist rule was producing chaos. Furthermore, in 1950, immediately after the

56

promulgation of the Indian Constitution, Parliament passed a Preventive Detention Act. The provisions of this bill and its successors will be discussed more fully in the next-to-last chapter; but suffice it to say here that the 1950 Act permitted the detention without trial of any person who law enforcement authorities determined to their own satisfaction was going to act in a manner, inter alia, "prejudicial to the defense of India, the security of the state, the maintenance of public order . . ."[38] There was no need to prove that a detainee was guilty of past or present criminal activity. Of the 10,000 persons who were detained under the Act of 1950, over half were communists who had engaged in violence in 1947 through 1949 and who the Indian government feared would do so in the future.[39] At times, pro-Chinese communists, Mizo and Naga rebels in northeast India, and communist-led Naxalites all felt the lash of preventive detention laws. Furthermore, as a glance at the facts of Kedar Nath v. State of Bihar[40] will remind the reader, a few communists who "on the soapbox" urged violence have been sentenced under Section 124A of the Indian Penal Code making it illegal to excite disaffection toward the government of India; and this law could be used against communists more frequently in the future.

The various communist organizations are not the only groups which have been perceived by Indians as threatening the survival of the country's political system. For example, the north Indian state of Jammu and Kashmir has a Moslem majority, and many Pakistanis feel that India seized Kashmir by force of arms and that it has ignored a United Nations resolution calling for a plebiscite to determine the state's future. Most Indians, though, feel quite strongly that Kashmir should remain part of India; and view any demand that it be made independent or given to Pakistan as as much a threat to the preservation of India as is a call for violent communist revolution. Thus, Sheikh Abdullah, the leader of the Moslem Kashmiris (and quondam friend of Prime Minister Jawaharlal Nehru) spent

13 of the 17 years prior to 1971 in jail under
federal or state Preventive Detention laws because
of his view that India should hold a plebiscite on
Kashmir.[41] More generally, it is a violation of
Section 2 of the Criminal Law Amendment Act of 1961
to call into question the country's territorial
integrity.

Article 50 of the Brezhnev Constitution provides that "In conformity with the interests of the
working people and for the purpose of strengthening
the socialist system, citizens of the USSR shall be
guaranteed freedom of speech, press, assembly,
meetings, street processions and demonstrations."
(Article 125 of the Stalin Constitution was almost
identical.) This book will not consider the Soviet
Union of the late 1930's, when Stalin's purges
jailed or killed millions. What it will analyze
here is the attitude of the Soviet state since the
downfall of Nikita S. Khrushchev in 1964 toward
those whom it views as threats to the security of
the regime. Actually, a good number of these individuals have no desire to overturn the Communist
regime by force; but it makes sense to treat of
them in this section because the Soviet government
views them as potential counterrevolutionaries.
One episode epitomizes the Soviet Union's repressive approach to such persons, the trial in
February, 1966, of two writers, Andrei Sinyavsky
and Yuli Daniel. The case is over fifteen years
old, but the jurisprudence is current. (The tran-
script of this trial was smuggled to the West,
translated into English, edited by Max Hayward, and
published as a book entitled On Trial.)[42]

Both Sinyavsky and Daniel wrote certain works
that the Soviet authorities viewed as "anti-Soviet"
and a threat to national security, the latter at
times using the pseudonym of Nikolai Arzhak and the
former that of Abram Tertz. Among the works of
Daniel which angered the regime was a novel entitled This Is Moscow Speaking. This satire commences with a decree of the Presidium of the
Supreme Soviet declaring a "Public Murder Day" on

58

which all Soviet citizens would have the right to
kill any other citizen except policemen and
soldiers. On the big day, there is actually very
little killing, and the Central Committee of the
Communist Party later issues a letter deploring the
lack of bloodshed. Daniel's hero, a war veteran,
dreams of killing those who were responsible for
the excesses of Stalinism and who still enjoy
positions of power. In his monologue describing
the dream he makes the following remarks.

Hatred gives one the right to murder . . .
And what about the fat faced masters of our
destiny, our leaders and teachers, true sons
of the people . . . The best friends of Soviet
gymnasts, writers, textile workers, colorblind
persons and madmen? What should be done with
them? Should they be forgiven? What about
1937? . . . No, no, no, they must be treated
differently. Do you remember still how to do
it? The fuse . . . pull out the pin . . .
throw . . . And these people? I've seen them
before! Only then they had belts with the in-
scription Gott mit uns on the buckles, caps
with Red Stars, knee boots . . . ; over the
body runs a Studebaker, two Studebakers, eight
Studebakers, forty Studebakers, and you lie
there flattened like a frog; we've had all
that before! I got up from the bed, went to
the window, and wiped my sweaty forehead with
the curtain.[43]

Sinyavsky, a critic of the doctrine of
"socialist realism" that the Communist Party wants
Soviet writers to adopt, wrote a novel <u>Lyubimov</u>
(translated into English as <u>The Makepeace Experi-
ment</u>), in which one Tikhomirov discovers that he
has hypnotic powers. He uses these to remove the
small town of Lyubimov from Soviet reality and sets
up his own regime there. He controls the population by hypnotizing people into believing that they
are already prosperous, that water is champagne and
that inedible red pickles are sausages. One of the
passages in this fantasy mentions Lenin baying at

the moon, while a sentence in his critique <u>On Socialist Realism</u> says that a cult of Leninism is impossible because "Lenin is too much like an ordinary man and his image is too realistic: small, bald, dressed in civilian clothes."[44]

At worst, Daniel's <u>This Is Moscow Speaking</u> indicates to the unseen audience of the novel that it might not be too tragic if some of the Stalinist relics who still infest the Soviet government were to be shot; though, based upon the last sentence of the above-quoted monologue, it is more likely that all he means is that they should be retired without violence even though they are little more than murderers themselves. At worst Sinyavsky is asserting that Lenin is a mortal man like the rest of us and that the Soviet government occasionally feeds its subjects doses of over-optimism. Yet both of them were tried and convicted under Section 1 of Article 70 of the Criminal Code of the Russian Republic, which provides that:

> Agitation or propaganda carried out with the purpose of subverting or weakening the Soviet regime or in order to commit particularly dangerous crimes against the state, the dissemination for the said purposes of slanderous inventions defamatory to the Soviet political and social system, as well as the dissemination or production or harboring for the said purposes of literature of similar content, are punishable by imprisonment for a period of from six months to seven years and with exile from two to five years, or without exile, or by exile from two to five years.[45]

Daniel received a five year jail sentence; Sinyavsky, one of seven years.

The Sinyavsky-Daniel trial is not an isolated instance of what happens in post-Khrushchev Russia to those whom the regime views as threats to its existence. On January 22, 1967, five young people, including Viktor Khaustov and Vladimir Bukovsky,

demonstrated peacefully in Pushkin Square in
Moscow to demand the release of Sinyavsky and
Daniel and the repeal of Article 190(1) and 190(3)
of the Criminal Code of the R.S.F.S.R. Article
190(1) outlaws "the systematic dissemination by
word of mouth of deliberately false statements
derogatory to the Soviet State and social system,
as also the preparation or dissemination of such
statements in written, printed or any other form
. . ."; while Article 190(3) makes illegal the
organization of, or active participation in, group
activities involving a grave breach of public
order, or clear disobedience to the legitimate demands of representatives of authority. Khaustov
and Bukovsky (now in exile) were both convicted
for violating this Article 190(3) against which
they protested (and which could cover soapbox
orators whose words threaten violence), the former
going to jail for three years and the latter being
sentenced to a forced-labor camp for the same
length of time.[46]

In 1970 the Soviet writer Andrei Amalrik was
arrested and charged with violating Article 190(1).
His supposedly defamatory material appeared in his
Will the Soviet Union Survive Until 1984? in which
he says that the country will be torn apart by
ethnic animosities, economic inertia, and war with
China. He was convicted in November, 1970, and
sentenced to three years' confinement in a labor
camp.[47] Four Soviet dissident intellectuals,
Aleksandr Ginzburg (now also in exile), Yuri
Galanskov, Aleksei Dobrovolsky and Vera Lashkova,
were arrested in 1967 for publishing Phoenix, an
underground journal, and also for gathering and
smuggling out of the country a collection of
materials (the White Book) on the Sinyavsky-Daniel
trial. Phoenix contained Sinyavsky's article What
is Socialist Realism? which was critical of the
Soviet practice of allowing the publication only
of literature that adopts a "realistic style" and
that shows the Soviet system in an optimistic
light. It also included an article entitled A
Description of Events at the Pochaevsky Monastery

in our Days, which opposed bitterly the government's persecution of the Orthodox Church and the
closing of one of its monasteries. Though it contained no call for an overthrow of the Soviet regime, Ginzburg and his co-defendants were convicted
under Article 70 of the Criminal Code of the
Russian Republic: he received five years and
Galanskov seven years in a labor camp.[48]

In addition to the above provisions of the
Criminal Code of the RSFSR (and analogous legislation in other republics), the Soviet authorities
have various other laws which can be used against
actual or potential "subversives." Critics of the
system have been convicted under an "anti-parasite"
law which had as its original purpose the punishment of people who refuse to work without any excuse;[49] while the government has put other
political suspects into mental institutions or
arrested them for "ordinary" crimes like rape.[50]
It has about a thousand dissenters confined in
psychiatric hospitals now; and Amnesty International contends that beatings and involuntary drug
injections are common in these facilities.[51] One
scholar estimates that there are now tens of
thousands of political prisoners in the U.S.S.R.
while Amnesty claims that there are at least ten
thousand.[52]

To be fair to the Soviet political system,
dissidents are hardly ever sentenced to death in
this post-Stalinist era. Also, not every alleged
anti-communist who is tried under one of the above-
mentioned laws will be convicted. Thus, according
to Robert Conquest, "A personal diary with an anti-
Soviet content" was held not to fall under the
range of speech proscribed by the Article 70 under
which Sinyavsky, Daniel and many others have been
convicted; and the same result was reached in a
case involving "deliberately incorrect statements
and opinions about the official activities and way
of life of individual leaders."[53] Moreover,
though it may not criticize the regime, even the
official press reveals numerous instances of

bureaucratic ineptness and dishonesty. More importantly, censuring governmental policies, even important governmental policies, is often tolerated; but the writer must refrain from making his condemnation appear to be an attack on such fundamental principles as the "'leading role of the Communist party,' the principle of socialism, the work of the central party organs and central party officials, the wisdom of Lenin and Marx. . . . and so forth."[54] In 1980, the government even allowed the publication of an article praising the anti-communist poet Boris Pasternak, who was reviled by the regime just before his death in 1960.[55]

The governing French Socialists have allowed the French Communist Party (PCF) four Cabinet positions and will probably continue to enter into electoral alliances under which they support some PCF parliamentary candidates in runoff elections. Thus the French state's current policy toward the PCF is encouragement of diversity, giving some thinking of voting for the PCF the assurance that a vote for it will not be wasted.

France has no loyalty-security program such as that in effect in the United States under President Eisenhower's Executive Order 10450.[56] To ban the members of a political party such as the PCF from public employment would run counter to the fervently held French tradition, enshrined in the 1789 Declaration of Rights, that all Frenchmen are equal before the law and thus are equally admissible to all public employment according to their capacities and without any other distinction than that of their virtues and talents. The well-known decision of the Council of State in Barel[57] put an end to an abortive attempt to rid the French bureaucracy of communist influence. In 1953 several communists were denied permission to participate in the competitive examination for entry into the École Nationale d'Administration, the institution whose graduates staff the higher ranks of the civil service, including the Council of State itself. The would-be candidates were able to demonstrate to the satisfaction of the Council that they had been turned away simply because they were communists. That body then annulled for excess of power the decision refusing to let them participate. It emphasized that to remove individuals from the lists of candidates solely because of their political opinions would violate the principle of the equality of the access of all Frenchmen to public employment and public offices. Similar to Barel was Guille.[58] M. Guille was the "inspector" of the academy of Haute-Marne at the same time that he was a communist municipal counsellor. The government abolished his administrative position and forced him into classroom teaching on the ostensible ground that the law did not require the employment of inspectors of academies. The Council of State, in annulling the decision ending his post, went on the narrow theory that it was not one that the government could abolish freely in the interests of the service.

But it would be misleading to state that France tolerates disloyalty among its civil servants. "Untrustworthy" civil servants who have not done anything to subject them to disciplinary action have been transferred from sensitive to non-sensitive positions within the same "cadre": Guille, supra, prevents shifting them to another "cadre."[59] Moreover, all civil servants owe a duty of "reserve" with respect to their conduct on and off the job, the violation of which can result in their being disciplined or discharged. The higher the rank of the civil servant, the more necessary it is that he respect this duty.[60] As a commissaire du gouvernement of the Council of State has remarked: "In his job, the State can demand of the bureaucrat that he abstain from any act suitable to create a doubt, not only of his neutrality, but also of his loyalty to institutions."[61] Even outside working hours, he has this duty of reserve that "ought to be respected in the measure of the

64

responsibilities which he assumes in social life by virtue of (his) rank in the hierarchy and the nature of (his) functions."[62] The Council has considered as violating the duty of reserve an inspector of an academy who attacked the political system of Martinique without taking the necessary precautions to see that his remarks did not get published in an Algerian newspaper.[63] The leading decision on this duty is Teissier.[64] Here the Council permitted the discharge of the Director of the National Center for Scientific Research because he refused to disavow a statement, circulated by an organization of which he was head, attacking in "scandalous" and "odious" terms the expulsion of Polish professors teaching in France. M. Teissier lost his job when he told the National Minister of Education that though he did not personally participate in the drafting of the document, his opinion on the issue was a matter solely for his conscience.

Before World War II numerous extreme right-wing groups sprung up on French soil in response to the rise of Mussolini and Hitler, the economic dislocations caused by the Great Depression, and the entry of the Communist Party into the Popular Front government of 1936. These and older right-wing organizations found sympathy among those who had never accepted the legitimacy of the French Revolution and among professional anti-Semites or those whose businesses were being threatened by Jewish competition. The most influential of the older groups, the Action Française, arose to defend those army officers whose unfairness toward the Jewish Captain Alfred Dreyfus was being attacked by the liberal press and liberal intellectuals such as Emile Zola; and in its early days received support from devout Roman Catholics who felt that the Republican government was persecuting the Church. Most of the far-right groups (henceforth referred to as the "Leagues") that existed in France during the 1930's did seek the violent overthrow of the Republican regime and its replacement by an authoritarian state.

In reaction to street riots precipitated by the Leagues, Parliament passed a law on January 10, 1936, providing that the executive branch of government may dissolve organizations that meet one of the following three criteria:

1. They provoke armed manifestations in the streets.

2. They appear to be private militias or combat groups.

3. They have as a goal the attack on the integrity of national territory or the attempt to overthrow by force (<u>attenter par la force</u>) the Republican form of government. Those who participate in the maintenance or the reconstruction of a dissolved group can be fined and jailed.

On February 13, 1936 an automobile carrying Socialist Deputy Georges Monnet, Mrs. Monnet and soon-to-be-Premier Socialist Deputy Léon Blum crossed the end of a funeral procession marking the death of Jacques Bainville, a figure of importance in the Action Française. Blum's car was surrounded by a group that attacked the Socialists. This was enough for the Cabinet: it dissolved the Action Française immediately, and other right-wing groups were soon afterwards disbanded.

The Law of 10th of January 1936 has often been considered by the Council of State. Of course, the Council cannot invalidate it as unconstitutional, but it can and does decide whether the executive's dissolution of a particular group is consistent with the statute's terms. The leading case on the matter is <u>Pujo</u>,[65] in which the Council upheld the dissolution of the Action Française and some of its subsidiary groups. The Council maintained that the 1936 law legitimates, among other things, the crushing of all groups which advocate the violent overthrow of the Republican form of government even when these groups do not attempt to put their ideas into execution.

66

It was clear that the Action Française believed in
the restoration of the monarchy by all means,
especially the use of force. Charles Maurras, its
leader, was quoted as saying that "It is necessary
to constitute a royalist state of mind, and in
order for this spirit to be fired, one must strike
a 'coup de force' to reestablish the monarch; the
coup de force is legitimate. . . . Having condemned
the regime let us work to execute it." In Parti
National Populaire[66] the Council sustained a dissolution of the Parti National Populaire (PNP)
pronounced by the executive on June 18, 1936. The
PNP claimed that it was a political party and thus
not covered by the law of January 10, 1936. The
Council asserted that it was not a genuine political party, but simply a front for the fascist
league called the Jeunesses Patriotes, definitely
a combat group and thus subject to abolition under
the statute. According to the leaders of the PNP
itself, it was the "living expression" of the
Jeunesses Patriotes. As it was in reality nothing
but the Jeunesses Patriotes, who were keeping
their militants ready for use when the time was
ripe, it could itself legally be outlawed.

The law of January 10, 1936 is alive and well
in France of the present day. After the student-
worker riots and strikes of May 1968, the government of President Charles de Gaulle used it to ban
eleven left-wing groups and one right-wing student
group.[67] In 1973 the executive outlawed the extreme left-wing Communist (Trotskyist) League and
the rightist Ordre Nouveau. The League had on
several occasions clashed violently with the police
and attempted to physically prevent a meeting of
the Ordre called to protest illegal immigration.
Early in 1974 the government banned two Breton
Liberation Groups that had bombed government buildings. In 1974 it dissolved the Peasant Front for
the Liberation of Corsica and in 1975 it ended the
legal existence of Action for the Rebirth of
Corsica.[68] In 1980, the fascist, anti-Semitic
group known as FANE was disbanded.[69] The majority
of the bans of 1968 were given the imprimatur of

the Council of State in several decisions handed down July 21, 1970. For example, in Krivine et Frank[70] it sustained the actions against the Communist Revolutionary Youth and Internationalist Communist Party groups on the ground that they had provoked armed demonstrations in the streets by tracts, posters, and orders to their militants.

The major French statute on freedom of association is the law of July 1, 1901. This recognizes as legal, inter alia, "undeclared" and "declared" associations. Many political groups are "declared" associations. These have judicial personality and receive it simply by depositing a notice (déclaration) and the articles of association at the prefect's office. When they deposit this notice, they must be given a receipt.

The Council of State in January, 1971 sustained in Geismar[71] a governmental decree of May 27, 1970, dissolving the Maoist La Gauche Proletarienne on the ground that it had provoked armed demonstrations. In protest, several French intellectuals formed a new group called "The Friends of the Cause of the People" and filed with the Paris prefect the papers required by the 1901 law. Had things gone normally, the founders would have been handed the receipt and The Friends would have been a "declared" association with legal personality. However, the prefect, acting on the instructions of Raymond Marcelin, the Minister of the Interior, refused to issue the receipt on the ground that The Friends were simply a reincarnation of the dissolved La Gauche Proletarienne. To back up Marcelin's probably illegal act, Parliament enacted a law which gave the prefect with whom the notice was filed the right to withhold the receipt and forward the documents to the Public Prosecutor (Procurateur de la République) in any case in which it appeared that the association had an immoral or illicit purpose or was an attempt to reconstitute an illegal association. It was this bill that the Constitutional Council invalidated in July, 1971 on the ground that it contravened freedom of association, a fundamental principle recognized by the laws of the Republic (the 1901 law) and thus enshrined in the Preamble to the Constitution of the Fifth Republic.

The famous law of July 29, 1881, provides in its Article 1 that the press is free. However, there are numerous articles (some added subsequently to 1881) in that law (henceforth referred to as the Press Law of 1881) that derogate from the freedom of the press and that cover certain purely oral as well as written or graphic statements. Article 24.3 makes it a crime to apologize for murder, theft, war crimes or for collaboration with the enemy. This paragraph was used in 1977 to fine editors who criticized police behavior in a "shootout"; in 1978 to convict an Alsatian who asserted that Hitler's murder of the Jews was a myth; and in 1980 to jail a neo-Nazi anti-Semite.[72] In Min. Publique c. Malliavin[73] a Vichy supporter received a fine for protesting the issuance of five postage stamps honoring the heroes of the Resistance. M. Malliavin declared strongly that the Vichy and neo-fascist victims of the vengeance of the Resistance were men of striking merit as outstanding as the Resistance heroes. The Court of Appeals of Paris asserted that this declaration was not a simple plea for the rehabilitation of the collaborationists but an apology for their crimes--and thus a violation of Article 24.3. In the eyes of the court, to declare men such as Action Française leader Charles Maurras on a par with the heroes of the Resistance was a "revolting comparison."

Article 24, clause 1 of the Press Law punishes any direct provocation to certain crimes against the security of the state, as defined by the Penal Code, while Article 25 makes illegal all provocations addressed to soldiers with the intent of getting them to ignore their military duties and the obedience they owe their commanders. On the whole, these two Articles have been interpreted narrowly by the French courts, since they are viewed as restrictions upon the fundamental freedom of the press. Thus in Jauneau et Vigne[74] the Correctional Tribunal of Beauvais decided in 1950 that it was no violation of Article 24 clause 1 to say that France was committing atrocities in its attempt to put down the nationalist rebellion in Vietnam and that peace there was inevitable. There was no provocation here to a determinate act constitutive of a crime against the security of the State: for conviction, the prosecution would have had to prove that the defendants had urged people to adhere to a group that was trying to demoralize the army. The Correctional Tribunal of Montpellier refused to convict a man prosecuted for violating Article 25 who had written an article stating that it was necessary to explain to the soldiers and conscripts the necessity to end the Vietnamese war. The court could not discover here any appeal to the commission of a military infraction.[75]

Nonetheless, convictions under Article 24, clause 1 and Article 25 are not unknown. In Finkelstein,[76] for example, a defendant was fined for distributing to students a tract saying that the government wants to keep them in poverty and drag them into the dirty war in Indochina. It urged the students not to go to the war and to support the dockers who were refusing to handle arms destined for the Far East. According to the Court of Appeals for Nancy, Finkelstein did violate Article 24, clause 1, since he was provoking the students to participate in an enterprise of demoralizing the army, a crime against state security. And during the Algerian war the publisher of a book written by a deserter from the French army was fined for provoking soldiers to disobedience. The book discussed desertions by the author and others.[77]

Article 14 of the Press Law is used for a variety of purposes, including the banning of certain books and newspapers that the government deems subversive. It provides that the government

may interdict the distribution and sale of any
publication of a foreign origin or originally
written in a foreign language. A work written in
French but originally published in another country
falls within the scope of Article 14. Moreover,
the administrative tribunal cannot question the
decision that the ban on such a book is necessary
to preserve public order.[78] Article 14 was thus
allowed to bar a journal edited and printed in
France in French that exactly reproduced the most
important revolutionary texts of a revolutionary
Cuban journal that itself had been banned in
France. The Council of State thought that for
practical purposes the French journal was the same
publication as the Cuban, and thus that the former
as well as the latter could be outlawed under
Article 14.[79]

One can sum up this section by stating that
the British approach to subversive speech and the
peaceful activities of subversive groups and individuals is usually tolerant; the Soviet repressive; and the American, Indian and French tolerant
but proportionately less so than the British. The
fact that, for example, American communists now
run for public office has to be weighed against
the pervasive infiltration of unpopular groups by
federal and local police and the difficulty their
members still encounter in obtaining public jobs.
The Indian legitimation of several Communist
parties and its ruling parties' habit of concluding electoral alliances with these marxist groups
have to be balanced against its sporadic preventive detentions of thousands of extreme
leftists and of individuals who have called into
question the sanctity of the country's boundaries
of the moment. And the French Communist Party is
strong; but small extremist groups may be banned--
and their leaders jailed for apologizing for
murder.

C. Criticism of the Government and of Public Officials

This section deals with the individual who sheds doubt upon the ability of a public official to do his job properly or who, without calling for violent overthrow or provoking a riot, makes it known that he believes that the existing system is not a success and should be replaced by another. To give an example from the United States, it is concerned with the person who is saying that the Supreme Court is coddling criminals or that President Reagan is paranoid; but not with the Communist or Klansman who urges his followers to overthrow the government or commit sabotage or arson.

The United States Supreme Court feels strongly that "the right . . . to praise or criticize governmental agents and to clamor and contend for or against change . . . is . . . one of the very agencies the Framers of our Constitution thoughtfully and deliberately selected to improve our society and keep it free."[80] This philosophy was applied in the leading case of New York Times v. Sullivan.[81] The New York Times had published an advertisement at the request of a group called the "Committee to Defend Martin Luther King and the Struggle for Freedom in the South." The advertisement asserted that:

> In Montgomery, Alabama, after students sang "My Country, 'Tis of Thee" on the State Capitol stops, their leaders were expelled from school, and truckloads of police armed with shotguns and teargas ringed the Alabama State College Campus. When the entire student government protested to state authorities by refusing to re-register, their dining-hall was padlocked in an attempt to starve

them into submission. .Again and again the
Southern violators have answered Dr. King's
peaceful protests with intimidation and
violence. They have bombed his home almost
killing his wife and child. They have
assaulted his person. They have arrested
him seven times--for "speeding," "loitering,"
and similar "offenses." And now they have
charged him with "perjury. . . ."

The plaintiff in this libel action was the man in
ultimate charge of the city police of Montgomery,
Alabama. He asserted that this advertisement
accused him of inflicting upon King and the students of Alabama State College the several
injustices it described. As it was admitted that
he had had no hand in them, the Supreme Court of
Alabama affirmed a $500,000 verdict in his favor
in an Alabama trial court.

The Supreme Court of the United States reversed this judgment. It held that a public
official cannot recover for a damaging untruth
about his official conduct "unless he proves that
the statement was made with 'actual malice'--that
is, with knowledge that it was false or with reck-
less disregard of whether it was false or not."[82]
The Court also added that no malice could be found
in this case even though the New York Times had
never bothered to check its files before accepting
the ad--and also remarked in passing that mere
attacks on the government cannot under the U.S.
Constitution be made the basis of a libel action,
for the law of "seditious libel" has no place in
American jurisprudence.

As a result of New York Times v. Sullivan,
therefore, one who lies about a public official
cannot lose in a libel action brought against him,
unless the official can prove that the falsehood
was malicious, which is difficult though not impossible to do. (The Supreme Court defends the
result in New York Times on the ground that if a
newspaper or speaker can be successfully sued for

73

libel, it will not publish the truth about the conduct of governmental officials for fear that
juries will find it false.) Great Britain has not
adopted the rule of the New York Times case. As a
consequence, one who tells a lie about a public
officer there will be liable to him even though
the untruth was uttered in a sincere belief that it
was accurate. Thus in Dingle v. Associated Newspapers, Ltd.[83] the town clerk of Manchester wrote a
letter to the shareholders of a cemetery corporation telling them that the city wanted to buy their
property for conversion for park or educational
uses and that it was offering them the price of ₤1
per share. In fact, this was a very generous
offer, but the London Daily Mail published an
article implying that the town clerk, the chief
executive officer of a British city and thus a
"public official" within the New York Times rule,
knew that the shares were worth a good deal more.
The clerk sued the Mail for libel and recovered
₤4,000, making it clear that a public official
whom someone falsely criticizes may recover damages
as easily as can a defamed private party. It is
generally believed, incidentally, that the relatively strict British policy epitomized by Dingle
has inhibited the press from reporting corruption
involving officials.[84]

If one attacks a member of Parliament in the
press or in a speech, not only may he be subject to
a successful libel action, but, moreover, there is
a chance (much less now than a few years ago) that
he will be adjudged in contempt of the House to
which the individual he criticizes belongs. One
guilty of a contempt of the House of Commons may be
sent to jail, though it is most probable that he wil
escape with a reprimand. The House of Commons has a
Committee of Privileges which decides whether or
not a contempt has been committed. Mere criticism
of policy will not give rise to a contempt citation; only allegations of dishonesty or corruption
on the part of MP's that are not made with an intent to reveal the truth will result in citations
of this sort. In other words, an assertion that

the Government is too favorable to the large private banks would not cause the author to be cited
for contempt. However, an accusation that the
Prime Minister wanted to weaken the British Broadcasting Corporation because a company in which he
had stock was planning to set up a television station would have led to the imposition of this
punishment if made before 1968--unless the speaker
or writer could have proven that he made the
charge, whether true or false, not for political
reasons or to revenge a grudge but to put an end
to the alleged corruption. The 1967-68 Committee
of Privileges declared that a critic ought to be
adjudged in contempt of the House only when
judicial remedies such as libel suits are inade-
quate or when the comments obstruct a Member in
the performance of his Parliamentary duties.
That this additional requirement provides real
protection for those who make disparaging comments
about MP's is seen in the decision of the 1976-77
Committee on Privileges not to inquire into an
allegation made by a Tory MP in a speech circulated to the press that thirty of his Labour
colleagues were "undercover agents for alien
political creeds."[85]

An actual event may indicate even more
clearly what sort of criticism of Parliament
would have given rise to a contempt citation before 1968. The British Government imposed petrol
(gasoline) rationing in December, 1956, after the
attack on Egypt and the closing of the Suez Canal.
When the newspaper The Sunday Express heard that
some MP's and candidates for Parliament were entitled to extra petrol allowances it lamented that

Tomorrow a time of hardship starts for
everyone. For everyone? Include the poli-
ticians out of that.
Petrol rationing will pass them by.
They are to get prodigious supplementary
allowances.
Isn't it fantastic?
The small baker, unable to carry out his

rounds, may be pushed out of business. The one-man taxi company may founder. The parent who lives in the country may plead in vain for petrol to drive the kids to school.

But everywhere the tanks of the politicians will be brimming over. . . . there is not a speak of protest (from Parliament)!

If politicians are more interested in privileges for themselves than in fair shares for all, let it swiftly be made plain to them that the public do not propose to tolerate it!

The Committee of Privileges said that the article contended that Members of Parliament were entitled to an unfair allocation of petrol against which they did not protest because of self-interest. The editor of the paper was summoned to appear before the House where he made a lengthy apology and so received only a reprimand.[86]

In the United States articles such as the one appearing in the Sunday Express about Parliament's allegedly refusing to subject itself to the petrol rationing it imposed on the ordinary Englishman are constitutionally protected. In the first place, the United States Supreme Court said over fifty years ago that Congress cannot itself adjudge one guilty of contempt of Congress when all that he has done is write a letter or article attacking it or some of its members.[87] Nor could Congress constitutionally pass a bill providing that defamatory or scandalous remarks about itself or its members made outside the halls of Congress are punishable as a contempt after a trial by a court. In Garrison v. Louisiana,[88] a "child" of New York Times v. Sullivan, the Supreme Court held that untrue statements about public officials could not (except where made with malice) constitutionally be made the basis for criminal libel prosecutions. And it would be ridiculous to allow one to be sent to jail for vituperative remarks about Congressmen and Senators by the simple device of switching the label of the crime for which he was prosecuted from "criminal libel" to "contempt of Congress."

The British law with respect to verbal attacks on judges has also become much more tolerant in recent years, as the following two cases attest. (We are talking about out-of-court criticisms of the judiciary. In no country could someone in the courtroom get away with screaming insults at the judge.) In the 1920's, the magazine The New Statesman published an editorial about a defamation action tried before one Avory, J., in which the defendant was Dr. Marie Stopes, an ardent advocate of birth control and a very unpopular figure. The editorial contended that "an individual owning to such views as those of Dr. Stopes apparently cannot hope for a fair hearing in a Court presided over by Mr. Justice Avory--and there are so many Avorys." The editor of The New Statesman was then adjudged guilty of contempt of court. The opinion justifying his conviction, R. v. Editor of the New Statesman,[89] said that he was guilty of a contempt because what he had written "imputed unfairness and lack of impartiality to a judge in the discharge of his judicial duties."

Then in the 1960's conservative politician Quintin Hogg wrote an article in Punch about certain decisions of the Court of Appeal in gambling cases. He referred to these as a "strange example of the blindness which sometimes descends on even the best of judges." The Court, he contended, has made the gambling laws unworkable; but it lambastes the police for not enforcing these statutes and Parliament for passing them. "Everyone, it seems, is out of step except the courts." The Court of Appeal dismissed an application to find Hogg in contempt of court. Lord Denning, Master of the Rolls, said that:

We will never use this (contempt) jurisdiction as a means to uphold our own dignity. Nor will we use it to suppress those who speak against us. We do not fear criticism, nor do we resent it. For there is something far more important at stake. It is no less than freedom of speech itself. It is the right of every man, in Parliament or out of it, in the press or over the broadcast, to make fair comment, even outspoken comment, on matters of public interest.[90]

I see no way to reconcile R. v. Editor of the New Statesman (still not formally overruled) and this decision!

The U.S. Supreme Court would say that comments such as those penned by the editor of the New Statesman and Quintin Hogg are constitutionally protected under the First Amendment. Thus in Pennekamp v. Florida,[91] the Miami Herald had published a series of editorials accusing several judges who had quashed indictments in rape, assault and gambling cases of using technicalities to turn the court into refuges for criminals. Justice Stanley Reed, writing for the Supreme Court, admitted that the editorials did not state "objectively" the attitude of the judges and that they had "deliberately distorted" the facts but nonetheless reversed the contempt convictions on the ground that they did not represent a clear and present danger to the administration of justice in Florida.

Before the proclamation of the state of emergency in 1975, the Indian approaches to criticism of the government were, on the whole, tolerant. Opposition parties and the press freely attacked the policies of the Nehru and Gandhi regimes. In 1975, however, a high court judge in Allahabad found that Prime Minister Gandhi had violated the electoral law in her successful 1971 campaign for a parliamentary seat. Angered at the threatened loss of her position as Prime Minister because of a technicality, and perhaps seizing upon the situation as a pretext to silence divisive political movements and leaders, she had President Fakhruddin Ali Ahmed declare a state of emergency in June of 1975. Soon, several thousand opposition politicians were detained without trial under the 1971 preventive detention law known as the Maintenance of Internal Security Act.[92] Twenty-six extremist groups were banned; and the government imposed by regulation stringent controls over the press. Newspapers and magazines were told not to print rumors or anything likely to bring the government or the Prime Minister into hatred or contempt. Some were forced to submit their issues for advance approval. As a consequence, most news that was printed was information favorable to the regime.

In other steps taken to implement the state of emergency, the government issued an ordinance making it unnecessary to disclose to those detained under the law why they had been arrested; outlawed public demonstrations; and pushed through the Thirty-Ninth Constitutional Amendment Act that, among other things, deprived the courts of the power to consider electoral cases involving the Prime Minister, the President, and the Speaker of the House. (This section is now repealed.) Another portion of this Amendment, that retroactively declaring the disputed election valid, was declared unconstitutional--though she was simultaneously held not to have violated the electoral statute.[93]

The government then enacted a law making it illegal to publish anything "defamatory of the President, the Vice-President, the Prime Minister, or any member of the Council of Ministers, the Speaker of the House or the governor of a state." The administration could, furthermore, ban news about "any activity prejudicial to the interests of the sovereignty and integrity of India and security of the state." Newspapers that violated this law (known as the Prevention of Publication of Objectionable Matter Act) could be shut down. The press stopped reporting anti-government demonstrations, political arrests, and opposition speeches--even when they were made in Parliamentary debates.[94]

Suddenly Mrs. Gandhi dropped another bombshell. In January, 1977, she announced that Parliamentary elections would take place the following March. She ended the state of emergency regulations imposing censorship on the press, and permitted opposition political parties to start campaigning. An oddly associated group of four parties, the Hindu supremacist Jana Sangh, the "opposition (old Guard) Congress" Party headed by Mr. Moraji Desai, the centrist Bharitya Lok Dal, and the Socialist Party formed a coalition group called the Janata Party.

To the amazement of Mrs. Gandhi, the Indian people, and the entire world, Janata won the election and Mr. Desai succeeded Mrs. Gandhi as Prime Minister. The new administration repealed the Prevention of Publication of Objectionable Matter Act and amended the Constitution to limit the President's power to declare a state of emergency.[95] This, of course, makes it more difficult for a political leader to silence critics of the government; and it is once again proper to say that criticism of the government is tolerated in India. What Mrs. Gandhi's return to power in the 1980 elections augurs for political dissent only time will tell.

In any event, the Indian law relating to attacks on public officials is still not as tolerant as the American. Out-of-court attacks on judges accusing them of dishonesty and corruption may be punished as contempts if they tend to interfere with the proper administration of the law even if they do not create a clear and present danger of such interference. Thus, in Advocate General v. Seshagiri Rao,[96] the defendant, a ninety-two year old man, sent a letter to judges about a case that he had lost. In that letter, he accused them of incompetence and bias in favor of the rich. The defendant was convicted for contempt, though his punishment was limited to a small fine because of his age and poor health. The High Court of Andrha Pradesh said "That these allegations amount to contempt of court admits of no doubt. They constitute an attack on the competence and integrity of the judicial officers. The consequences of such an attack on their character is to destroy the confidence of the people in courts, seriously impair judicial administration, and bring the action of justice itself into disrepute. It makes no difference that the attacks were made not during the pendency of a proceeding but after its disposal."

Critics of the Indian state and national Parliament and their members may be cited for contempt of Parliament. This happened to Mrs. Gandhi in 1977 for calling "preposterous" the remarks of a Lok Sabha (lower house) member. The Times of India in 1953 referred to an event in the Bombay State legislature as a "performance in its malice and vituperation . . . unworthy of the legislature of what was once a premier State. But perhaps it is too much to expect elementary good manners and good taste from those who know no standards and observe none." The Bombay House and its Committee on Privileges found the editor and paper guilty of contempt, asserting that the criticism in the editorial exceeded the bounds of decency and fair comment and was calculated to undermine the prestige and authority of the House. As a result, the editor was ordered to apologize.[97]

India does not follow the rule of New York Times v. Sullivan that criticized public officials can recover in libel cases only where the untrue statement is made "with malice." In one lower court case,[98] the defendant's newspaper published an article stating falsely that a woman called to a police station for questioning had been sexually assaulted by the policeman in charge of the station. The plaintiff, the subinspector who was in charge of the station at the time this incident

81

allegedly occurred, was permitted to recover damages even though the defendant contended that the statement was "privileged" (i.e., protected from recovery in a libel action) because the conduct of the police is a matter of public interest. An American court would not have considered the libel here malicious, and thus not have allowed recovery, because the defendant did believe the statement to be true.

Indians who vent their anger against a public official may also be subject to prosecution for criminal defamation (i.e., criminal libel or criminal slander) under Sec. 499 of the Indian Penal Code. This outlaws the making of an imputation against the character of another that one knows or can reasonably be expected to know would harm him. The Section itself contains several exceptions. Exception 9 provides that it is not defamatory to demean the reputation of another when the attack is made in good faith for the protection of any person or for the common good, while Exception 5 declares that there is no crime when the attack is made in good faith concerning the official conduct of a public official. Truth is not in and of itself a defense;[99] though it is relevant for the purpose of proving good faith.

Section 499 prosecutions of persons who reprimand public officials are not uncommon, though the courts are often willing to give the defendant the benefit of the doubt. Bibhuti Bhusan v. S. Kumar[100] provides a good idea of how the courts approach these prosecutions. The defendants here were the editor and publisher of a weekly paper in the town of Purulia. They charged that an individual who had been Commissioner of the Purulia municipality between 1951 and 1958 and Chairman of that municipality between 1958 and 1960 had remained in arrears on his taxes between 1951 and 1958, a period while he was still Commissioner. They added (1) that at the time of the recent municipal elections the Commissioner-Chairman still had not paid all his taxes, a fact that should have resulted in the disqualification of his nominating petition; and (2) that he overcame an objection by his opponent to the petition by wrongfully alleging that he owed the city nothing. The trial court found, in convicting the defendants, that the Commissioner had settled his tax bills but that this payment had never been entered in the municipal records. Moreover, no objection to the petition had ever been raised. On appeal, the Calcutta High Court reversed the decision as to one part of the article but not as to the other. The good faith that a defendant must exercise in order to escape a defamation charge was defined as having good reasons, after using due care, to believe that his allegations are true. The assertions about the Commissioner's being in arrears on his taxes were made in good faith, as so defined, for the municipal records themselves indicated that he owed the city money. The High Court commented that it is good that the acts and conduct of public men be "probed, criticized and exposed before the public gaze. The public has a right to know the strength and foibles of its public men. . . ." However, the contention that the Commissioner overcame the objection to his nominating petition by lying was found not made in good faith and thus defamatory. The due care that is a constituent of good faith was lacking because the newspapermen had never bothered asking the opponent who allegedly had brought the objection whether one had in fact been made. Instead, they relied on the assertion of a third party that a challenge had been entered.

In the Soviet Union, the regime at present makes little distinction between criticism of the government and high-ranking politicians on the one hand and subversion on the other: consequently, people who criticize governmental policy and the leaders of the Soviet Communist Party are as likely to be repressed as actual subversives. For proof, the reader should simply glance again at the Soviet cases noted when comparing treatment of subversives --none of these situations really involved people who wished to overthrow the government by illegal means; and all of the defendants were simply out-spoken critics of past and present governmental policy.

The major aspects of French law relating to the right to criticize public officials are found in certain articles of the Press Law of 1881 and the interpretations thereof. Article 30 prohibits the defamation (diffamation) of the courts, the army, and corps of civil servants. Article 31 is designed to protect the reputation of individual public officials. It punishes defamations against one or several members of either chamber of Parliament, a public official, a depositary or agent of the public authority, or a citizen charged with a public mandate. Charges under Article 31 cannot be brought unless the defamation relates to the official conduct of the politician or bureaucrat. Article 32, paragraph 1 provides for the punishment of those who defame a private party or a public individual in his private role. Article 33 makes illegal the uttering of insults (injures) to other people. The difference between injure and diffama-tion can best be illustrated by the following example. If one were to call M. Mauroy, the Prime Minister of France, a "fascist pig" he would be guilty of uttering an insult (injure); while an assertion that M. Mauroy was using his official po-sition to enrich himself in real estate specula-tions would be a defamation culpable under Article 31. Truth is a defense to defamation but not to insult.[101] When one is prosecuted for defamation or insult, he may be fined and jailed and have to pay civil damages to the person he slandered or insulted. However, prosecutions under Article 30 and 31 can be brought only at the request of cer-tain public officials: for example, a prosecution for defaming a public official may be initiated only at the request of the Minister who heads the Department where he works.

From time to time, prosecutions for defaming or insulting public officials (including courts and judges) are brought under one or another of the

84

above articles. Not untypical is a decision issued in June of 1975. Several newspapers called an examining magistrate (<u>juge d'instruction</u>) an "assassin" because a Portuguese national he had had detained pending trial committed suicide in prison. The trial court found that the magistrate had been defamed in respect to his capacity as a public official and thus that the defendants had violated Article 31. One paper had to pay him $6,000 in damages and was fined $500.[102] A magazine that published an editorial in which Pierre Messmer, the Minister of State for Overseas Departments, was referred to as "Messmer (S.S.)" was fined under Article 33 for insulting a public official. Calling a Frenchman a member of the S.S. is, according to the court, just that sort of invective that Article 33 bars.[103] An individual wrote an article quoting a line from the Marxist hymn <u>The International</u> saying that if these cannibals (the army) persist in making heroes of us, they will soon see that our bullets are for our own guns. The author added that the army was rushing to drown itself in the blood of popular revolt. For his pains, he was convicted of violating both Article 30, prohibiting the defamation of the army, etc., and Article 25, outlawing provoking soldiers to disobedience. To rub salt into his wounds, the Court of Cassation abandoned the usual judicial scepticism about Article 25 and declined to build into it what an American would call a clear and present danger standard for determining guilt.[104]

On occasion the courts will allow a defendant prosecuted for one form or another of defamation to escape by proving that he acted "in good faith" though what he said was partially or wholly untrue. The criteria that determine when this defense can be successfully raised are quite hazy. Mere belief in the truth of what one says is not enough: a journalist to benefit from it will in the normal case have had to make some attempt to verify the accuracy of his sources. Literary and artistic critics and persons who evaluate their subordinates can often invoke it; and it permits a certain

85

amount of puffery during election campaigns about the defects of candidates for public office. Recent decisions saw the good faith defense failing a journal that accused Nanterre police of systematic brutality against Algerian youth but exculpating those who had published a newspaper article accusing a trade union of weaning magistrates from their professional loyalties.[105]

During the Presidency of General Charles de Gaulle there was much discussion of Article 26 of the 1881 Press Law. This provides that "The Offense to the President of the Republic is punished with an imprisonment of three months to a year and/or a fine. . . ." Nowhere is the "Offense to the President" defined in the statute itself, but as the instances to be discussed shortly will make clear, it consists of directing certain insults against him. During the Third and Fourth Republics, where the President was a mere figurehead whose impotence shielded him from criticism, the law was employed only on nine occasions.[106] However, in the first nine years of de Gaulle's Presidency under the Constitution of the Fifth Republic it was used 350 times. One author was fined for writing that the General gets carnal pleasure from appearing in crowds; another had to pay for calling him a mixture of Cyrano and Machiavelli.

The courts have had a difficult time determining just what criticism of the President falls under the ban of Article 26. There is language to the effect that it consists not of simple raillery or irreverence but of imputations which hurt the honor and dignity of the President. Thus to refer to the President as a despotic turkey (dindon) is no violation.[107] In Moreux, Lionel[108] the Correctional Tribunal of the Seine said that there could be no conviction for referring to Gaullism as a plague: this attacks a political movement but not the honor and dignity of the President. However, the same article was a violation of Article 26 insofar as it claimed that de Gaulle

86

had, by freeing Algeria, amputated the national territory. This charge accused him of the crime of maladministration and thus attacked his honor.

Even though de Gaulle has passed away, Article 26 cannot yet be said to be a dead letter. The author of an article in the newspaper Combat was fined for writing that President Pompidou decided not to commute the death sentences of two men after he saw a public opinion poll in favor of capital punishment. The writer's offense was that he let it be believed that the President did not make his decision alone.[109] President Giscard d'Estaing said that France should become a country of political and intellectual asylum and that no newspaper would be confiscated merely because it attacked the President. He kept his word and never invoked Article 26 during his term of office. (In 1980, however, a magazine was forced to ink over a cover showing a nude Mme. Giscard seated on an Arab emir's knee and averring that France would never lack oil while Giscard offered his wife to the emirs!)[110] What use President François Mitterrand will make of Article 26 remains to be seen.

The state-controlled television networks, the only ones in France, are well known for keeping dissenting views off the air. During the referendum of October, 1962 that legitimated the direct election of the President, the five main opposition parties were granted a total of 50 minutes of radio-TV time for the entire campaign.[111] During the widespread troubles of May, 1968, RTF (the name of the only TV network then existing) said that all was calm. The government suppressed a two-hour report on undergraduate unrest, an action that continued its tradition of deciding what could and could not go on the air.

President Giscard maintained political control of TV and radio, though he held the reins more loosely than did de Gaulle. In 1974 a reorganization of the RTF into three networks produced pro-Government broadcasters as heads of each. The head of station Europe 1, located in Paris and partly owned by the French state, was fired because the station had "mocked" the Government. Interviews with critics of friendly foreign countries (e.g., Morocco, Guinea) were barred from the TV screen; while Mitterrand as Socialist leader spoke over illegal private radio to protest Government domination of the electronic media during the 1979 European Parliamentary elections.[112] Now President, he has promised to liberate radio-TV from political domination.

A device much used during the Algerian War to repress newspapers and magazines critical of the Government's Algerian policy of the moment was Article 30 (formerly Article 10) of the Code of Criminal Procedure. This authorizes certain officials to take all measures, including seizure of personal property, to determine whether a crime against state security has been committed. The Article was frequently used as a pretext to prevent the distribution of issues of newspapers and magazines containing columns attacking this or that French action vis-à-vis Algeria. Even on the French mainland there were 269 seizures of newspapers and magazines between 1955 and 1962; practically all of these were carried out under Article 30.[113] Most of the disputes over the validity of the Article 30 seizures were decided in the ordinary rather than the administrative tribunals; and the former were much more reluctant than the latter to find them illegal.[114] Thus the Court of Appeal of Paris legitimated an Article 30 seizure of France-Observateur as a preliminary step in a judicial prosecution. The issues contained articles on the misconduct of the French military in Algeria and on the uselessness of military action there. According to the Court, the purpose of this seizure was in fact to get evidence about the crime of demoralizing the army, though no prosecution was ever brought.[115] "At most, fifteen percent of seizures in metropolitan France were followed by indictment."[116] The one time a seized newspaper did recover damages the case was reversed on appeal.[117]

Thus the Americans tolerate governmental criticism; the British, French, and Indians tolerate it but somewhat less than the Americans; and the Soviets repress it, arguably on a massive scale. In the light of the rather lengthy description of French statutes which are used to discipline those who express displeasure with governmental policies or officials it might seem surprising to conclude that the French tolerate here. But those who are familiar with French newspapers and magazines will recognize that they often take the government to task: in fact, this is one reason why it attempts to dominate the nation's TV sets. The Communist L'Humanite circulates freely and Le Canard Enchainé specializes in directing satirical barbs against French politicians. Though it often mocked de Gaulle rather bitterly, he was supposed to have read it regularly.

D. Sexually Oriented Materials

Political discourse and pornographic speech are in different ballparks. Thus every nation except Denmark bans speech, action and writing it defines as "obscene." However, the definition of "obscene" varies greatly from country to country.

Up until June, 1973, a plurality of the United States Supreme Court adopted the following rule. A work could be considered obscene only if each of these three elements was present:

(a) the dominant theme of the material taken as a whole appeals to a prurient interest in sex;

(b) the material is patently offensive

because it affronts contemporary community standards relating to the description of representation of sexual matters; and

(c) the material is utterly without redeeming social value.[118] This test is very tolerant, permitting just about anything dealing with sex to be published, since a good lawyer can show that most any material treating of sex has some therapeutic or aesthetic merit. And, in fact, the Court not only passed such classics as _Lady Chatterley's Lover_[119]--it had before it the film version--and Henry Miller's _Tropic of Cancer_,[120] but also paperbacks and periodicals entitled _Lust Pool_, _Shame Agent_, _High Heels_, and _Spree_.[121]

In the 1973 case of _Miller v. California_[122] the Court in a 5-4 decision promulgated new guidelines for determining obscenity. A work can be considered obscene if and only if the following factors are all present:

A. The average person, applying contemporary community standards, would find that the work, taken as a whole, appeals to a prurient interest in sex.

B. The work depicts or describes, in a way the community deems patently offensive, sexual conduct specifically described by the applicable state law and

C. The work taken as a whole lacks serious literary, artistic, political or scientific value.

This test is stricter with material dealing with sex than the one described in the previous paragraph. In the first place, some works with social value can now be held obscene. Also, the finder of fact, in determining whether the material appeals to prurient interest or is patently offensive, is to use the standards of his community. This means, admitted the Court, that what cannot be declared obscene in New York City may constitutionall

be held so in Maine, because something that a New
Yorker would pass off with a shrug of his shoulder
might strike a citizen of Maine as patently offensive and appealing to prurient interest. Nonetheless, the test is a tolerant one. Under its
phraseology, no work with serious literary,
artistic, political or scientific value can be declared obscene and, therefore, it seems to protect
any book, article, film, painting, or sculpture
that is praised by a reputable literary critic,
art critic, political journalist or scientist.
Certainly, Miller did not destroy the nation's
pornography industry. New York City's Times
Square is notorious around the globe; while in
Chicago establishments are tolerated where "for a
price, a woman employee will whisper sexual fanta-
sies into a customer's ear while he views a hardcore pornographic film."[123]

     For a long while the leading case on
obscenity in Britain was R. v. Hicklin.[124] Here
the Queen's Bench Division sustained an order
issued by the Wolverhampton magistrates for the
destruction of a work called The Confessional
Unmasked, which carried lurid extracts from what
were called Roman Catholic publications. The
Court held that "the test of obscenity is to deprave and corrupt those whose minds are open to
such immoral influences and into whose hands publications of this sort may fall." As Harry Street
points out,[125] many judges, instead of requiring
that the work as a whole be considered, encouraged
prosecuting counsel to emphasize to the jury the
book's most lurid passages and to quote them out
of context. Also, some, though not all, judges
thought that a book would be obscene if it would
corrupt a virginal teenager even though it would
have no effect whatsoever on the average adult.
Street quotes a judge in 1954 making the following
remarks: "A book which would not influence the
mind of an Archbishop might influence the minds of
a callow youth or girl just budding into womanhood .
. . It is a very comforting thought that juries
from time to time take a very solid stand against

91

this sort of thing and realize how important it is for the youth of this country to be protected and that the fountain of our national blood should not be polluted at its source."[126]

The Obscene Publications Act of 1959 is at present the major piece of British legislation concerning erotic material. Under Section 1 an article (i.e., a writing or a physical object) is declared obscene if its effect is "taken as a whole, such as to tend to deprave and corrupt persons who are likely, having regard to all relevant circumstances, to read, see or hear the matter contained or embodied in it." Section 4 says that no offense is committed "if it is proved that publication of the article in question is justified as being for the public good on the ground that it is in the interest of science, literature, art or learning, or other objects of general concern." Also, expert evidence can be introduced about whether the book really has social, political, scientific, or literary merit. The Act reverses Hicklin, or at least the repressive judicial interpretation of Hicklin, in the following respects:

1. No book can be declared obscene merely because it contains a few sexually-oriented passages.

2. No book can be declared obscene merely because it might by some mischance fall into the hands of a fourteen-year old: to determine whether the book has a tendency to "deprave and corrupt," look to the group that is most likely to read it.

3. Even if a book is obscene as defined in the Act, it cannot be banned if its aesthetic, etc., merit makes its publication beneficial to the public.

However, an author, publisher and/or distributor of a book who could not be prosecuted successfully under the Obscene Publications Act of 1959 may on occasion be jailed for the common law (judge-made) crimes of outraging public decency or of agreeing to corrupt public morals. Street mentions a case in which one who published a booklet containing the names and addresses of prostitutes was convicted under both the 1959 Act and the latter common law offense, and perhaps 30 persons were fined or imprisoned between 1962 and 1972 for that particular crime.[127]

The first major case under the 1959 Act was the prosecution of the Lawrence novel, <u>Lady Chatterley's Lover</u>. When the prosecutor tried to read just the "sexiest" parts of the work to the jury, he was interrupted by the trial judge, Mr. Justice Byrne, who emphasized that the act requires the jury to read the book as a whole. The jury rendered a general verdict of not guilty.[128] A second important decision is <u>R. v. Calder and Boyars</u>.[129] The defendant here, a well-known publishing company, issued an American novel by Hubert Selby entitled <u>Last Exit to Brooklyn</u>, which contains graphic and realistic descriptions of homo- and other sorts of human sexuality in an American slum. The publisher unsuccessfully contended at the trial that the tendency of the book was not to drive the reader into an acceptance of homosexuality, but, on the contrary, to shock him into a rejection of it. However, on appeal the conviction was reversed because the trial judge did not give the appropriate interpretation of the Act in his charge. Salmon, L.J., emphasized that to determine whether the publication of an "obscene" work is for the common good, the jury must consider on the one hand the number of readers they believe would be corrupted by the book, the strength of its tendency to deprave, and the nature of the resulting depravity. On the other, they should assess the strength of the literary, sociological or ethical merit which they consider the book to have. They should then weigh all these factors together and decide whether on balance the publication was proved by the defendant as being for the public good.[130]

Since works such as <u>Lady Chatterley's Lover</u>
have obtained an imprimatur under the British Obscene Publications Act, one may conclude that the
British rules regarding obscenity are tolerant, as
a whole. However, it is not at all impossible
that a writer or artist will run afoul of these
precepts. For example, in 1974, 702 prosecutions
were brought under the Obscene Publications
Act.[131] Also, in Britain, a work can be obscene
under the 1959 Act even though it does not treat
of sex. (The definition of obscenity there, unlike the American, refers only to "tend to deprave
and corrupt," and does not require any "appeal to
prurient interest.") The leading decision is <u>John
Calder v. Powell</u>,[132] involving an attempt to seize
<u>Alexander Trocchi's Cain's Book</u> as obscene. The
magistrate's court granted the police the requisite warrant and the decision was upheld on
appeal. The book did not revolve about sex
natural or unnatural, but dealt with the life of
an aging New York junkie and emphasized the favorable effects of drug taking. So, concluded Lord
Parker, there was sufficient evidence showing that
it "tended to deprave and corrupt" and thus was
obscene within the meaning of the 1959 Act.

The agencies with the power to censor films
in Britain are local authorities, especially justices of the peace. These local authorities are
guided by a private agency known as the British
Board of Film Censors. The Board determines in
the first instance whether a film may be shown at
all and, if it may, whether it should be exhibited
as a U, A, AA or X film. U films are those suitable for all ages; A films are open to all, though
the rating indicates to parents that the film may
be unsuitable for young children; AA films are
banned to children under fourteen; and X films may
not be exhibited while anyone under sixteen is in
the movie house. (The American motion picture industry adopted a similar system in the 1960's.)
At times, the local authorities are more lenient
than the Board: Cambridge allowed the exhibition
of Marlon Brando's <u>The Wild One</u> though the Board

94

wanted it banned. There are other occasions when the local authorities will outlaw a film the Board approves. The Board is in practice more worried about horror and violence than about sex and is not well disposed to movies which depict living persons unfavorably. Thus, it refused to grant a certificate to Operation Teutonic Sword because it said unfavorable things about General Speidel of the German army. Once in a while it will delete a portion of a film showing the royal family or which seems sacrilegious; but on the whole it permits a serious film to be seen by adults in its unexpurgated version. However, in 1971, it withheld a certificate from Andy Warhol's Trash, a movie emphasizing drugs and transvestism.

There is no censorship of legitimate theater in Britain or the United States. Of course, if a play is obscene, its producer and actors may be prosecuted for a violation of the general obscenity laws. In Britain, the 1868 Theatre Act ending theater censorship in that nation extends the 1959 Obscene Publications Act to the theater, and this means that theater obscenity probably includes too much violence as well as excessive sex.[133]

Turning to India, though Hindu tradition has its "lusty" side, with at least one of its classics, the Kama Sutra, achieving fame in the West as an "how to do it" manual and with some Hindu temples formerly having priestesses who doubled as prostitutes, Hinduism is at present a religion which considers the body at best unimportant and at worst evil. This feeling is mirrored in the practical sphere by the development of an extremely puritanical attitude toward sex. Sexual relations between couples engaged to be married are viewed as abhorrent, and it is rare to see a couple strolling down the street hand in hand.

Thus, it is not surprising that Article 19(2) of the Constitution of India permits the government to limit freedom of expression in the interests of "decency or morality." And S. 292 of the Indian Penal Code makes it a crime to sell, rent, distribute or exhibit any obscene book, pamphlet, paper, drawing, painting, representation or figure. In the leading case of Udeshi v. Maharashtra[134] the Supreme Court of India noted that obscene material is offensive to modesty and decency and thus is not within the free speech protected by Article 19(1). It then tried to determine what S. 292 meant by obscene and also whether the book Lady Chatterley's Lover was obscene under the Court's interpretation. The Court essentially adopted the Hicklin test: material is obscene if its tendency is to deprave and corrupt persons into whose hands it may fall. Hidayatullah, J. did say that a stray sexually-oriented passage would not make a book obscene but continued that that result was perfectly consistent with Hicklin since a stray passage would tend to deprave and corrupt no one. However, though the total work should be considered, the obscene matter may be analyzed by itself to see whether it is so decidedly obnoxious that it is likely to deprave and corrupt those into whose hands the book is likely to fall. Furthermore, an obscene work was not to receive constitutional protection on the grounds of "public good" unless the aesthetic or social merit far outweighed the obscenity. (A 1969 amendment to Section 292 allows the publication of obscene works if such would further the "common good.")

As for the application of this definition of obscenity to the Lawrence novel, a lengthy quotation from the opinion is much more satisfactory than a paraphrase:

(The gamekeeper Mellors) . . . explains to Constance (Chatterley) the entire mystery of eroticism and they put it into practice. There are over a dozen descriptions of their sexual intimacy. The gamekeeper's speech and vocabulary were not genteel. He knew no

96

Latin which could be used to appease the
censors and the human pudenda and other
erogenous parts are freely discussed by him
and also named by the author in the descriptions. The sexual congress each time is
described with great candidness. . . . The
rest of the story is a mundane one. There
is some criticism of the modern machine
civilization and its enervating effects and
the production of sexually inefficient men
and women and this, according to Lawrence,
is the cause of maladjustment of sexes and
their unhappiness . . .
No doubt he wrote a flowering book with
pistils and stamens standing but it was to
quote his own words again "a phallic novel,
a shocking novel," . . .
This is where the law comes in. The law
seeks to protect not those who can protect
themselves, but those whose prurient minds
take delight and secret sexual pleasure
from erotic writings. . . .
The poetry and music which Lawrence attempted to put into sex . . . cannot sus-
tain (the book) long and without them the
book is nothing . . . When everything is
said in its favour we find that in treating
with sex the impugned portions viewed
separately and also in the setting of the
whole book pass the permissible limits
judged of from our community standards and
as there is no social gain to us which can
be said to preponderate, we must hold the
book (obscene).[135]

It will not astound the reader to hear that,
in a country whose Supreme Court can worry about
an individual's getting pleasure from thinking
about sex, there is film censorship. Furthermore,
the censor bars nudity--even the bellybutton must
be covered. Kissing on the lips was first permitted in 1978. To give the audience a bit of an
extra thrill, the director has to insert cabaret
scenes totally unrelated to the plot but showing

the dancers wriggling and shaking--with their bellybuttons concealed from view.[136] However, the exhibitors of a film sanctioned by the censor may not be prosecuted under Sec. 292 of the Penal Code.[137]

Since literature and art in the Soviet Union are supposed to inspire its citizens to work hard for their country and to put the nation and its people in a favorable light; and since nothing can be legally published in the Soviet Union until it is approved by the editors of the state-owned publishing houses, regional or city Party Committees, and the state censorship board (Glavlit); it is hardly surprising that most works published there contain little in the way of explicit descriptions of sexual activity. Glavlit is expressly permitted to ban writings which have a pornographic character--as well as those, to revert for a moment to the theme of the next-to-last section, which contain agitation or propaganda against Soviet authority or the dictatorship of the proletariat.[138] As a weapon against those whose works slip by the watchful eye of the censor or have their works published underground, there is a law which makes it illegal to produce and disseminate objects of a pornographic character. The courts have not yet interpreted this act, whose violation can result in a three-year jail sentence.[139] However, there is little indication that the state publishing houses are about to violate it. For example, an edition of the letters of Anton Chekhov deleted the work "backside" from the sentence "My entire backside is covered with mosquito bites."[140] Movies that contain too much explicit sex, violence or inappropriate political messages may not be shown to the average citizen, though certain members of the elite are permitted to watch them.[141] However, more experimentation in art, literature, film and music is permitted now than a decade ago.[142]

There are several weapons available to French governments that desire to suppress the

publication of erotic material. The first is
Article 293 of the Penal Code. This makes it a
crime to make, operate, sell or give writings,
posters, engravings, photographs, paintings or all
other objects "contrary to good morals." A newspaper article describing and illustrating homosexual graffitti on urinals is punishable under
this clause.[143] However, explicitly though
regretfully taking into account changing standards
of sexual morality, a court held that it was not a
violation of Article 283 to operate a "sex shop"
forbidden to minors but selling books, films,
erotic dolls and suggestive lingerie.[144] Some say
that an erotic work of real worth is not now within the ambit of the articles;[145] but the relevant
judicial decisions do not yet go this far. The
leading case is Min. Publ. c. Pauvert.[146] M.
Pauvert was prosecuted and convicted under this
law for having published in a limited edition a
work of the Marquis de Sade entitled Juliette Or
The Prosperity of Vice. Pauvert admitted that the
works of this author contain numerous scenes of
debauch and violence. He added, however, that De
Sade has scientific value as a precursor of
psychologists of the unconscious such as Freud,
Kraft-Ebbing and Havelock-Ellis. In a rather
jumbled opinion, the court rebutted M. Pauvert by
looking to his intent: this could not have been
to further scientific knowledge since his advertising was not limited to psychological or medical
journals. Also, the fact that he was aware of the
"outrageous character for morals" of the book by
itself establishes culpable intent: much of the
opinion is a marshalling of shocking passages to
show that M. Pauvert must have been aware that de
Sade's book had such a character.

No film may be shown in France except upon
the issuance of a certificate by the Minister of
Cultural Affairs advised by a Commission for the
Control of Films set up by a law of July 3, 1945.
This commission consists of seven representatives
of the government, seven of the film profession,
and eight "neutrals" drawn from various walks of

99

life. The Commission may recommend the issuance of a certificate permitting the general exhibition of the film or of one prohibiting it from being shown to minors below certain ages. It may suggest modifications and cuts or the refusal of any certificate. In past years it actively censored sexually-oriented films as well as movies showing the French military in a bad light. The movie Les Sentiers de la Gloire, dealing with desertion from the army during World War I, was not exhibited in France until 1975, 18 years after it was made: the producers never even presented it to the Commission because they knew that it would be futile to do so.[147] The French government said that year that it would no longer impose restraints on "political" films and that the producers of such films would be entitled to the state financial aid that is available to all French filmmakers.[148] As another step in President Giscard d'Estaing's campaign to "liberalize" French life, the Commission began granting licenses to sexually-oriented films such as Deep Throat, The Devil in Miss Jones, and the French-made L'Exhibition. The only ground on which it will deny a license now is incitation to violence: it will let even "hardcore" pornographic films be shown but grant them an "X" rating. Even though there is a special and rather heavy tax on the production and exhibition of X-rated films and their makers lose certain government subsidies, they are shown in over a hundred theaters.[149]

There is no formal system of theater censorship. However, the local authorities have on occasion banned plays that they believe are likely to disturb the peace.[150] More frequent until recently were their attempts, under their statutory power to preserve order, to bar films to which the Control Commission had given a certificate. The legality of these decrees was often considered by the Council of State, which in about half the cases upheld the mayor. The leading holding is Films Lutetia.[151] Here the Council sustained a proscription imposed by the mayor of Nice on three films that had been granted certificates by the Commission. The Council developed the laconic formula that the local authorities could interdict any film that threatens serious trouble or that, by reason of the immoral character of the film and local circumstances, is prejudicial to public order; and said without any proof that because of the immoral nature of these films and the local circumstances, they were prejudicial to public order. The threat to "public order" which may because of local circumstances justify the banning of the film is not necessarily coterminous with the "threat of serious troubles" that might also legitimate a taboo by the mayor. In fact, local circumstances which have been found by the administrative tribunals to justify a proscription by the local authorities include not only a wave of strong protests emanating from diverse local milieux or their spokesmen but also the location in a city of a large number of schools or the fact that during certain times of the year, a town is a haven for religious pilgrims. The "local circumstances" test results, of course, in a situation wherein the Council can allow a ban in some towns and annul it in others. Thus on the very same day the Council upheld 9 of 13 local bans on the film Les Liaisons Dangereuses.[152]

The law of July 16, 1949 allows the Minister of the Interior to forbid the sale to minors of 18 years or younger of all publications of whatever nature that present a danger for youth on account of their pornographic or licentious character or on account of their emphasis on crime or violence. Though he cannot bar its sale to adults, he can and sometimes does make it illegal for any book seller to expose to view in the interior or exterior of his shop or kiosk any writing whose emphasis on sex or violence threatens youth. Moreover, he can and does declare it criminal to advertise such a book, thus making it even less likely that anyone will buy it. When three works issued by a publisher are restricted during the same year under this 1949 law, further publications

101

of his must be submitted to the Minister of the
Interior for prior approval, which can be delayed
for three months. Between 1959 and 1965 more than
40 magazines and 500 books were affected by the
law.[153] It is somewhat less commonly invoked now
and was never consistently applied: no action was
taken against the American Playboy but the sale to
minors and public display of its French counterpart Lui was forbidden.[154] On one occasion, the
Council of State annulled a ministerial decision
taken under the act. Société les Editions du
Fleuve Noir[155] declared illegal a ministerial in-
terdiction of a book entitled Une Fille Tranquille
because the prohibition did not say that the book
was dangerous to youth because of its pornographic
character, but condemned it merely because of its
general atmosphere, its absence of morality, and
the indigence and vulgarity of its style.

The 1949 law was one of the weapons brought
against the well-known publisher Maurice Girodias.
His monthly magazine Olympia had to be submitted
to the Minister of the Interior each month. This
official in turn often banned it, though it met
with no problems in the United States or Great
Britain. Some of the works published by him were
proscribed under Article 14 of the Press Law of
1881 which, as seen earlier, allows the government
to ban writings published in a foreign language or
appearing first in French but of "foreign origin."
For example, the English-language editions of
Vladimir Nabokov's Lolita and Jean Genet's
Lady of the Flowers were not permitted to be sold
in France even though the French editions freely
circulated.[156] In Min. de l'Intérieur c.
Girodias[157] the Council of State sustained the
Article 14 ban on some of Girodias' books. It
asserted that it can be applied whether or not the
publisher may be subjected to a criminal prosecution and that the administrative tribunal cannot
consider whether the "foreign" book in fact presents a danger to public order. Eventually, his
brushes with the law (which also involved his
prosecution for committing an outrage to good

morals) resulted in his being sentenced to jail
for six years, though he actually served only two
days of his term. Disgusted, he left Paris for
London. However, after the death of President
de Gaulle, he returned to Paris feeling that the
climate there was now more favorable.

Of the countries discussed, the United States
has the rules relating to obscenity that are most
tolerant, though Britain's and France's standards
also fall into the tolerant category. In the
United States, no work of serious value can be held
obscene; while in England and India the social
value must outweigh the lewdness before the work
can be published or exhibited with impunity. In
the United States, France and Britain, the trier of
fact usually must look to the work as a whole; in
India (and perhaps in England in the case of newspapers and magazines), one passage can cause the
whole work to be declared obscene. In Britain but
not in the United States, the courts have begun to
define as obscene writings emphasizing certain matters other than sex, and the common law crimes of
outraging public decency and agreeing to corrupt
public morals are still viable. But in France,
America and Britain the "banned in India" Lady
Chatterley's Lover (both in book and film version)
is by now regarded as mild stuff. Since India outlaws the publication of a book so widely considered
a good example of the writing of one of the most
important authors of the twentieth century, as well
as for the other reasons noted above, its rules relating to obscenity must be considered repressive.
And the Soviet Union's policy here must be similarly characterized, since its censor will allow
few, if any, sexually-oriented works or passages to
be printed. As for France, the continued
possibility (more theoretical than real)[158] of
local film censorship to preserve order is one factor compelling the conclusion that France's rules
relating to obscenity are less tolerant than those
of the United States, especially when it is realized
that producers of "hardcore" (not "softcore") pornographic films licensed by the Film Control

103

Commission may nonetheless be prosecuted under Article 283 for outrages against good morals.[159] Moreover, Article 283 still stands as a genuine threat to those desiring to sell or exhibit serious but in spots lewd books, magazines, or objets d'art; and there remains the real possibility of book censorship under the law of July 16, 1949 and Article 14 of the 1881 Press Law.

FOOTNOTES TO CHAPTER II

[1]372 U.S. 229 (1963).

[2]372 U.S. at p. 237. Terminiello v. Chicago is cited 337 U.S. 1 (1949).

[3](1902) 1 K.B. 167.

[4]Certain British courts have an expansive view of when speech is likely to occasion a breach of peace. For example, a man was fined for walking about with the letters ACAB embroidered on his jacket. For those few in the know, ACAB stood for "All Coppers Are Bastards." The incident is described at p. 47 of Paul O'Higgins, Censorship in Britain (London: Nelson, 1972).

[5](1963) 2 Q.B. 744.

[6]R. v. Malik, (1968) 1 All E.R. 582.

[7]The Times (London), October 18, 1980, p. 2. Beauharnais v. Illinois, 343 U.S. 250 (1952) permits an American state to outlaw racialist speech ("group libel") even though it creates no clear and present danger. India, France and the Soviet Union also have enacted "group libel" legislation.

[8](1951) All India Rep. Patna 12.

[9](1962) All India Rep. S. Ct. 955; (1962) Supp. 2 Sup. Ct. R. 769.

[10](1962) Supp. 2 Sup. Ct. R. 809.

[11]May 19, 1933, Recueil Lebon (henceforth abbreviated "Rec.") 541; Dalloz (henceforth abbreviated "D.") 1933.3.54.

[12]February 5, 1937, Rec. 153; D. 1938.3.19.

[13]December 23, 1936, Rec. 1151; D. 1938.3.22.

[14]June 19, 1953, Rec. 298.

[15]See Claude-Albert Colliard, Libertés Publiques, 3rd ed. (Paris: Dalloz, 1968) at pp. 568-71 and 5th ed. (Paris: Dalloz, 1975), pp. 642-658 for a good summary of the law about the authorities' power to bar demonstrations.

[16]February 19, 1964, Rec. 113.

[17](1936) 1 K.B. 218.

[18]283 U.S. 697 (1931).

[19]403 U.S. 713 (1971).

[20]See Cox v. Louisiana, 379 U.S. 536 (1965); Shuttlesworth v. Birmingham, 394 U.S. 147 (1969).

[21]One candidate for public office in Britain obtained an injunction ordering a magazine not to defame him. The Times (London), March 6, 1980, p. 2.

[22](1957) All India Rep. S. Ct. 896. On Sec. 144's, see David Bayley, The Police and Political Development in India (Princeton: Princeton U. Press, 1969), p. 266. Section 144 was upheld in Babulal Parate v. Maharashtra, (1961) All India Rep. S. Ct. 884, the Supreme Court expressly refusing to use the clear and present danger test to determine its validity.

[23]April 8, 1935, Rec. 1226; D. 1935.3.25.

[24]New York Times, December 12, 1979, p. A15. In 1980 the police barred a private meeting of 20 Jewish scientists who had lost their jobs. New York Times, December 1, 1980, p. A11.

106

[25] 341 U.S. 494 (1951).

[26] 354 U.S. 298 (1957).

[27] John Roche, The Quest for the Dream (Chicago: Quadrangle Paper, 1968), p. 229.

[28] 395 U.S. 444 (1969).

[29] Baggett v. Bullitt, 377 U.S. 360 (1964).

[30] Elfbrandt v. Russell, 384 U.S. 11 (1966).

[31] 22 Cox Crim. Cas. 1 (1909).

[32] See Geoffrey Wilson, Cases and Materials on Constitutional and Administrative Law (Cambridge, Eng.: Cambridge U. Press, 1965), pp. 321ff for a description of the case.

[33] New Statesman 95:728, June 2, 1978; 96:189, August 10, 1978; 99:158, February 1, 1980. Also, a 1976 anti-terrorism law bans membership in terrorist organizations such as the "Provisional" branch of the Irish Republican Army. Harry Street, Freedom, the Individual and the Law, 4th ed. (Harmondsworth, Mx.: Penguin Books, 1977), p. 35.

[34] Harry Street, Freedom, the Individual and the Law, 2nd ed. (Harmondsworth, Mx.: Penguin Books, 1967), pp. 210-11.

[35] Ibid., pp. 234-43.

[36] Note, The National Security Interest and Civil Liberties, Harv. L. Rev., 85:1130, 1160 (1972); Herbert Hyman, England and America: Climates of Tolerance and Intolerance 1962, at pp. 227, 240, 242 of Daniel Bell (ed.), The Radical Right (New York: Doubleday, 1963).

[37] Harvard Law Review, op. cit., pp. 1162-63; New York Times, September 9, 1976, p. 1.

[38]Bayley (1969), op. cit., p. 27.

[39]David Bayley, The Policy of Preventive Detention 1950-63, Indian Journal of Public Administration, Vol. 10, pp. 235, 243 (1964).

[40](1962) All India Rep. S. Ct. 955.

[41]New York Times, January 10, 1971, p. 10; January 2, 1968, p. 8. In 1973 he entered national politics as a spokesman for all Indian Moslems. New York Times, August 26, 1973, p. 2. He again became Chief Minister of Kashmir in 1975 and was reelected in 1977.

[42]New York: Harper and Row, 1966.

[43]Ibid., pp. 18-20.

[44]Ibid., pp. 14, 24.

[45]Ibid., pp. 41-42.

[46]Pavel Litvinov, The Demonstration in Pushkin Square (Boston: Gambit, 1969).

[47]New York Times, November 3, 1970, p. 1. The Amalrik book was published in paperback by Harper and Row, New York, 1971.

[48]Abraham Brumberg, The Rise of Dissent in the U.S.S.R., pp. 3, 7-8 of Abraham Brumberg, In Quest of Justice: Protest and Dissent in the Soviet Union Today (New York: Praeger, 1970) and the documents contained at pp. 93-182 of Ibid.

[49]Andrei Amalrik was himself convicted of violating this law, an event that forms the basis of his An Involuntary Journey to Siberia (New York: Harcourt, Brace, Jovanovich, 1970).

[50]Harvey Fireside, _Psychiatric Abuse in the USSR_, p. 1, unpublished paper delivered at the 1979 N.Y. State Political Science Ass'n. Convention; _New York Times_, August 15, 1980, p. A22.

[51]See its _Report on Torture_ (New York: Farrar, Straus and Giroux, 1975), p. 190. See also _The Times_ (London), July 26, 1978, p. 3.

[52]Richard Lowenthal, _The Return of Stalin's Mustache on a Higher Level_, _New York Times Magazine_, March 28, 1971, p. 26; Amnesty International, _Prisoners of Conscience in the USSR_ (London: Amnesty International, 1975), p. 53.

[53]Robert Conquest (ed.), _Justice and the Legal System in the U.S.S.R._ (New York: Praeger, 1968), p. 93.

[54]Jerry Hough and Merle Fainsod, _How the Soviet Union Is Governed_ (Cambridge: Harvard U. Press, 1979), p. 291.

[55]_New York Times_, September 19, 1980, p. 1.

[56]Mark Joelson, _Legal Problems in the Dismissal of Civil Servants in the United States, Britain and France_, Am. J. Comp. L. 12:149,168 (1963).

[57]28 May 1954, Rec. 308; D. 1954.594.

[58]Countil of State (henceforth abbreviated "C.E.") October 1, 1954, Rec. 496; D. 1955 Jurisprudence (henceforth abbreviated "J.") 431.

[59]Joelson, _op. cit._, p. 168.

[60]Long, Weil and Braibant, _Les Grands Arrêts de la Jurisprudence Administrative_, pp. 390-91.

[61]Quoted _Ibid._, p. 389.

[62]Quoted _Ibid._, p. 390.

[63]March 8, 1968, Plenel, Rec. 168. For a general discussion, see Long, Weil, and Braibant, op. cit., pp. 387-92.

[64]C.E., 13 March 1953, Rec. 133; D. 1953.J. 735.

[65]April 4, 1936; D. 1936.3.38.

[66]November 29, 1936; D. 1937.3.14.

[67]New York Times, November 1, 1968, p. 2.

[68]Le Monde, January 22, 1975, p. 10; July 31, 1975, p. 20; New York Times, August 28, 1975, p. 12.

[69]The Times (London), September 4, 1980, p. 3.

[70]July 21, 1970, Rec. 499. Assoc. Enbata, C.E. October 8, 1975, Rec. 494 upheld the outlawing of the Basque Liberation group Enbata because one of its goals was secession.

[71]C.E., January 13, 1971, Rec. 31.

[72]Le Monde, June 9, 1977, p. 18; December 21, 1978, p. 18; The Times (London), October 18, 1980, p. 4.

[73]D. 1959.J.552.

[74]Gazette du Palais (henceforth abbreviated "Gaz. Pal.") 1951.1.200.

[75]Teff et Bec Marceau, Gaz. Pal. 1950.1.370.

[76]Gaz. Pal. 1951.1.151.

[77]Times Literary Supplement, March 30, 1962, p. 217.

[78]C.E., July 13, 1973, Monus, Rec. 527.

[79]November 2, 1973, Librarie François Maspero, Rec. 611. 7

[80]Mills v. Alabama, 384 U.S. 214,219 (1966).

[81]376 U.S. 254 (1964).

[82]376 U.S. at p. 279.

[83](1961) 2 Q.B. 162, aff'd. (1962) 2 All E.R. 737.

[84]See Clancy Sigal, The British Way of Libel, Nation 230:242, March 1, 1980.

[85]See, generally, Madeline Robinton, Parliamentary Privileges and Political Morality in Britain, Political Science Quarterly, Vol. 73, pp. 179, 186 (1958). For the more recent developments, see The Times (London), December 22, 1976, p. 2.

[86]A discussion of this case can be found at p. 183 of Robinton, op. cit.

[87]Marshall v. Gordon, 243 U.S. 521 (1917).

[88]379 U.S. 64 (1964).

[89](1928) 44 T.L.R. 301.

[90]The case is R. v. Metropolitan Police Comm'r. ex parte Blackburn, (1968) 2 All E.R. 319. The quote is on p. 320 of (1968) 2 All E.R. However, in 1980 a judge recovered $60,000 in a settlement with The Economist, which had reported that his appointment was due to his Catholicism. New York Times, December 15, 1980, p. A9.

[91]328 U.S. 331 (1946).

[92]New York Times, July 5, 1975, p. 1.

[93]Smt. Indira Gandhi v. Raj Narain, (1976) 2 Sup. Ct. R. 347.

[94] New York Times, December 21, 1975, p. 1; January 4, 1976, p. 11; January 5, 1976, p. 3; January 30, 1976, p. 3; February 17, 1976, p. 7; April 4, 1976, p. 8.

[95] New York Times, March 29, 1977, p. 2; April 5, 1977, p. 3; Times of India (Bombay ed.), May 6, 1978, p. 8.

[96] (1966) All India Rep. Andhra Pradesh 167.

[97] W. H. Morris-Jones, Parliament In India (Philadelphia: U. of Pennsylvania Press, 1957), pp. 253-54.

[98] K. P. Narayanan v. Mahendrasingh, (1965) I.L.R. Nagpur Series 439.

[99] Nelson's Indian Penal Code, 6th ed. (Allahabad: Law Book Co., 1970), p. 2752.

[100] (1966) All India Rep. Cal. 473.

[101] Albert Chavanne, Diffamation Contre les Particuliers, pp. 6-7, Juris Classeur Pénal, Presse.

[102] Le Monde, June 25, 1975, p. 6. Those who heap scorn upon a court verdict may also run afoul of Article 226 of the Penal Code, which condemns attacking a judicial decision in such a way as to threaten the authority or independence of the judiciary. Thus in Coulouma, D. 1964.623, February 27, 1964, the Court of Cassation upheld the Article 226 conviction of a man who attacked a land condemnation decision that allegedly gave the owner too little compensation. His article said that landowners in the Fifth Republic, whether their land be developed or undeveloped, can be sure that the courts will not pay them. He also referred to the particular decision as a masterpiece of incoherence, extravagance and abuse of law rarely seen in the annals of French jurisprudence. Article 226 has, however, been invoked only four

112

or five times. New York Times, November 10, 1980, p. A4.

[103]"R . . .," Gaz. Pal. 1974.1.353.

[104]Case of Sallent, October 9, 1974, Gaz. Pal. 1975.1.200. In 1977 editors were fined under Art. 30 (as well as for apologizing for murder) when they criticized police behavior in a "shoot-out." Le Monde, June 9, 1977, p. 18.

[105]On the good faith defense see Albert Chavanne, Diffamation Contre les Particuliers, pp. 17ff, Juris Classeur Pénal, Presse. The Trade union case is Syndicat de la Magistrature, Sem. Juridique, 1978, Tab. Juris., p. 168; the police case is Proc. Gen. c. B and S, Gaz. Pal., March 18, 1979, p. 8.

[106]New York Times, March 10, 1968, p. 22.

[107]Albert Chavanne, Offense au Président de la République, p. 4, Juris Classeur Pénal, Presse.

[108]Gaz. Pal. 1966.1.349.

[109]New York Times, January 28, 1974, p. 6.

[110]Le Monde, February 3-4, 1980, p. 6.

[111]New York Times, October 27, 1962, p. 5; October 21, 1965, p. 2.

[112]Le Monde, September 7, 1978, p. 8; New York Times, November 28, 1974, p. 15; Economist, December 17, 1977, p. 51; July 15, 1978, p. 49; January 27, 1979, p. 35; Index on Censorship, Vol. 3, May-June, 1977, p. 67; The Guardian, August 10, 1979, p. 4.

[113]Martin Harrison, Government and Press in France during the Algerian War, American Political Science Review 58:273,274,277 (1964).

[114]Harrison, op. cit., p. 275; Long, Weil, and Braibant, op. cit., pp. 486-87.

[115]The case is S.A.R.L. des Editions de France Observateur c. Agent Judiciaire de Trésor, D. 1964.231.

[116]Harrison, op. cit., p. 274.

[117]Long, Weil, and Braibant, op. cit., p. 487.

[118]This test is found in A Book Named John Cleland's Memoirs of a Woman of Pleasure v. Attorney General of Massachusetts (the Fanny Hill case), 383 U.S. 413 (1966).

[119]Kingsley International Pictures Corp. v. Regents, 360 U.S. 684 (1959).

[120]Grove Press v. Gerstein, 378 U.S. 577 (1964).

[121]Redrup v. N.Y., 386 U.S. 767 (1967).

[122]413 U.S. 15 (1973). In FCC v. Pacifica Foundation, 438 U.S. 726 (1978), the Court held that the government could penalize the use of dirty albeit not per se obscene words over the air. Similarly, sending indecent but not obscene matter via the British mails violates the law, R. v. Stanley, (1965) 2 Q.B. 327.

[123]New York Times, May 19, 1974, p. 55.

[124](1868) L.R. 3 Q.B. 360.

[125]Street, op. cit., 2nd ed., p. 137.

[126]Ibid., pp. 134-35. Pinkus v. U.S., 436 U.S. 293 (1978), held that American juries should look to the effects of a work on adults (including gays and sado-masochists) but not on children.

[127] Street, op. cit., 2nd ed., pp. 145-46; The Times (London), June 22, 1972, p. 18.

[128] The case is described in Street, op. cit., 2nd ed., pp. 141-43.

[129] (1969) 1 Q.B. 151.

[130] (1969) 1 Q.B. at p. 172. A 1976 case, R. v. Staniforth, (1976) 2 All E.R. 714, Ct. of Appeal, held that its therapeutic effect upon deviants is not relevant to show that an obscene book furthers the public good.

[131] Street, op. cit., 4th ed., p. 149.

[132] (1965) 1 Q.B. 509.

[133] Graham Zellick, Violence As Pornography, (1970) Crim. L. Rev. (Eng.), pp. 188-95.

[134] (1965) 1 Sup. Ct. R. 65.

[135] (1965) 1 Sup. Ct. R., pp. 77ff. However, a description of a love affair is not per se obscene. C. K. Kakodkar v. Maharashtra, (1970) All India Rep. S. Ct. 1390.

[136] Wall Street Journal, January 24, 1977, p. 6. The censors can ban violence, glorification of crime, and attacks on ethnic groups as well as obscenity. See Current Events, March, 1974, Vol. 20, p. 46. India's film censorship (including labelling some films "for adults only") was sustained in K. A. Abbas v. Union, (1971) All India Rep. S. Ct. 481. Udeshi applies to films but, the Court added, the censor must seriously consider the film's value as an art work. The kissing dispute is discussed in New York Times, May 28, 1978, Sec. 1, p. 46.

[137] Raj Kapoor v. Laxman, (1980) All India Rep. S. Ct. 605.

[138] John Hazard and Isaac Shapiro, The Soviet Legal System (Dobbs Ferry, N.Y.: Oceana, 1962), p. 78; Lev Lifshitz-Losev, What It Means to Be Censored, New York Rev. of Books, June 28, 1978, pp. 43ff. The secret police and military sometimes act as censors; and theater censorship prevails. See Index on Censorship, August 1980, pp. 5, 23.

[139] Commission on Obscenity and Pornography, Report (New York: Bantam Books, 1970), p. 406.

[140] V. S. Pritchett, Hearing from Chekov, New York Rev. of Books, June 28, 1973, p. 3.

[141] New York Times, March 11, 1979, p. 4.

[142] New York Times, November 30, 1980, Sec. 4, p. E3.

[143] Le Monde, January 18, 1979, p. 10.

[144] The case is Gerard Nelly, Gaz. Pal. 1972. 2.558.

[145] See D. 1975 J. 243, Comments on Leguiader et autres, D. 1974 J. 242.

[146] January 10, 1957, D. 1957.J.259.

[147] Claude-Albert Colliard, État des Libertés Publiques en France en 1970-71, Human Rights Journal, 5:19, 29-30 (1972); New York Times, March 15, 1975, p. 5.

[148] New York Times, March 15, 1975, p. 5. As a result of this change, the first full-length film on the Dreyfus case reached the French screen in 1975. Ibid.

[149] Le Monde Dimanche, January 13, 1980, p. V (translated in Manch. Guard. Wkly., March 2, 1980, p. 13).

[150] Colliard, <u>Libertés Publiques</u>, 3rd ed., pp. 496-97; Herbert Lottman, <u>Interdit: Censorship in France</u>, <u>Wilson Library Bulletin</u>, 40:759 (1966).

[151] December 18, 1959, Rec. 693.

[152] Colliard, <u>Libertés Publiques</u>, 3rd ed., pp. 509-14; Long, Weil, and Braibant, <u>op. cit.</u>, pp. 477-80.

[153] Colliard, <u>Libertés Publiques</u>, 3rd ed., p. 433. <u>Index on Censorship</u>, October, 1980, pp. 56-58.

[154] Lottman, <u>op. cit.</u>, p. 762.

[155] January 3, 1958, Rec. 4.

[156] <u>New York Times</u>, March 18, 1962, p. 19.

[157] December 17, 1958, Rec. 968.

[158] Jean-Michel Marchand, <u>Cinéma</u>, Fasc. 267 of <u>Juris Classeur Administrative</u>, at pp. 10-11. However, in 1980 the Marseilles police prefect successfully pressured a theater owner to postpone a festival of antimilitarist films until after the anniversaries of the death of General de Gaulle and the 1918 Armistice. <u>Le Monde</u>, November 8, 1980, p. 13.

[159] Beytout et Soc. Nouvelle de Cinématographie, Ct. Cassation, <u>Sem. Juridique</u>, June 6, 1979, #19143.

CHAPTER III

CHURCH AND STATE IN THE
FIVE COUNTRIES

A. Freedom of Religion

The United States political system is extremely tolerant of religion, respecting the
command of the First Amendment (incorporated by
the Fourteenth) that it shall not abridge the free
exercise of religion. No individual can be denied
a government job simply because he belongs to a
particular faith or does not believe in God at
all.[1] Article VI, Section 3 of the Constitution
itself states that ". . . no religious Test shall
ever be required as a Qualification to any Office
or public Trust under the United States." In addition, the laws of many states make it illegal
for employers, trade unions, landlords or real
estate brokers to discriminate against anyone on
account of his religion. (These anti-
discrimination laws, whether banning discrimination
on racial or on religious grounds, are better
characterized as examples of "stimulation of
intergroup contact" than as "toleration.")

Just how far the Supreme Court of the United
States is prepared to protect religious practice
can be seen in the following cases. In Cantwell v.
Connecticut,[2] a Jehovah's Witness appealed his
conviction by a Connecticut court of crimes including breach of the peace. He had gone around
a Roman Catholic neighborhood in New Haven,
Connecticut and asked passers-by if he could play
his records. When somebody agreed to hear them,
he started the phonograph. The records contained
violent attacks on the Roman Catholic Church--one
Catholic listener felt like hitting Cantwell,

119

while another told him to get off the street before something happened to him. The Court made it clear that convicting him violated his freedom of religion, noting that this freedom protects not only mild pleading on behalf of one's views but even some exaggeration, falsehood and vilification of one's opponents. Had Cantwell been a political propagandist, his conviction probably would have been sustained on clear and present danger grounds.

In <u>Martin v. Struthers</u>,[3] the Court invalidated, as applied to Jehovah's Witnesses, an ordinance of the city of Struthers, Ohio forbidding door-to-door handbilling even though many people in that community worked in factories at night and slept during the day. However, a similar law as applied to sellers of secular magazines was held constitutional.[4] In <u>West Virginia Board of Education v. Barnette</u>,[5] it reversed a decision it had issued three years previously and held that a state could not compel Jehovah's Witnesses to salute the American flag in school when to do so would be in violation of their religious beliefs. Jehovah's Witnesses living in New Hampshire may tape over that part of their license plates proclaiming "Live Free or Die": making them display this slogan is unconstitutionally forcing them to infringe the rules of their creed.[6]

The most ticklish problems in the United States involving freedom of religion have arisen when an act commanded by one's faith violates state or federal legislation intended to promote health, safety, morality, or education and not to stamp out religious dissent. One example is the situation covered by the door-to-door salesman case noted above: another is presented by the anti-polygamy laws. As is well known, the Mormon religion used to permit its male adherents to have more than one spouse. In <u>Reynolds v. United States</u>,[7] the Supreme Court upheld the conviction of a Mormon who violated a federal anti-polygamy law. However, there have been important and numerous occasions when the conflict between unorthodox religious practices and the state's power to promote the health, safety, convenience, education and morality of its citizens has resulted in a defeat for the public authority and thus in toleration. One well-publicized example involved the Amish, a group of fundamentalist Mennonites who believe that education beyond the eighth-grade level is dangerous because it will expose their youth to worldly influences. The Supreme Court declared in Wisconsin v. Yoder[8] that when Wisconsin forced the Amish to send their children to high school, it violated their religious freedom.

The British as well as the United States approaches to minority religious groups are generally highly tolerant. Though it was not until 1824 that Roman Catholics were allowed to sit in Parliament and hold public office, and though it was not until 1858 that Jews who refused to swear that they were Christian could sit in Parliament and until 1871 that they could go to Oxford and Cambridge, as early as 1883 Chief Justice Coleridge was saying that Christianity was no longer automatically the law of Britain and that one could thus criticize the Christian faith without being guilty of blasphemy.[9] (In the United States, in State of Maryland v. West,[10] a statute making it illegal to curse or blaspheme God, Christ or the Trinity was invalidated as a violation of the "establishment" and "free exercise" clauses of the U.S. Constitution.) The Oaths Act of 1888 allowed atheists to take their seats in Parliament and, when witnesses in court, to affirm rather than swear. The House of Lords made it clear in Bowman v. Secular Society[11] that a bequest to a society to promote atheism was valid.

In 1966, the Home Office (which controls the London police) stated that it doubted that the offense of blasphemy would ever be prosecuted now.

121

Amazingly, in 1977 an editor was convicted of this very offense when he published a poem depicting Christ as a homosexual, attracting a Roman centurion as His body was being taken off the cross. In R. v. Lemon the Court of Appeal upheld the conviction and this decision in turn was approved by the House of Lords.[12]

Britain too is faced with the religion versus public health, order and/or morality conflicts that arise, for example, when a group claims that its members are under a religious duty to practice polygamy or to refrain from giving blood even to save a dying relative. The few pertinent cases have found against the group or its members. For instance, if someone is prosecuted for neglecting criminally someone in his care by refusing to give him the necessary medicine, he probably could not defend by saying that he objected to the use of medicine on religious grounds.[13] In R. v. Senior[14] a father was convicted under the Prevention of Cruelty to Children Act of 1894 of failing to give his infant child suffering from diarrhea and pneumonia adequate medical care. The defendant was in all respects a loving parent, and refused to fetch medical assistance merely because he was a member of a religious sect that objected to physicians and drugs. And a more recent holding refused to construe a statute to allow a Moslem teacher, without losing pay, to miss class to pray on Friday at a mosque.[15]

Like the United States, Britain has been troubled by the question of whether something is "religious." This definitional problem is bound to occur whenever a statute grants or takes away benefits from a "religious" group. (The best known such situation in America involves conscientious objection to war. The relevant statute exempted from the draft religious conscientious objectors only, but the Supreme Court in another example of tolerance extended the exemption to clearly felt conscientious objection to war on secular grounds.)[16] In Henning v. Church of Jesus

Christ of Latter Day Saints,[17] the question was whether the Mormon temple in Godstone, Surrey, was entitled to a property tax exemption. Subsection 2(a) of the Rating Act of 1955 gave such an exemption to places of public religious worship. There was no doubt that Mormon chapels are such. But the temple, unlike the chapel, is not open to the public, nor even to all Mormons, unless they possess the requisite spiritual qualities. The court held, therefore, that the temple was not entitled to the tax exemption, since it was really a private sanctuary for sacred rites rather than a place of public worship. Likewise, the Ethical Culture Society was denied a property tax exemption for one of its halls since the group does not believe in a Supreme Being. The Camden Borough Council then refused to grant it partial tax relief because it had rented the hall to rightwing as well as leftwing speakers.[18] A U.S. court declared Ethical Culture property exempt from tax.[19]

Until a few years ago, an exception to the policy of official religious tolerance in the United Kingdom was to be found in Northern Ireland. In local affairs, this region was until 1972 governed by its own Parliament. This "Stormont" legislature subjected Catholics in the North to certain subtle disabilities, though they worshiped openly and without any hindrance. There used to be a property qualification for voting in elections to local councils in Northern Ireland: to vote one had to be an owner or a renter or a spouse of an owner or a renter. This effectively disqualified many Catholics. Northern Irish Catholics often have in the household adult children or poor relations--on the whole Catholic families in Ulster are larger than Protestant because of Catholic objection to birth control--and these children and poor relatives were disenfranchised by the property requirements. Thus the town of Derry is 2 to 1 Catholic but had in 1969 thirteen thousand Protestant voters to only nine thousand Catholic. The Derry City Council consisted of 12 Unionists (the Ulster branch of the Tory party, and formerly the major political arm of Ulster Protestantism) and only 8 Nationalists (the then-major party of the Northern Irish Catholics). The Protestants also maintained their dominance of local government by use of a gerrymander technique to throw most Catholic voters into one election district. The local authorities often favored Protestants over Catholics when it came to allocating municipal jobs and apartments in public housing.

These facts are some of the material out of which the distrust and bloodshed that plagues Belfast and other Ulster communities is made. By 1981, over 2,000 persons had been killed as a result of sectarian violence. The legal discrimination is gone; but on the unofficial level Protestants and Catholics continue to confront one another in this small corner of the globe. At best, they are mutually suspicious; at worst they shoot each other, innocent bystanders, and any British soldier they feel is in their way.[20]

Indian society is much less secularized than American or English; and the dictates of religion still play an important part in the lives of a majority of Indian citizens. Moreover, the division of the Indian subcontinent into Pakistan and India was the product of extreme antagonism between Moslem and Hindu. Within the Republic of India itself, conflict between Moslem and Hindu has led to bloody riots in, e.g., 1968, 1978 and 1980.[21] Thus, like Ulster, India lives under the constant threat of religious civil war; and full-fledged religious civil war in India could lead to millions of deaths.

In addition to 60 million Moslems, there are in the country large communities of Buddhists, Christians, Sikhs, and Jains and smaller groups of Parsis (Zoroastrians) and Jews. All of these, including the Moslems, practice their religion openly without suffering, jail, fine, or other disability

124

at the hands of the state. A Moslem, Dr. Zakir Husain, was elected Vice-President of India in 1962 and President in 1967; and another, Fakhruddin Ali Ahmed, was chosen President of India in 1974. The government makes it easy for Moslems wishing to make the pilgrimage to Mecca to obtain foreign exchange.[22] On the whole, then, the approaches of the Indian political system toward claims of freedom of religion are tolerant; but there are some interesting exceptions to this general orientation. Similarly, Hinduism is basically a tolerant faith; but there are Hindu political parties and groups, including the Jana Sangh, that demand supremacy within India for the Hindu religion.

Hinduism's essential tolerance was one strand that went into weaving those clauses of the Indian Constitution dealing with freedom of religion and the relationship of state to organized religion. Another was Mohandas Gandhi's dislike of the caste system, and still another was the agnosticism (albeit a "reverent agnosticism") of men such as Jawaharlal Nehru, the Prime Minister of India during the first 17 years of its independence and an important participant in the framing of the Constitution. What emerged from all these threads was a piece of constitutional cloth that is extremely complicated. The American Constitution deals with religion quickly though powerfully in the First Amendment. The analogous part of the Indian Constitution is six sections long (Sections 25 through 30) and most of these sections contain several sub-paragraphs--and even these six sections do not exhaust what the Constitution has to say specifically about religion.

Of importance are some particular situations in which religious groups have claimed that a state or the national government, acting under its power to promote public health, welfare, and order, has treated them too repressively. Through the centuries Hinduism developed practices on a subcontinent-wide or local level which educated Indians regard as shocking. Thus some states have enacted legislation to ban animal sacrifice at Hindu temples and the dedication of young virgins to the temple (who often became temple prostitutes). There is no doubt about the constitutionality of these laws, which are valid under the clause of Article 25(1), the freedom of religion article, granting freedom of religion but providing that this freedom shall be subject to the demands of public order, morality and health.

Many Hindu temples have been donated lands and vast amounts of jewelry, money and other personal property in order to secure for the donor or testator health and prosperity in this world and reincarnation in his next life in a higher caste. Though the property is given to the temple deity or to the temple as an institution, in this imperfect world it has to be managed by men, usually the temple priests or trustees or temple guides. As of Indian independence many temples were being badly maintained, even though a good deal of property had been bequeathed to them, because the human beings who were supposed to use it for the benefit of the idol employed it dishonestly or wastefully. Article 26 consequently gives each religious denomination or any section thereof the right to establish and maintain institutions for religious and charitable purposes but subjects this right to control in the interest of public order, morality and health. Similarly, Article 25(2)(b) allows the state to provide for social welfare and reform notwithstanding the Constitution's grant of religious freedom.

Relying on these Articles the State of Madras passed in 1951 an act enabling a public commissioner to superintend and administer religious endowments to make sure that they were properly maintained. The commissioner had the right to enter temples and, under certain circumstances, to dismiss trustees of religious institutions and to appoint others in their place --or even to start administering the temple directly through one of his assistants. The

126

trustees of the temples had to submit reports to the commissioner and get his permission before any sale or mortgage of the immovable property of the temple could be permitted. Furthermore, surplus temple funds could be spent only in accordance with the purposes listed in the act and particular expenditures for these purposes had to be approved by a deputy commissioner.

In the decision that is called the Shirur Math23 case the Supreme Court sustained some and invalidated other parts of this act, which concerned Hindu temples only. The temple priests who asserted the act was invalid pointed to Article 26(b) giving each religious denomination the right "to manage its own affairs in matters of religion." The Court did strike the parts of the law giving the commissioner unrestricted right to entry and complete control over surplus income; requiring the temple heads to appoint a manager for the secular affairs of the institution; obliging the temple to pay up to 5 percent of its annual income to compensate the state for the services the government rendered; and granting the state the right to administer their property in accordance with law. However, it upheld those sections of the act allowing the commissioner to modify the budget of the religious institution and said that he could regulate the temple's expenditures on religious ceremonies even though the religious denomination itself had the right to determine what ceremonies were essential to the faith. In 1959 Madras passed a new law retaining the state's power to prevent abuse of temple funds but limiting the right of entry and giving the temple priests control over surplus funds. Other states, too (for example, Bombay, Orissa), have passed similar legislation.

Article 17 outlaws the practice of untouchability and Article 25(2)(b) allows the state to throw open Hindu religious institutions of a public character to all classes and sections of Hindus. The purpose of the latter is to make illegal the practice of excluding Harijans (untouchables) from Hindu temples: orthodox Hindus hold that Harijans must worship in the temple courtyard and cannot enter the temple itself. A Harijan in a temple is as welcome to a member of the Brahmin caste worshipping there as a side of roast pork on his Passover table is to an orthodox Jew!

A major Supreme Court case dealing with temple entry legislation passed pursuant to Article 25(2)(b) is Devaru v. State of Mysore.[24] This involved an act providing that untouchables "shall be entitled to enter any Hindu temple and offer worship therein in the same manner and to the same extent as Hindus in general." The temple in question was run by a sect called the Gowda Saraswath Brahmins, who contended that this law was unconstitutional under Article 26(b) granting each religious denomination the right to manage its own affairs in matters of religion. There is no doubt, of course, that Articles 25(2)(b) and Article 26(b) are in literal conflict, as the court itself recognized. To resolve them, it held the law valid insofar as it required the denomination to admit untouchables most of the year but invalid insofar as it prohibited the Gowda Saraswath Brahmins from excluding untouchables and other members of the general public from the temples while the sect's most sacred ceremonies were being held there. To revert to an earlier comparison, the Court's decision was analogous to a decision compelling Jewish synagogues to be open to gentiles Friday evening and Saturday, the usual times of workship, but allowing them to exclude outsiders during Rosh Hashana (New Year) and Yom Kippur (Day of Atonement) services!

Article 25(1) grants all persons the right to propagate as well as practice religion. However, Hinduism, like Judaism and unlike Christianity and Islam, is not a proselytizing faith. Furthermore, though Christian communities have existed in India since at least the fourth or

128

fifth centuries A.D.--and perhaps as early as 52 A.D.--Christianity became the religion of a significant number of Indians thanks to the efforts of European missionaries who did their work during the years of British rule. As a result, Christian missionaries are naturally viewed as agents of western imperialism and so are suspect in certain Hindu and radical quarters. In addition, these missionaries have been very active and successful among the Naga tribesmen of Assam demanding independence from India. As a consequence, they are viewed by some as carriers of treasonable doctrines.

Despite these suspicions, there were 5,700 foreign missionaries in the country in 1955. In that year, however, the Indian government began adopting a repressive approach toward them, deciding to admit only those who possessed special qualifications. Along with this restriction, it required missions to gain its approval before opening new centers, and institutions and missionaries from Commonwealth countries were no longer to be given special preference. In 1967, it ordered all foreign missionaries to leave Assam because they were suspected of stirring up a desire for independence among the hill people there, including the Nagas.[25] Thus, by 1972, there were only 3,000 foreign missionaries left in India.[26] Also, the states of Madyha Pradesh, Orissa and others have passed "anti-conversion" bills aimed mainly at Christian missionaries. The Orissa statute reads that "No person shall convert or attempt to convert, either directly or otherwise, any person from one religious faith to another by the use of force or by inducement or by any fraudulent means." Various Christian evangelists have been arrested under these laws, which have been sustained by the Supreme Court on the theory that the right to propagate one's religion implies the right to give an exposition of its tenets but not the right to convert.[27] Moreover, Hindu fanatics have beaten Christian missionaries and had them arrested on trumped-up charges, while local governments in Arunachal Pradesh have been accused of jailing converted Christians and of refusing to let Christians build churches.[28]

Another example of a repressive approach in the area of religion arises because the humble cow is to Hindus a sacred animal. Article 48 of the Constitution, whose wording is designed to make its capitulation to traditional Hinduism not too displeasing to more westernized, scientifically-oriented Indians, reads as follows:

> The State shall endeavor to organize agriculture and animal husbandry on modern and scientific lines and shall, in particular, take steps for preserving and improving the breeds, and prohibiting the slaughter, of cows and calves and other milch and draught cattle.

Most Indian states have passed cow slaughter bans under the protective umbrella of Article 48. This legislation is especially controversial because Indian Moslems slay cows on their festival of Bakr Id. In Quareshi v. Bihar,[29] the Indian Supreme Court was confronted squarely with the question of whether these bans were an unconstitutional infringement of the right to freely practice one's religion when applied to Moslems who wanted to sacrifice cows on that holiday. The Court, in upholding this legislation even under these circumstances, put itself in the position of a group of Moslem theologians. It found, first of all, that it is the duty of every free Moslem to offer a sacrifice on Bakr Id--the holiday is, after all, a festival of sacrifice. But, continued the Court, the sacrificed animal does not have to be a cow, though it admitted that Indian Moslems have been sacrificing this particular beast from time immemorial. The religious requirements of Bakr Id can be satisfied by the slaughter of a goat for one person or a camel for seven persons. It is true that a family might not be able to sacrifice seven goats, but the compulsion to offer up a cow

130

in that event is economic, not religious. And since cow slaughter on Bakr Id is not made obligatory by Islam, its prohibition under an otherwise valid law would not be considered to infringe the religious liberties of Moslems.

Another event which seemed to some Indian Moslems serious repression of their religious liberties involved Aligarh Moslem University, the intellectual center for Indian Moslems and, before independence, the source of the idea of a separate Moslem state of Pakistan. In 1951 the Indian government passed a law providing that non-Moslems could become members of the University "Court," the institution's governing body, and gave the President of India the authority to appoint the Vice-Chancellor, the real head of the college. Hindu extremists were interested in erasing the Moslem character of the University; but the government was motivated simply by a desire to insure that the University would adhere to the provisions of the Constitution forbidding institutions receiving state aid from requiring religious instruction of any student or discriminating in admission on account of religion, caste or language. In 1965 a riot erupted against the secularist Moslem Vice-Chancellor of the University. The rioters were conservative Moslem students protesting a proposal that would have the effect of reducing the percentage of Moslems in the medical and engineering colleges. The Vice-Chancellor was injured, and the Indian Minister of Education, himself a secularist Moslem, had the Union cabinet pass an ordinance that reduced the power of the University Court and vested more authority in the hands of the government-selected Vice-Chancellor.[30] The effect of the 1951 and 1965 reforms was, of course, to put Aligarh University under secular control. An American reader will inevitably be reminded here of the Dartmouth College Case,[31] in which the U.S. Supreme Court dealt unfavorably with an attempt of the Republican (i.e., Jeffersonian) government of New Hampshire to place a private college under public control against the wishes of

131

its trustees.

The Moslems who wanted to return Aligarh Moslem University to Moslem control brought suit in court to have the 1951 statute and the 1965 decree declared invalid. They relied on Article 30(1) of the Indian Constitution, which gives religious and linguistic minorities, "the right to establish and administer educational institutions of their choice." Their contention was that this statute and decree deprived the Moslem minority of the right to administer its own educational institution. The Indian Supreme Court, however, upheld the constitutionality of these laws.[32] It argued, first, that the only educational institutions which, under Article 30(1), minorities have the right to administer are those which they have established. Now, the Court continued, has the Moslem community established Aligarh University? The predecessor of this University, a college created under the auspices of another university, may have been set up by Moslems. But the establishment of Aligarh University took place when it was raised from college to University status. And this conversion, the Court contended, was the result of an act of the Indian Government in 1920, even though this act was admittedly passed at the behest of India's Moslems. Therefore, Aligarh Moslem University, the Court concluded, was established by the Government of India and not the Moslem community and that community has no constitutional right to continue to administer it.

To obtain Moslem political support, Prime Minister Desai in 1978 decided to let the University revert to Moslem control. Nonetheless, there are still factors creating Hindu-Moslem tension and making Moslems feel like second class citizens, including cow slaughter legislation; severe unemployment among educated Moslems; and the fact that Moslems are significantly underrepresented in government service.[33] Likewise insensitive to Moslem feelings is Mohammed Ali Khan v. Lucknow,[34] holding that a city can condemn a

132

mosque and adjacent cemetery for public purposes.
The High Court said that the taking does not
violate a Moslem's Article 25(1) guarantee of freedom of religion because he can pray in another
mosque. Moreover, the loss of the graveyard,
according to the opinion, deprives no living person
of freedom of religion.

Though the Soviet Union is the only one of
our countries that is officially atheist, Article
52 of the Brezhnev Constitution (formerly Article
124 of the Stalin Constitution), guarantees freedom
of conscience and of religious worship, as well as
freedom of anti-religious propaganda. The number
of religious groups in the U.S.S.R. is large. In
addition to Jews and Russian Orthodox, one finds
the sect of Russian Orthodoxy known as the "Old
Believers," the Armenian Church, Roman Catholics,
Roman Catholics of the Eastern Rite, various Greek
Catholic groups, Buddhists, Sunni Moslems, Shiite
Moslems, Karaites, Bahais, pagans, Baptists,
Methodists, Lutherans, Calvinists, Evangelical
Christians, Jehovah's Witnesses and others. The
Soviet Union has no reference to religion in its
census, and so one cannot know with any degree of
exactitude how many adherents its religious groups
and sects have. The government tends to play down
the number of believers in God in the U.S.S.R.
while foreign observers sympathetic to religion
imply that this number is substantial.

The Russian Orthodox Church is the religious
faith of a plurality of believers. One writer
estimates that there may be between 20 and 30 million practicing members of this Church; others
suggest a figure of 30-50 million.[35] The fate of
Russian Orthodoxy under Russian communism has been
a chequered one; and its future remains difficult
to predict. It was "disestablished" by the
Bolsheviks in early 1918, soon after they had come
to power. In February of 1922 the Government asked
the Orthodox churches to surrender all treasures
except for those used in the sacraments in order
that the government could become financially able

to purchase food for the people who were starving in the widespread famine raging at the time. When priests resisted this decree, they were arrested and quite a few of them were killed. Perhaps over 8,100 Orthodox priests, nuns and monks were murdered by the Soviet government in 1922.

Between 1926 and 1937, when the Stalin Constitution was introduced, priests of all faiths were disenfranchised and excluded from membership in trade unions and teaching; and their children were not admitted to universities. In 1929, as part of its campaign to collectivize the countryside and destroy the kulaks, the Government intensified its repression of the Orthodox Church. Thousands of churches were forcibly closed; hundreds were actually destroyed; heavy taxes were imposed on the parishes; bell ringing was prohibited and bells were melted down for industrial use; and numerous priests, bishops, and ordinary believers were exiled and often killed. The persecution lasted until 1932. The regime then moderated its attacks until 1937; in that year, the Orthodox Church, like most of the institutions of Soviet society, including the Communist Party itself, suffered massive repression through Stalin's purges. Many of its leaders were executed; and by the outbreak of war there were not more than 100 churches in the country open to worshippers.[36]

During World War II, the Soviet regime felt the need for support from the Church in the struggle with the Nazis; and the individual Orthodox churches asked their parishioners to go to the defense of the motherland. In September, 1943, Russian Orthodoxy received its reward in the form of less repression. It was allowed to elect its own Patriarch and open a few seminaries; it received recognition as a judicial person; and it was handed back some churches. After 1955, the Church leaders helped Soviet foreign policy by holding frequent meetings with Christian leaders in the West. In 1959, for reasons which are not

134

too clear, the Khrushchev government began a new era of massive repression of the Church. Churches were closed, taxation of priests was increased, and the profit made from the sale of candles was declared illegal speculation--up till that time, the parishes had obtained a good deal of income from selling candles. Perhaps only half the Orthodox churches in the country in 1959 were still in use by 1962. Monasteries and seminaries were padlocked and some church officials and priests were jailed for "economic crimes" or preaching religious doctrines which endangered the public welfare. This particular persecution ended in 1964 and the Orthodox church and the Soviet state once again exist in an uneasy modus vivendi.[37]

The Soviet Union and the Roman Catholic Church are for several reasons natural enemies. Both are international movements which at times claim that their world view is absolute truth. Furthermore, the Catholicism of Soviet nationalities such as the Poles and the Lithuanians is believed to hinder their acceptance of Communist philosophy. Between 1919 and 1925 the government imprisoned numerous members of the Catholic hierarchy. The massive repression that hit Orthodoxy between 1929 and 1932 did not spare the Catholic Church: priests were exiled and churches were closed; and many other members of the Catholic clergy were persecuted as spies in the purge trials of 1937. After World War II, the Soviets jailed or exiled about half the Catholic clergy in Latvia and Lithuania and put to death over a thousand Ukrainian Catholic priests. Following Stalin's death, most of the priests exiled in the immediate postwar period were amnestied, together with most other political prisoners. Though they freely conduct mass, Catholic priests in Lithuania are still being arrested for teaching catechism to children and preparing them for first communion. Government officials in that S.S.R. can shut churches at will.[38]

There is a nationwide Baptist organization
known as the "All-Union Council of Evangelical
Christian/Baptists" (AUCECB). AUCECB has remained
loyal to the Soviet state, exhorting its members
to work diligently for the Soviet Union and, as a
result, has received concessions such as being
allowed to print the Baptist edition of the Bible
in limited quantities for the first time since the
1929 persecutions.

However, reform Baptists (those opposed to
the AUCECB), who do not differ from the AUCECB on
theological matters, are more assiduous proselyt-
izers and demand less AUCECB and state control
over individual Baptist churches. This gets them
into trouble under several sections of the Soviet
criminal law. Article 227 of the Criminal Code of
the Russian Socialist Federated Soviet Republic--
there are similar laws in the other republics--
provides that persons guilty of the following
activities may be jailed or exiled for up to five
years:

> Organizing or directing a group, whose
> activity, although carried on with the
> appearance of preaching religious beliefs
> and performing religious ceremonies, is
> related to causing harm to the health of
> citizens or with any other infringements
> of the persons or rights of citizens, or
> with inducing citizens to refuse calls to
> social activity or performance of civic
> duties, or with inducing minors to enter
> such a group.

Article 142 of the Criminal Code of the RSFSR,
which also has counterparts in the other Soviet
Republics, makes it illegal to violate the laws on
the separation of church and state. An edict of
the Presidium of the Supreme Soviet of the RSFSR
describes the following activities as among those
violating these laws:

> Compulsory collection of taxes and

contributions for the use of religious
organizations and clergy; preparation for
the purpose of mass distribution, or mass
distribution of appeals, letters, leaflets,
and other documents exhorting refusal to
observe legislation on religious denominations; commission of fradulent acts for the
purpose of arousing religious superstitions
in the masses of the population; organization and conduct of religious meetings,
processions and other ceremonies of the
denomination, violating public order;
organization and systematic conduct of
classes to teach religion to minors in violation of the regulations established by
law . . .

Soviet law also requires that all religious associations be registered with the state and declares
that religious associations that violate the law
will not be permitted to register. It is the
local church that has to register with the authori-
ties--not the central church authority.

A proselytizing community of reform Baptists
can easily run afoul of one or another of the above
rules. First, they refuse to register. Next, they
can be deemed to have contravened the Presidium's
edict by teaching Sunday or Bible classes or by
preaching in public places, and by claiming that
this world is not of much importance they can be
held to have violated Article 227. In fact, the
reform Baptist groups were attacked in the press
and hundreds of reform Baptists were tried and convicted during the 1960's for failing to observe one
or another of these measures.[39] The following episode, involving four people convicted in Rostov-On-
Don of violating Article 142 by organizing a street
procession, mimeographing literature and running a
Sunday school, needs no comment.

Under the pretext of freedom of conscience and without the knowledge of the
local authorities, the defendants organized

137

a street procession by their co-
religionists in the city and a baptism in
the Don on 2 May, 1966. These violated
public order and aroused the legitimate
indignation of the local residents. The
defendants set up their own printing press,
where they illegally mimeographed literature steeped in a spirit of hostility
towards Soviet conditions and sometimes
containing open exhortations to believers
not to submit to Soviet legislation.

The defendants also have it on their
conscience that they organized a Baptist
Sunday School for children, where ignorant
and fanatical "teachers" taught the "word
of God" to children of between eight and
eleven, persistently and systematically
inculcating upon them a religious outlook
on life. . . .[40]

A substantial percentage of the political prisoners in the Soviet Union are now reform Baptists
and Jehovah's Witnesses, another proselytizing
sect. Also found in the jails are Pentacostals,
who hold religious classes for minors and refuse
military service.[41]

However, not every religious activity engaged in by a reform Baptist or other religious
dissenter will result in his losing his freedom:
the Soviet courts have, on occasion, released
Reform Baptists whose activities clearly did not
run counter to the various rules described above.
Hazard, Shapiro, and Maggs describe the following
case involving four Reformers who had been jailed
in a lower court for violating Article 227. What
these defendants, T., S., M., and A., did was to
leave the "regular" Baptist community in their
town, begin to conduct religious services in their
home, and distribute materials on religious matters. The Presidium of the Supreme Court of the
Tatar Autonomous SSR reversed the conviction. It
pointed out that severing oneself from one's

religious community is not a crime, since the state is not supposed to interfere with the internal affairs of a church. Moreover, under Article 124 of the USSR (Stalin) Constitution, freedom to conduct religious services is protected and therefore the defendants did no wrong in holding religious services in private homes and municipal apartment houses. The mere act of distributing pamphlets on religious topics is not a crime--Article 227 relates only to religious teaching which injures the health of citizens or induces them not to perform their civic duties.[42]

All the laws cited above apply to all religious groups, not only to reform Baptists or Catholics. (In essence, they limit churches to conducting religious services; and prevent them from proselytizing, performing fundamentalist rites such as "speaking in tongues," forming discussion groups, and conducting Sunday schools and other religious classes.) Thus they constitute weapons that the state uses against various denominations. The government holds additional power over religious groups because (as seen) no congregation may be organized without its consent; and because the churches are dependent on its permission for the printing of Bibles and other publications and the acquisition of real estate and personal property such as candlewax. No churches are constructed in new cities; and Bibles are printed infrequently and in limited editions and hardly ever appear in bookstores. However, the most potent device the polity uses against persons who have religious beliefs and display them publicly is a very simple one: no member of the Communist Party of the Soviet Union may take part in religious ceremonies.[43] Since political power and professional success require Party membership, Soviet citizens who wish to be overtly religious are almost automatically denied access to important offices and jobs.

When the Bolsheviks came into power, one of the customs of the Russian Empire that they wished

139

to eradicate was anti-Semitism. Many of the early leaders of the Soviet Union in the years immediately succeeding the Bolshevik revolution, for instance Kamenev, Zinoviev, and Trotsky, were non-religious Jews. As late as 1929 Jews were only 1.82 percent of the population of the Soviet Union but furnished the Communist Party with 4.34 percent of its membership, making them the third largest ethnic group in the party. But even during the early days of Bolshevism, overtly religious Jews suffered from disabilities similar to those afflicting other religious groups in the Soviet Union. They were subject to propaganda to work on the Sabbath and on Jewish Holy Days such as Yom Kippur. In the early 1920's, Jewish religious schools were closed and persons who continued to teach the Jewish religion were jailed. During the years 1929-1932 many synagogues as well as churches were shut. In 1938 some rabbis were imprisoned on the charge that they were Nazi spies!

After World War II, Stalin turned against displays of Jewish ethnicity as well as against the Jewish faith and closed down Yiddish publications, schools, and theatres; imprisoned some Jewish leaders; and had several Yiddish writers executed--the Jews who bore the brunt of this pogrom were not practicing Jews. Soviet textbooks during the last years of Stalin's life omitted all mention of even ancient Israel, while anti-Semitic cartoons and articles attacking "rootless cosmopolitans" (i.e., Jews) appeared in Soviet newspapers. In 1952, several Jewish doctors were arrested and accused of using improper methods of medical treatment to shorten the lives of various Soviet leaders. In 1953, after Stalin's death, the doctors were released and the government admitted that the evidence against them had been fabricated by the police. Between 1953 and 1959 not only the doctors but most of the Jews incarcerated between 1947 and 1952 were freed, the government confessing that most of them should not have been arrested in the first place. In addition, the regime allowed the publication of several thousand copies of a Jewish prayerbook. In 1959, however, the campaign against Judaism recommenced, with the state closing down many synagogues and punishing persons who baked matzot.[44] A campaign against "speculators" in the early 1960's was anti-Semitic: Jewish offenders were referred to by nationality and a majority of those eventually executed were Jews.

Many Soviet Jews now desire to emigrate to Israel. The Soviet Union does not want to lose the services of its Jewish scientists, antagonize the Arabs, or see other minority groups begin clamoring to leave; and so it initially allowed only a couple of hundred Jews each year to go. In 1969 two thousand departed for Israel, but in 1972, 30,000 did. In 1975, the emigration figure fell to 12,000, despite the signing of the Helsinki Declaration that year calling for freer movement of people and ideas. Since then, however, 100,000 have left for a total of a quarter of a million since the emigration process began. The flow of Jewish emigrants now varies significantly from year to year, varying with the constantly fluctuating willingness of the authorities to issue exit visas.[45]

At present, there are only forty or fifty synagogues in the U.S.S.R., a decline from three thousand in 1917. Moscow has perhaps 400,000 to 500,000 Jews; but only one synagogue and two smaller prayer houses. Passover services at the Moscow synagogue have been disrupted by police. There are no Jewish religious schools nor any schools where Jewish children may learn Yiddish or Hebrew, though the government permits a handful of young people to study abroad for the rabbinate. Two Yiddish periodicals are published, which support the Soviet Union on political issues. One of these circulates in an area that was one of the great pre-war Soviet experiments, the Jewish Autonomous Region in the Far East. The chief city of this region is Birobidzhan--of its 56,000

141

inhabitants only 17,000 are Jews and there are probably no more than 25,000 Jews in the whole region. The only books about Judaism available to Soviet Jews are critical of the Jewish religion and traditions; and it is still difficult for religious Jews to get the flour they need to bake unleavened bread for Passover. Very few Jewish prayerbooks (and very few Moslem Korans) are presently being printed; and the Jews and Roman Catholics, unlike the Orthodox, Moslems, Buddhists, and Baptists, are denied the right to have a central organization. Anti-Zionist books full of anti-Semitic stereotypes were printed with government blessing in 1978, while the number of Jews in universities is falling proportionally and absolutely. (In 1967 and 1968 there were 111,900 Jews in Soviet universities; by 1975-1976 there were only 66,900. In 1977 Moscow University admitted no Jews.)[46] If both parents are of Jewish nationality, the children are considered so too, even though the entire family are devout Christians.[47]

Yet, as is indicated in a dispassionate analysis by Bernard Gwertzman in the New York Times of the position of Soviet Jewry,[48] the Soviet Government can make some good arguments in defense of its position that there is little official anti-Semitism in the Soviet Union. Though some assimilated, non-practicing Jews (the majority of Jews in the U.S.S.R.) do meet discrimination in employment, many of them live very well and have good jobs. Jews are overrepresented in law, medicine, science, engineering, journalism, writing, art, and music. One guess for recent years (the exact dates unspecified) is that 14.7 percent of all medical doctors in the Soviet Union were Jews; while the analogous figure for lawyers and judges was 10.4 percent; for actors, musicians and artists 7.7 percent; and for writers 8.5 percent.[49] Jews account for 14 percent of the doctorate holders and 6 percent of the scientific personnel in the country. Yiddish drama was permitted to make a comeback in Moscow until fire

142

regulations forced the closing of the theatre.
The anti-Semitic books of 1978 were criticized in
the press in 1979; while a surprising number of
Jews received Lenin prizes in 1980.[50] (The fate
of Soviet Jews, like that of Soviet political
dissenters, seems to vary with the extent of the
influence of the "liberals" in the Communist
Party's ranks.)

In summation, those who contend that the
Soviet policies toward freedom of religion are
massively repressive are correct, but only for
certain periods of Soviet rule; the early 1920's,
the period of collectivization from 1929 through
1932, the Stalinist purges of the late 1930's, and
the large-scale anti-Orthodox campaign of the
Khrushchev era. For the other years of Soviet
control (including the past decade), the government's position on freedom of religion probably
can best be characterized on balance as simple repression. Though believers are let alone, on the
whole, they are denied entry into positions of
responsibility and, moreover, Jews and Reform
Baptists have at one time or another even during
these periods of "moderation" been subject to
serious limitations on the exercise of their faith.

In France, unlike the rest of the countries
discussed in this volume, the vast majority of
people belong, nominally at least, to one faith.
This is, of course, the Roman Catholic. There are
about 800,000 Protestants--under 2 percent of the
population; 550,000 Jews, many immigrants from
North Africa; and perhaps a million Moslems,
practically all of whom came from Algeria, Tunisia
and Morocco. Article 2 of the French Constitution
declares that France "shall respect all beliefs"
and, as seen, the Declaration of the Rights of Man
of 1789, incorporated by the Preamble to the Constitution, proclaims in its Article 10 that "No
one may be disturbed for his opinions, even religious." These constitutional clauses are now
fully respected, as is the oft-cited Article 1 of
the law of December 9, 1905 on the Separation of

143

Church and State which provides that "The Republic assures the liberty of conscience. It guarantees the free exercise of religions (<u>cultes</u>)."

The present state of tolerance of religion in France (as extensive as that prevailing in the United States and Great Britain) is to some extent a child of this century and was rudely interrupted as recently as the 1940's. Moreover, with one exception, it has not been members of minority sects who during the past two centuries have complained about governmental persecution, but, rather, the Roman Catholic Church and its clergy; and even today title to Catholic churches built before 1905 remains in the state.[51]

Under Pierre Waldeck-Rousseau's Prime Ministry the law of 9 July, 1901, relating to the formation and dissolution of associations, was enacted. As was seen in a prior chapter, this permits a group of persons to form an association with judicial personality upon the formality of a declaration filed with the prefect. Title Three, however, provided special, rigorous rules for religious orders. Article 13 declared that no religious congregation could be formed without an authorization given by a law which determined the conditions of its functioning. Article 16 provided punishment for the formation of religious congregations without authorization; while Article 18 specified that congregations existing at the time of the law which had not received an authorization had three months to do so or they would be dissolved and their property liquidated. Article 13, requiring that no religious congregation could be formed without governmental approval, applied to most of the men's and some women's congregations then existing in France, as only five (not including the Jesuits, Dominicans or Assumptionists) had been authorized prior to the passage of the 1901 law. In early 1902 Waldeck-Rousseau was succeeded as Prime Minister by the violently anti-Catholic Emile Combes, who had once been a seminarian himself. Combes's first move against

144

the Church was to close 2,500 schools run by nuns
in authorized orders. These schools themselves
had not tried to obtain authorization--nor, given
the language of the statute, was there any need
for them to have done so--but the Prime Minister's
twisted interpretation was that each school was a
separate religious order that needed separate
authorization. Most of the orders that applied
for authorization were not granted it and so had
to disband. Some monks were expelled from their
property by force and many went into exile abroad.
His next step was to pass a law on July 7, 1904,
which outlawed religious orders devoted to teaching and proclaimed that no member of a religious
order could teach, whether or not the order was
authorized. The property of the orders destroyed
under the laws of 1901 and 1904 was confiscated
by the state and often sold in fraudulent trans-
actions for ridiculously low prices. About 12,000
schools belonging to religious orders were closed
and over 600 persons were found guilty of having
violated the 1904 law. Much of this work was accomplished before Combes retired as Prime Minister
in January, 1905. For the sake of national unity,
the government at the start of World War I
ordered the prefects not to enforce the 1901 and
1904 statutes against the orders; and now any
group of persons can form a teaching or other
religious order without penalty and members of
religious orders may teach.

The December 9, 1905 law on Separation of
Church and State, whose Article 1 guarantees the
free exercise of religion, has other provisions of
interest. Article 4 of the law mandated that the
individual churches of all faiths were to be
managed by new organizations called "religious
associations" (associations cultuelles), which had
to be set up within a year. The religious associations were to have the right to use the church
(title to which was in the state) rent-free and
manage the property and revenues of the church.
The Protestants and Jews had no trouble founding
religious associations. However, the Catholic

145

Church violently objected to them as their lay composition posed a significant threat to its hierarchical organization and created the possibility that the churches would be managed by schismatics.

After Combes left office, the state yielded when it passed a law on March 28, 1907 providing that churches were to be placed at the disposal of the faithful even though the worshippers had not set up a religious association. In 1924 Pope Pius XI allowed the creation of "diocesan associations," which in practice now perform for the Catholic churches the functions of the "religious associations" mentioned in the 1905 law.[52] But by 1924 the War had to some extent healed old wounds: how deep these were in the period 1898-1914 is vividly illustrated in the following quotation.

> The intransigence of the republican regime was matched by that of the Pope who excommunicated every deputy who had voted the separation laws. Faithful Catholics were driven into a political ghetto. Regular attendance at mass by army officers (reported by Freemasons converted into amateur spies) became a hindrance to promotion. A feeling of being besieged from outside the walls of their faith was given expression in many Catholic publications of the period. The faithful saw no other way than the overthrow of the existing political regime to overcome their isolation.[53]

All this in a supposedly Catholic country!

The Council of State proved of help to the Church in this struggle against the state. As will be remembered, the law of July 7, 1904 outlawed religious orders exclusively devoted to teaching. In Soeurs de La Visitation Sainte Marie de Troyes et autres[54] the Council held that the following congregations were not banned by the law:

146

1. One that in addition to teaching also offered shelter to women who wanted to live far from the world in the exercise of Christian virtue.

2. Two that also sheltered the poor and sick and were used by women who wished to make retreats.

3. One that was also devoted to the contemplative life. Also, in a whole series of cases arising between 1907 and the creation of the diocesan associations in 1924, the Council made it clear that the Catholic churches reserved for the faithful by the law of 1907 were in practice to be controlled by the parish priest if he had submitted to the ecclesiastic hierarchy and if he were in communion with his bishop.[55]

However, the Council did not always take the side of the Church. Thus, in Commune de Saint Dezery[56] it declared that a prefect could not rent a church to a priest; the law of 1905 and its successors regulated the conditions under which churches were to be at the disposal of the faithful and did not permit the state to lease the church to a curé. And in Abbé Bouteyre[57] the Council sustained a decision of the Minister of Public Education not to let a priest sit for an examination (concours), success in which would entitle him to teach in a public secondary school. The Council's opinion is laconic, but the commissaire du gouvernement whose report formed the basis of its decision felt that the Minister could reasonably decide that a priest could not observe the neutrality in religious matters required of teachers in public secondary schools and that secondary school students were not sophisticated enough to be able to judge of the religious propaganda he might spread in his classroom.[58]

The tradition of militant anti-clericalism, so foreign to the Anglo-American world, persisted on the local level in France through the immediate

post-World War II years. It produced numerous in-
cidents in which mayors antagonistic to the
Catholic Church attempted to prevent church
parades through the streets of their villages. As
seen previously, the basic law regulating parades
and processions on the public way is the decree-
law of October 23, 1935, which requires the spon-
sors of all public parades and rallies to file a
"prior declaration" with the local authorities.
According to the "Paganon Circular" the mayor,
subject to reversal by the prefect, can prohibit
the event if it threatens public order. The
decree-law itself exempts from the requirement of
a prior declaration events "on the public way con-
forming to local traditions." Most of the
ceremonies that "conform to local traditions," in
a country such as France, are processions of the
Roman Catholic Church, including parades on church
holy days such as All Saints' Day and the Assumption. The Council of State has issued many
decisions holding that pageants on days such as
these do indeed so conform and do not threaten
public order.[59] Thus the requirement of prior
notice is waived for them and more importantly,
they cannot be banned. For example, in Rastouil[60]
the Council ordered the mayor of Limoges not to
bar an Eastertime parade. This ceremony was traditional in the area: no other procession had
traditionally been celebrated on the streets of
that city for the past 80 years. Moreover, there
was no showing that this ban was needed to maintain order.

        The Council of State has shown itself will-
ing to defend religious practice from the actions
of anticlericals in other areas too. In Pasteau[61]
it declared illegal an action of the Minister of
National Education firing a school hygienist because she was religious. In Jamet[62] the local
school administration refused to promote a woman
from "apprentice" to "certificated" instructor in
a school because she attended a "group of confessional character" during her leisure hours.
The action of the administration was annulled, as

it could not establish that she would depart from the duty of strict neutrality imposed upon every public employee. To say that a religious person does not have the ability to be a good public school teacher is an idea entirely foreign to French legislation. In a more traditional "religion vs. police power" situation, the Council overturned a municipal decree banning methods of slaughter used by Jewish "Kosher" butchers.[63] Contrary to these tolerant decisions is Joudoux et Riaux.[64] Here the Minister of the Interior used Article 14 of the 1881 Press Law, allowing the banning of works of foreign origin, to forbid the sale of The Watchtower, the magazine of the Jehovah's Witnesses. The Council sustaining the decree said that The Watchtower may induce certain persons to refuse military service and, in any event, the Minister's determination that a foreign book may threaten the public order cannot be questioned in a case before it.

When the Germans conquered France in 1940 and set up the puppet Vichy regime headed by Marshal Henri Phillippe Pétain, the hour of French anti-Semitism had come. The government enacted legislation and decrees in 1940 and 1941 preventing Jews from holding public office, from exercising certain professions, and from engaging in certain businesses and holding certain types of property. Algerian Jews were also deprived of citizenship. The regime soon handed Jews over to the Germans: first non-citizens, then foreign-born Jewish citizens, and lastly, a few native-born French Jews. Many of the Jews so deported died in Hitler's gas chambers. (In fairness, it must be noted that since World War II the French Jewish community has flourished.)

The Council of State (purged of its Jewish membership) continued to function throughout the Vichy era and rather bravely issued some decisions protecting persons of Jewish descent, though it was of course in no position to prevent the deportations or protect most of those who lost their

149

job, business or property. In <u>Darmon et autres</u>[65] it annulled a decree of the governor general of Algiers limiting the number of Jewish students who could enroll in primary and secondary school. Such a decree could be justified only by a law; and no relevant statute existed. In <u>Consorts Weill</u>[66] it wrestled with an attempted state con- fiscation of real estate owned by two Jewish brothers, Jean and Curt Weill. The seizure of Curt's property was upheld: under the relevant 1941 legislation Jewish real property could be taken if, as Curt, the owner neither farmed the land nor lived in the buildings. However, Jean inhabited the buildings and farmed the lands and thus the regime could not obtain his share of the estate. In <u>Époux Auerbach</u>[67] the Vichy Commis- sioner for Jewish Affairs tried to name an administrator for an apartment in Paris belonging to the Auerbachs, a Jewish family. Mrs. and Mrs. Auerbach could not actually reside in Paris be- cause of the German occupation. Nonetheless, the Council declared that this apartment should be deemed their personal residence. Thus, since the law of 1941 providing for the appointment of an administrator of Jewish property excepted personal residences, the naming of one here was void for excess of power.

The Vichy law of June 2, 1941, supplement- ing the law of October 3, 1940 which initially placed restrictions on Jews, defined a Jew as any- one with 3 or 4 Jewish grandparents or with two Jewish grandparents and who practiced the Jewish religion on June 25, 1940. Thus, the definition of "Jew" had a religious as well as a racial ele- ment. The Council issued several decisions on the question of whether appellants before it were Jewish under the terms of the 1941 act. In one case it found that a M. Bloch-Favier could under law be discharged as a Jew from his teaching posi- tion: his two fathers were Jewish and his two grandmothers were considered Jewish because of their patronymic name. Thus the state had proven M. Bloch-Favier's Jewishness. However, on the

same day it decided that one M. Lévy, who also had
two uncontestably Jewish grandparents, was not a
Jew and thus could not be prevented from taking an
examination for a civil service position. M. Lévy
had the luck to have saved his certificate of baptism as a Roman Catholic; nor could it be proven
that he had ever renounced the Catholic faith.
Thus he was not one of those half-Jews who had the
misfortune of being a practicing Jew in 1940 and
so was not a Jew under Vichy law.[68]

B. Establishment of Religion

The phrase "established religion" is vaguer
than "freedom of religion." It may connote a
situation such as that which prevailed in Spain
during the Spanish Inquisition where non-Catholics,
or Catholics who were suspected of being half-
hearted in their devotion to the faith, were executed or banished by the secular authorities. It
may mean a situation where those who reject the
state-supported religion stay out of jail but find
it difficult to get permission to worship openly
and to conduct schools. It may refer to a state
of affairs where there is complete religious toleration but where one religion is declared the
official church and receives some assistance not
accorded other faiths. Finally, it may describe a
situation in which all faiths are tolerated, there
is no official church, and the state grants financial and/or other help to all religions according
to a formula which is generally considered equitable.

The very first clause of the First Amendment
to the United States Constitution provides that
"Congress shall make no law respecting an establishment of religion. . . ." However, the Roman
Catholic Church, which maintains the largest
though not the only system of elementary and
secondary schools in the country under religious
sponsorship, has seen the costs of operating these

151

institutions increase greatly over the past two
decades and has had to close many of them. It has,
therefore, looked with some success to the federal
and state government for financial aid to keep the
rest of the system alive. The Supreme Court of
the United States in 1947 confronted the issue of
aid to parochial schools in Everson v. Board of
Education.[69] This arose out of a New Jersey statute that permitted local governments to reimburse
parents of public and parochial school children
for the fares they spent going to and from school
on public transportation. The Court, in an oft-
quoted phrase, said:

> The "establishment of religion" clause of
> the First Amendment means at least this:
> Neither a state nor the Federal Government
> can set up a church. Neither can pass laws
> which aid one religion, aid all religions,
> or prefer one religion over another.
> Neither can force nor influence a person to
> go to or to remain away from church against
> his will or force him to profess a belief
> or disbelief in any religion. No person
> can be punished for entertaining or pro-
> fessing religious beliefs or disbeliefs,
> for church attendance or non-attendance.
> No tax in any amount, large or small, can
> be levied to support any religious activi-
> ties or institutions, whatever they may be
> called, or whatever form they may adopt to
> teach or practice religion. Neither a
> state nor the Federal government can,
> openly or secretly, participate in the af-
> fairs of any religious organizations or
> groups and vice versa. (Emphasis mine)

The Catholic Church was alarmed by the underscored
phraseology. If these words are taken literally,
they forbid any sort of governmental assistance to
parochial schools, direct or indirect, even for
secular purposes only. For example, the aid
granted to the parents in the statute involved in
Everson is in an economic sense a use of tax funds

152

to support the Roman Catholic Church. If this aid
were not given the parents, the Church would probably have to reimburse the parents for their fares
if it wanted to retain its students. And this
subsidy would mean that the Church would have less
money to spend on bibles, altars, and sacramental
wine. However, the Court held that the Act here
was constitutional as "public welfare" legislation
designed to protect the health and safety of
parochial school children: it was not, it said,
the use of tax monies to support religion.

The hierarchy was not irrational in fearing
Everson. In Lemon v. Kurtzman,[70] the Court overturned a Rhode Island law under which the state
supplemented the salaries of teachers of secular
subjects in parochial schools; and a Pennsylvania
law under which the state reimbursed parochial
schools for teachers' salaries, textbooks, and instructional materials used in the teaching of
secular subjects. Both measures violated the
establishment clause because they gave rise to
"excessive entanglement" between government and
religion. Under both, the government had to
watch the church schools continually to see that
the subsidized teachers did not teach religion in
their classes and, moreover, under the Pennsylvania law, the money went to the church school
directly, not to the student, the parents, or the
teacher. In a series of 1973 cases, the Court invalidated state programs granting parochial
schools money for maintenance and repair of school
facilities; allowing state income tax credits to
parents of parochial school pupils to compensate
for their tuition payments or reimbursing parents
for such payments; and paying church schools for
the expenses they incurred in performing a state-
mandated function such as test-giving when the
tests were prepared by teachers at the school.[71]
The majority felt that all these programs were unconstitutional because their primary purpose and/
or effect would be the furthering of religious
institutions and religion. For example, the
school could use the state grant for maintenance

153

to repair the school chapel while the financed tests could possibly be employed for purposes of religious education or indoctrination. (By the time this book is published, federal tuition income tax credits may well be available to parents of church and private school pupils.)

But the post-Everson Court has not been completely antagonistic to governmental attempts to aid educational institutions operated by religious bodies. On the same day as Lemon v. Kurtzman was announced, Tilton v. Richardson[72] allowed the federal government to grant money to church-related colleges for construction of buildings to be used for secular purposes. In Board of Education v. Allen[73] the Court sustained a law of the state of New York requiring local public school boards to lend secular textbooks to parochial school pupils. The statute was upheld on the ground that since the loaned books were secular, the bill would not promote the teaching of religion but simply insure that parochial school pupils received a decent education in secular subjects, a "public welfare" goal at which the state can legitimately aim. So despite Everson's broad language and cases such as Lemon v. Kurtzman, government in the United States can and does provide a fair amount of aid to parochial schools for secular purposes, especially where the pupils or the parents are the direct recipients of that aid. Some of this money comes from the federal government under the often-amended Elementary and Secondary Schools Education Act of 1965. This requires public school districts getting aid under the program to make available guidance, remedial reading and speech therapy programs to non-public school pupils; and mandates these districts to lend students textbooks, films, maps, and globes.

The Supreme Court may soon decide the constitutionality of the 1965 Education Act. In the light of Meek v. Pittenger[74] and Wolman v. Walter[75] one can predict with confidence that some though

154

not all of it will be sustained. In these decisions, the Court said that while a state could
continue to supply textbooks to parochial students, it could not loan their schools
instructional materials such as periodicals,
photographs, maps, charts, tape recorders, and
laboratory equipment. Nor can it lend the students wall charts and slide projectors. The state
may provide remedial instruction for non-public
school children; but only when such instruction is
not furnished at the private school. However, it
may provide diagnostic services at the school itself and subsidize standardized tests prepared by
a secular agency. This means that Jane O'Brien, a
hypothetical fifth- grade student at Our Lady of
Good Counsel Elementary School who is having difficulty reading Dr. Seuss, can have the city Board
of Education administer a test to her at Good
Counsel to determine the grade level of her reading but must schedule her remedial reading class
anywhere but at Good Counsel or other religious
schools!

    Most states in the United States have some
form of what is generally referred to as Sunday
Closing legislation or "Blue Laws." These vary
widely from state to state, but all require certain businesses to close completely or refrain
from selling certain products on a Sunday. The
Supreme Court legitimated these "Blue Laws" in
McGowan v. Maryland.[76] It admitted that they
originally were designed to aid the Christian religion by insuring that people would have nothing
else to do on Sunday, the Christian Holy Day, than
go to church. However, it declared that these
laws have a primarily secular purpose now: they
assure that there will be at least one day during
the week when the family breadwinner can rest and
be with his family and friends. This secular purpose could not have been attained by allowing each
business to choose for itself what day of the week
it would close, for under such circumstances different members of the family and their friends
might have different days free and so could never

get together. The Blue Laws are especially hard on "Sabbatarians," persons such as Orthodox and Conservative Jews and Seventh Day Adventists whose holy day is Saturday, because they in effect force them to close on both days of the weekend, the time of the week that is most profitable for small business. However, in Braunfeld v. Brown,[77] the Court said that refusing to exempt Sabbatarians does not violate their freedom of religion; if the state were to be required to permit these people to shut on Saturday rather than on Sunday, the police would have to check business closings on two days of the week and Sabbatarians would get an economic windfall from being open on Sunday when the doors of their competitors were locked. Some states do allow Sabbatarians to refrain from work on Saturday rather than Sunday even though this exception is not constitutionally mandated.

The controversial cases of Engel v. Vitale[78] and School District v. Schempp,[79] which their opponents claim contribute to the moral decline of America by "getting God out of the public schools," declare it an unconstitutional establishment of religion for the state to require prayers to be read or said in public schools. These ceremonies are invalid even though students who do not wish to participate in the prayers may leave the room, even though the teacher has the choice of what parts and versions of the Bible he wishes to read, and even though the prayer is a "nondenominational" one. The Supreme Court said in Schempp that a law violates the establishment clause if either its purpose or its primary effect is to promote religion; and school prayers fall on both these counts. However, the "purpose of furthering religion" test of Schempp is not rigidly adhered to. Witness, for example, the phrase "In God We Trust" on coins, the insertion of the words "under God" in the Pledge of Allegiance to the Flag, prayers in legislative chambers and the hiring of chaplains for those institutions.

Unlike the United States, parts of Great

Britain have established churches. In England the established church is the Anglican (Church of England); in Scotland it is the Presbyterian; and there is no established church in either Northern Ireland or Wales. What does it mean to say that England and Scotland have established churches? First of all, the Sovereign is the head of the Church of England and of the Church of Scotland. Second, the bishops of the Church of England have seats in the House of Lords. Third, the Sovereign must consent to the appointment of Anglican bishops, but the state does not pay the salary of Anglican ministers. Parliament has the ultimate say over approving or disapproving changes in Anglican Church doctrines, though it has no similar power vis-à-vis the Presbyterian Church. In practice, Parliament, a body with a good number of non-Anglicans, non-Christians, and even non-believers, is usually content merely to ratify the decisions the Church takes with reference to these matters. But in 1927 and 1928 the House of Commons rejected a revised Book of Common Prayer as too oriented to Roman Catholicism.

The English, unlike the Americans, do not resort to indirections to keep religious schools afloat. The Education Act of 1902 declared that "voluntary" as well as "county" (the equivalent of American public) schools would receive financial aid from the government; and both types still get these subsidies. Most "voluntary" schools are established and maintained by religious groups such as the Anglicans or Roman Catholics.

In both public (i.e., county) and voluntary schools, the day must begin with collective worship, which in the public schools must be "non-denominational." Religious instruction must be given in both sorts of schools, except that in Scotland it is not mandatory. What this means is that religion may be taught as truth during the period of religious instruction, which is not permissible in the American public schools. However, in the public school the religious instruction is

to be given in accordance with a nondenominational
syllabus agreed upon by the teachers, local
churches, and the local educational authority.
(In the English context, "nondenominational"
usually means nondenominational Christian. For
example, most syllabi stress the life of Jesus.)
In the voluntary school, which was of course set
up to give education in a particular religion,
whether the religious instruction is to be in the
faith of the group which founded the school or in
accordance with an "agreed syllabus" depends
largely upon the extent to which the school is dependent upon governmental aid. Also, though in
voluntary schools receiving a state subsidy most
teachers are appointed by the local education
authority, these institutions retain some control
over the hiring and firing of those who are to
teach religion in their classrooms. In all
schools, a parent can withdraw his child from
prayer and religious education.[80]

England, like the United States, has its
Sunday Closing laws. These require certain businesses to be closed on Sunday while permitting
others to be open, but in some cases for certain
hours only. (Shops in holiday towns are treated
more leniently by this legislation.) Jews may in
some cases open on Sunday; and a tribunal exists
to determine whether a particular tradesman is
really a Jew.[81]

There is nothing in the Indian Constitution
that is an exact copy of the command of the U.S.
First Amendment that "Congress shall make no law
respecting an establishment of religion." However, there are certain Articles in the Indian
Bill of Rights designed to insure that no one
faith will be preferred in certain important
areas. Thus Article 27 reads that "No person
shall be compelled to pay any taxes, the proceeds
of which are specifically appropriated in payment
of expenses for the promotion or maintenance of
any particular religion or religious denomination." Article 28(1) says that "No religious

158

instruction shall be provided in any educational institution wholly maintained out of state funds." Article 28(3) allows parents of children in educational institutions recognized by the state or receiving state aid to excuse them from participating in religious instruction or worship there. Article 30(2) provides that "The State shall not, in granting aid to educational institutions, discriminate against any educational institution on the ground that it is under the management of a minority, whether based on religion or language." Article 30(2) makes it impossible to read Article 27 to hold that the state cannot constitutionally subsidize a school controlled by a religious community.

The state governments of independent India, following the British example both at home and in India, will give aid to schools run by any religious faith. This receipt of aid has not proven an unmixed blessing. Certain states go beyond inspection of the school to see that it meets academic standards and demand that a certain number of state representatives serve on the school's board of trustees; and some states have obtained some control over the hiring and firing of teachers at these schools. The Communist government that ruled the state of Kerala from 1957 to 1959 passed a bill giving the state sweeping power over the private schools (mostly Roman Catholic and Hindu) located there. Under the bill all teachers' salaries at these institutions would be paid by the government and they would be eligible for state-funded pension and insurance plans. However, all fees collected by the management were to be transferred to the government; teachers were to be appointed from a list prepared by the state; and the state could take over any school for five years if its performance were subpar. In the Kerala Education Bill case,[82] the Supreme Court of India upheld most of the act except for those provisions which enabled the state to take over the management of state-aided schools entirely, provisions which violated the right guaranteed by

Article 30(1) to religious and linguistic minorities to establish and administer educational institutions of their choice.[83] However, subsequent decisions have retreated a bit from this decision and have made it clearer that public aid to denominational schools is not to be the prelude to absolute government control or even to the power of the government to select the majority of the student body. Thus in <u>Reverend Sidhrajbai Sabbaj v. Bombay</u>[84] the Supreme Court overturned a state order compelling teacher training schools operated by religious sects to reserve 80 percent of their places for students selected by the government. The Court said that the right of minority groups (in this case, a Presbyterian Society) to manage their schools was "absolute" and any regulation of these schools would be invalid unless "conducive to making the institution an effective vehicle of education for the minority community or other persons who resort to it. . . ."

As noted above, Article 28(1) bans religious instruction in schools wholly supported by the state. This runs counter to the British practice and is consistent with the U.S. Supreme Court's decision in <u>Schempp</u>. However, many Indians conceive of education and religion as closely intertwined, and so there exists a great deal of pressure to bring some form of nondenominational religious instruction into the governmental schools. Article 28(1) says nothing about banning prayers and certain schools hold an assembly at which a nondenominational prayer is said. This practice is, of course, outlawed for America by <u>Schempp</u>.[85]

The famous Bolshevik decree of January, 1918 disestablished the Russian Orthodox Church; and Article 52 of the Brezhnev Constitution reads "In order to guarantee freedom of conscience for all citizens, the church in the USSR has been separated from the state and the school from the church. The freedom to hold religious services and the freedom of anti-religious propaganda is

160

acknowledged to all citizens." (Article 124 of the Stalin Constitution was similar.) However, it is arguable that there is more establishment of religion in the Soviet Union than in any of the other four countries. As the last sentence of Article 52 (which guarantees freedom of anti-religious but not of religious propaganda) indicates, the religious faith that is established in the Soviet Union is atheism, the doctrine that there exists no supernatural being or beings which in some way are above the laws of nature. The religious persecution and bans on religious teaching noted previously are obviously attempts to hinder the dissemination of religious views and insure that the atheist position is the only one to which most Soviet citizens are exposed. Persons who want responsible jobs would be ill-advised to worship openly. Soviet schools teach atheism and, at times, actively discriminate against those students who avow religious faith. A state-sponsored League of Militant Godless was very active during the 1930's preaching atheism throughout the country and publishing atheist journals. Since World War II other state-controlled groups carry on the same tasks.

The Soviet state has at times established religion in the more traditional way of preferring one faith to another. It has already been indicated that the Roman Catholics and the Jews, alone among the major religious groups, are not permitted to have a central organization. The Soviet government has on several occasions crushed Orthodox churches which claimed "autocephalous" status, i.e., independence from the Russian Orthodox Church. The Ukrainian Autocephalous Church was destroyed in the 1930's with the arrest and exile of all the Church bishops and of many ordinary priests. After World War II the Soviet Government forced the Estonian Orthodox Church to rejoin the Russian Orthodox Church by the simple expedient of arresting its leader and many of its priests and then ordering its governing Synod to repent of its disagreement with the Russian Church. In Latvia,

161

the Latvian Orthodox Church renounced its independent status when Soviet troops occupied the
country in 1940; and a budding Byelorussian autocephalous Orthodox Church met the same fate in the
30's as the Ukrainian.[86]

France ranks with the United States and the
U.S.S.R. as a nation whose fundamental laws
clearly separate church and state. Article 2 of
the Law of December 9, 1905 on Separation of
Church and State provides that "The Republic
neither pays the salaries (of the ministers of)
nor subsidizes any denomination." The cost of
operating the churches was, henceforth, to be
borne by the religious associations discussed in
the last section. The state surrendered its right
to nominate bishops and the bishops and arch-
bishops lost certain privileges. However, it continued to hold title to existing Catholic Church
buildings; and municipalities are still responsible for the maintenance of the church buildings
they own. The 1905 law forbids religious signs
and emblems from being placed on public monuments
and the erection of religious emblems in ceme-
teries (which are municipally controlled) except
that the tombstones themselves may be shaped like
a religious symbol such as a cross. Article 2 of
the 1958 Constitution declares the country a secular (laïque) Republic. As a result of this
proclamation, though Sunday Closing Laws exist because of trade union pressure, ". . . the church
has the same standing as the sports car club," and
there are eliminated "religious symbols in public
places and prayer and Bible reading in public
schools. No one swears on a Bible or invokes a
putative deity's help in fulfilling his public
obligations; they are simply not permitted. If
the National Assembly opened with a prayer each
day, it would be dissolved by sheer abstention.
In short, religion is a private, not a state
matter."[87]

Not quite! As in Britain, the United States,
and even India, the most important dispute in the

sphere of Church-State relations concerns state aid to non-public schools. Laws of 1881 and 1882 sponsored by the anti-clerical Minister of Education Jules Ferry created free public primary schools which are to be "secular." That is, the doctrines of no particular faith are to be taught there, though teachers are to inculcate their students in the principles of patriotism and traditional morality and the schools are to close one day a week so that parents who desire this can arrange for their children to have a religious education. Though until 1941 instruction in morality could include instruction on one's obligation to God, one's duty to God could not be defined as that duty as filtered through the prism of the doctrines of a particular sect, and many socialist and anti-clerical teachers did not even promulgate the nonsectarian deism initially permitted by the 1882 law on the secularization of the primary school.[88] Thus French parents who wish their children to have a religious education and who feel that this cannot be satisfactorily acquired on the one weekday each week the public schools are closed must send them to non-public schools.

These private schools enroll about 15-20 percent of the student population and are almost all Catholic.[89] The Loi Falloux of 1850 permits the communes, departments and French state to subsidize up to one-tenth of the annual expenses of non-public secondary schools. The major source of state aid to non-public primary schools is the Loi Debré of December 31, 1959, a slightly belated Christmas present which was the first major domestic legislation of the Gaullist Fifth Republic. Private (including secondary and technical) schools desiring aid from the state may enter into a contract of association (contrat d'association) or a simple contract (contrat simple) with it. Under the latter, the state pays the salaries of the teachers if the latter have the requisite academic and other qualifications. The schools that enter into a simple contract remain freer in

163

determining their hours and their teaching methods
though their quality and instruction must conform
to the "fundamental principles of the state." A
contract of association may cover some or all of
the classes in a school. The state defrays here
not only the salaries of the teachers in the
covered classes but the social welfare charges
that are the responsibility of their employers.
It also pays for the materials used by the pupils.
In return, the classes must be open to children of
all religions and must follow the hours and to
some extent the teaching methods of public education. Moreover, the state will supervise the
school's finances. Disputes over the application
of any part of the _Loi Debré_ are to go first to
special "conciliation committees" composed of
representatives of the prefect, public education,
private education, and respected citizens. By
1977 35,000 simple contracts and 61,500 contracts
of association had been signed: about 98 percent
of the nation's private schools are now benefitting
from the _Loi Debré_.[90] (Many municipalities also
aid private schools.)

On the whole, the _Loi Debré_ seems to have
been effectuated rather smoothly. By 1977 the
total amount of state aid to private schools was
about 6 billion francs (i.e., $1.2 billion).
Nonetheless, the Council of State has decided
quite a few cases involving state conflicts with
private schools receiving or desiring governmental
assistance. In one the Minister of Education rejected a simple contract with a technical school on
the ground that its classes were too small. This
decision was annulled because he refused to submit
his decision to a conciliation committee.[91] On
another occasion his failure to enter into an
agreement with a secondary school was invalidated
in the face of his insistence that its teachers
were not good enough; they had the certificates required by a decree of 1960 implementing the law.[92]
On the other hand, he could validly refuse to contract where the technical school was unsafe, dirty,
and featuring a mediocre faculty and excessively

164

small classes.[93] Likewise a prefect could turn down a simple contract where the classes were smaller or larger than the size specified in the 1960 decree.[94] And the state may compel the principal of a school under a contract of association to retire at 65.[95]

Except for aid to Catholic schools, the principle of separation of Church and State is in France pretty well accepted by now. (The current Socialist government may nationalize the private schools. Already, a few Socialist town councils have ended the local subsidy to religious schools.) The general distribution of contraceptives was legalized in 1974 and the abortion laws were liberalized the same year and in 1979, while in 1975 Parliament passed a measure further loosening restrictions upon divorce. The constitutionality of the abortion reform law was upheld by the Constitutional Council.[96] Thus the French government itself, dominated until 1981 by parties certainly not anti-religious, has managed to overturn much of the legislation the Church traditionally has favored.

In the United States, the sum of the policies of the political system with respect to state support of religion falls on the side of tolerance. The courts have tried to insure that the amount of state aid going to religious institutions, even for secular purposes, is strictly limited, which leaves the atheist, agnostic or member of a church which does not receive public aid not subject to much in the way of compulsory contributions to support institutions whose creed he cannot accept. On the other hand, the churches' lobbyists usually squeeze enough funds from the public treasury to keep most of their schools open: this respects the claims of those who believe that it is their religious duty to educate their children in a religious school. Also, the school prayer decisions free the American non-believer from having to take part in ceremonies at variance with his own point of view. In Britain, France and India, the most important

165

approach of the political system in the area of
state support of religion encourages diversity.
The broad support granted in these nations to
denominationally-controlled schools makes it relatively simple for these denominations to keep
these schools open, which in turn makes it easier
for them to propagate their doctrines. It is
necessarily true that state support of religious
schools forces taxpayers who have no religious
faith, or who belong to a sect that maintains no
schools, to pay money for the operation of institutions whose creed they reject and thus ignores
their claim to be free from the necessity of doing
this. But this infringement upon religious freedom is not very great, and so the British, French
and Indian policies supporting religious education
can still be considered as encouragement of
diversity rather than repression. The approaches
of the U.S.S.R. in the way of state support of
religious groups are mostly repressive. For example, those who overtly depart from the official
"religion" of atheism are barred in practice from
many desirable positions. Also, some faiths
(Judaism, Roman Catholicism) are more unequal than
others. And in the past, massively repressive
steps were taken; for example, the destruction of
the "national" Orthodox churches was sometimes
accompanied by large-scale arrests.

FOOTNOTES TO CHAPTER III

[1] Torcaso v. Watkins, 367 U.S. 488 (1961).

[2] 310 U.S. 296 (1940).

[3] 319 U.S. 141 (1943).

[4] Breard v. Alexandria, 341 U.S. 622 (1951).

[5] 319 U.S. 624 (1943).

[6] Wooley v. Maynard, 430 U.S. 707 (1977).

[7] 98 U.S. 145 (1879).

[8] 406 U.S. 205 (1972).

[9] R. v. Ramsay and Foote, 15 Cox Crim. Cas. 231, 238 (1883).

[10] 9 Md. App. 270, 263 A 2d 602 (1970).

[11] (1917) A.C. 406.

[12] (1978) 3 All E.R. 175 (Court of Appeals); (1979) 1 All E.R. 898 (House of Lords).

[13] Street, op. cit., 4th ed., p. 189.

[14] (1899) 1 Q.B. 283.

[15] Ahmad v. I.L.E.A., (1977) 3 Weekly L.R. 396.

[16] Welsh v. U.S., 398 U.S. 333 (1970).

[17] (1962) 3 All E.R. 364.

[18] The Times (London), February 20, 1980, p. 14.

[19]Wash. Eth. Soc. v. D.C., 249 F 2d. 127 (D.C. Cir. 1957).

[20]These paragraphs on Ulster are based mainly upon Liam dePaor, Divided Ulster (Harmondsworth, Mx.: Penguin Books, 1970); John Darby, Conflict in Northern Ireland (New York: Barnes and Noble, 1976); David Holden, A Bad Case of the Troubles Called Londonderry, New York Times Magazine, August 3, 1969, p. 10.

[21]New York Times, August 15, 1980, p. A3; America, 121:315 (1969); Economist, September 30, 1978, p. 70.

[22]Times of India (Bombay ed.), June 10, 1979, p. 4.

[23](1954) All India Rep. S. Ct. 282.

[24](1958) All India Rep. S. Ct. 255.

[25]Christian Century, 204:1653 (1967). In 1978 a missionary who had worked in India for forty years was expelled allegedly for fomenting rebellion among a tribal group. The Tablet (London) 233:144, February 10, 1979.

[26]Liberty, July-August, 1972, p. 23.

[27]See Liberty, November-December, 1970, p. 18. The case is Rev. Stainislaus v. State of M.P., (1977) 1 S. Ct. Cas. 677.

[28]R. H. Lesser, The Evangelization Crisis in India, The Catholic World, Vol. 211, pp. 166ff (1970); The Statesman, May 21, 1979, p. 1.

[29]21 Sup. Ct. Journal 975 (1958).

[30]For an account of the Aligarh University dispute, see Theodore P. Wright, Muslim Education in India at the Crossroads: The Case of Aligarh, Pacific Affairs, Vol. 39, p. 50 (1966).

[31] 4 Wheat 518 (1819).

[32] Azeez Basha v. Union of India, (1968) All India Rep. S. Ct. 662.

[33] New York Times, October 25, 1973, p. 2; New Statesman 97:110, January 26, 1979; Staten Island Advance, December 26, 1979, p. 35. Moslems also complain of police harshness and discriminatory curfews. New York Times, August 28, 1980, p. A5.

[34] (1978) All India Rep. All. 280.

[35] Walter Kolarz, Religion in the Soviet Union (New York: St. Martin's, 1962), p. 37; Manchester Guardian Weekly, October 8, 1978, p. 13.

[36] This discussion of the troubles of Russian Orthodoxy is based upon Nikita Struve, Christians in Contemporary Russia (New York: Scribner's, 1967), Ch. 3-9, 19.

[37] This paragraph is based on Struve, op. cit., Ch. 13; Kolarz, op. cit., pp. 51-72.

[38] This paragraph is based on Kolarz, op. cit., Ch. 5; The Tablet (London) 233:610, June 23, 1979; New York Times, September 27, 1971, p. 5; November 27, 1971, p. 10; November 28, 1977, p. 6; December 14, 1977, p. A3.

[39] New York Times, June 24, 1979, Sec. 1, p. 3; Michael Bordeaux, Religious Ferment in Russia (New York: St. Martin's Press, 1968), pp. 3-6.

[40] This episode is quoted on p. 166 of Ibid.

[41] New York Times, February 3, 1975, p. 7; September 5, 1979, p. All. Seventh Day Adventists are fined, jailed, or threatened with losing their children because they reject military service. New York Times, October 16, 1977, Sec. 1, p. 8. Perhaps 2,000 Christians are in jail for practicing

their faith. _Economist_, April 16, 1977, p. 58.

[42] Case excerpted on p. 84 of Hazard, Shapiro, and Maggs, _The Soviet Legal System_, rev. ed. (Dobbs Ferry, N.Y.: Oceana, 1969).

[43] Merle Fainsod, _How Russia is Ruled_ (Cambridge: Harvard U. Press, 1961), p. 319.

[44] What has preceded in these two paragraphs is based on Trudie Vocse, _Twenty Four Years in the Life of Lyubia Bershadskaya_, _New York Times Magazine_, March 14, 1971, p. 27ff; Kolarz, op. cit., Ch. 12, p. 231; Fainsod, op. cit., p. 319, 495; _New York Times_, January 5, 1971, p. 3; Zvi Gitelman, _The Jews_, in _Problems of Communism_, September-October, 1967, pp. 92ff.

[45] _New York Times_, July 27, 1971, p. 13; January 2, 1972, p. 14; August 14, 1972, p. 1; January 24, 1973, p. 2; September 28, 1973, p. 35; January 16, 1975, p. 18; January 3, 1976, p. 1; January 21, 1976, p. 8; December 26, 1978, p. A9; April 4, 1979, p. 1; February 14, 1981, p. 24; _Economist_, August 6, 1977, p. 42.

[46] What has preceded in this paragraph is based on William Korey, _Anti-Zionism in the USSR_, _Problems of Communism_, November-December 1978, pp. 63ff; Ben Ami, _Between Hammer and Sickle_ (Philadelphia: Jewish Publication Society, 1967), Ch. 3; _New York Times_, December 7, 1970, p. 9; January 5, 1971, p. 3; February 14, 1971, p. 9; March 30, 1975, p. 5; January 22, 1976, p. 8; January 7, 1979, p. 12; _New Statesman_ 99:618, April 25, 1980. See generally Lionel Kochan (ed.), _The Jews in Soviet Russia Since 1917_ (London: Oxford University Press, 1970); Salo Baron, _The Russian Jew_ (New York: Macmillan, 1976), Ch. 11-19.

[47] Ben Ami, op. cit., pp. 23-24, 143-44.

[48] January 5, 1971, p. 3.

[49]Alec Nove and J. A. Newth, The Jewish Population, pp. 125, 150 of Kochan (ed.), op. cit.

[50]New York Times, July 7, 1974, p. 2; December 26, 1978, p. A9; July 11, 1980, p. A2.

[51]Jacques Georgel, Polices Administratives, Police des Cultes, p. 12, Juris Classeur Administration.

[52]The appropriate bishop has some say in determining the membership of these associations.

[53]Henry Ehrmann, Politics in France (Boston: Little Brown, 1968), p. 49.

[54]April 3, 1908, D. 1909.3.89.

[55]Colliard, Libertés Publiques (3rd ed.), pp. 342-43 notes some relevant cases.

[56]March 1, 1912, D. 1914.3.46.

[57]May 10, 1912, Rec. 553; D. 1914.3.74.

[58]See Long, Weil, and Braibant, op. cit., p. 109.

[59]Colliard, Libertés Publiques (3rd ed.), pp. 347-50, 568-71; Long, Weil, and Braibant, op. cit., pp. 87-88.

[60]December 3, 1954, Rec. 639.

[61]C.E. December 8, 1949, Rec. 464.

[62]C.E. March 3, 1950, Rec. 247; Gaz. Pal. 1950.2.6.

[63]Assoc. Israélite de Valenciennes, March 27, 1936, Rec. 383.

[64]C.E. June 4, 1954, Rec. 346.

[65] C.E. January 21, 1944, D. 1944.J.65.

[66] C.E. January 19, 1944, D. 1944.J.65.

[67] C.E. January 31, 1943, D. 1944.J.66.

[68] For a good summary of the statutes, decrees and cases concerning the Jews in Vichy France, see La Definition Légale du Juif au Sens des Incapacités Légales, Revue du Droit Public, 1944, pp. 74ff.

[69] 330 U.S. 1 (1947). The following quote is from pp. 15-16 of 330 U.S.

[70] 403 U.S. 602 (1971).

[71] Committee for Public Education v. Nyquist, 413 U.S. 756 (1973); Sloan v. Lemon, 413 U.S. 825 (1973); Levitt v. Committee for Public Educ., 413 U.S. 472 (1973).

[72] 403 U.S. 672 (1971).

[73] 392 U.S. 236 (1968).

[74] 421 U.S. 349 (1975).

[75] 433 U.S. 229 (1977).

[76] 366 U.S. 420 (1961).

[77] 366 U.S. 599 (1961).

[78] 370 U.S. 421 (1962).

[79] 374 U.S. 203 (1963).

[80] This paragraph is based on Street, op. cit., 2nd ed., p. 202; W. O. Lester Smith, Education in Great Britain, 4th ed. (New York: Oxford U. Press, 1964), pp. 126-29; Religious Education, Vol. LXIV, January-February, 1969 (whole

issue); Richard Gross (ed.), British Secondary Education (London: Oxford Univ. Press, 1965), pp. 38-39.

[81]This paragraph is based on Street, op. cit., 2nd ed., p. 206.

[82]In Re Kerala Education Bill, (1958) All India Rep. S. Ct. 956.

[83]Article 30(1) obviously can be used to encourage diversity. Thus in a well-publicized decision, D.A.V. College, Bhatinda, v. St. of Punjab, (1971) All India Rep. S. Ct. 1731, the Supreme Court held invalid a regulation of the Sikh-dominated Punjabi government ordering all colleges in the state to give exams in the Sikh Gurumukhi script as applied to a college run by a Hindu group which felt obliged on religious grounds to use the Deva Nagari script.

[84](1963) All India Rep. S. Ct. 540.

[85]Much of this and the previous several paragraphs are based on Donald Smith, India as a Secular State (Princeton: Princeton Univ. Press, 1965), Ch. 12.

[86]This paragraph is based on Kolarz, op. cit., Ch. 3.

[87]Charles Markmann, Freedom à la Française, The Civil Liberties Review, Spring 1975, pp. 73, 76.

[88]Adrian Dansette, Religious History of Modern France, Vol. 2 (New York: Herder and Herder, 1961), pp. 50-55, 259-61.

[89]Colliard, Libertés Publiques (3rd ed.), p. 389.

[90]Georges Burdeau, Les Libertés Publiques, 4th ed. (Paris: R. Pichon et R. Durand-Auzias,

1972), pp. 338-39; Colliard, <u>Libertés Publiques</u> (3rd ed.), pp. 398-404; <u>Le Monde</u>, June 8, 1977, p. 16.

[91]C.E. March 8, 1968, Min. de l'Éduc. Nat. c. Syndicat de la Métallurgie Auboise, Rec. 171.

[92]C.E. October 2, 1968, Min. de l'Éduc. Nat. c. Moulignier, Rec. 469.

[93]C.E. November 27, 1968, Min. de l'Éduc. Nat. c. Centre Menager et Technique "La Providence à Valence," Rec. 598.

[94]C.E. March 11, 1966, Leriche et Sacre, Rec. 206.

[95]C.E. November 24, 1978, Messières de Beaudiez, Rec. 839.

[96]<u>Le Monde</u>, January 15, 1975, p. 8.

CHAPTER IV

RACE AND ETHNIC RELATIONS IN
THE FIVE COUNTRIES

Conflict between racial or ethnic groups inhabiting the same country is commonplace and
actually or potentially polarizing. One group may
exploit another; another may try to secede; while
yet others might turn to revolutionary activity.
Whether this type of conflict is polarizing or not;
in fact, whether such conflict prevails at all, a
government must take some stance regarding the
politically weak groups under its jurisdiction, as
these will be making explicit or implicit requests
to be allowed to carry on the activities that the
group dominating the political system performs as a
matter of course. This stance can be classified
under one or another of the five types of approaches to civil rights and liberties claims used
in the previous chapters: toleration, encouragement of diversity, stimulating intergroup contact,
repression, and massive repression.

A. The United States

There is room to discuss the treatment of
only one minority group by the American political
system, and this must be the American black.
White-black relations are one of the major chal-
lenges facing America's politicians today, and
they must be handled intelligently in order to insure the full development of the potential of the
American black and the peaceful functioning of the
country's social system. As Tom Wicker said a
decade ago in his Introduction to the Bantam
Edition of the Kerner Commission's report on the
black urban riots of the 1960's, ". . . the

175

rioters are the personification of (the) nation's shame, of its deepest failure, of its greatest challenge. They will not go away. They can only be repressed or conceded their humanity, and the choice is not theirs to make. They can only force it on the rest of us, and what this Report insists upon is that they are already doing it, and intend to keep on."[1]

As every reader knows, the United States Civil War of 1861 to 1865 led to the end of legalized slavery in the United States. The Thirteenth Amendment to the United States Constitution, adopted in 1865, says in Section I that "Neither slavery nor involuntary servitude, except as a punishment for crime whereof the party shall have been duly convicted, shall exist within the United States." More important for the Negro in the past three decades, however, has been the Fourteenth Amendment, ratified in 1868, whose Section I provides in part that no state shall "deny to any person within its jurisdiction the equal protection of the laws." Also, note should be taken of Amendment XV, whose Section I holds that "the right of citizens of the United States to vote shall not be denied or abridged by the United States or by any State on account of race, color or previous condition of servitude."

Despite these Amendments, the era of slavery was followed by a period of legally sanctioned and required racial segregation of the black. There is no space here to describe slavery and segregation, both of which as practiced in the United States were examples of massive repression. The first institution within the national government to enter the lists against legally-required segregation was the U.S. Supreme Court in several cases decided in the 1930's, '40's, and '50's.[2] Then in 1954, in Brown v. Board of Education,[3] it turned definitively to a policy stimulating intergroup contact. Here it held that segregated education was inherently unequal and thus violative of the Equal Protection clause of the Fourteenth Amendment. It

176

found that legally-required segregation makes the forcibly-segregated group feel inferior and that this feeling of inferiority, in turn, affects its ability to learn. This decision, which was soon made applicable to all public facilities, was followed a year later by a second <u>Brown v. Board of Education</u>,[4] in which the Court, aware of the widespread southern hostility to mixing of the races, held that total integration of formerly segregated systems was not immediately required. However, local school districts were required to make a "prompt and reasonable start toward full compliance" and to proceed toward the development of a racially non-discriminatory school system with "all deliberate speed."[5]

The emphasis in the desegregation of the south's schools was more on deliberation than on speed. School systems in the large border cities of Washington, St. Louis, and Baltimore eliminated legally-required school segregation within a couple of years of <u>Brown</u>. In much of the Deep South, however, "massive resistance" to <u>Brown</u> became the slogan, and state governments passed laws to make integration extremely difficult. Thus, to quote C. Van Woodward:

> Mississippi and South Carolina amended their constitutions to enable their legislatures, counties or school districts to abolish the public schools, and Georgia entertained a similar amendment. Alabama provided permissive legislation enabling the state and its subdivisions to discontinue public schools and turn over public money to aid private education . . . These measures were accompanied in some states by various provisions for leasing or selling of school buildings and property to private individuals.[6]

One of the troubles confronting those who wanted racial integration of the south's schools was that only the judicial branch of the

government of the United States was committed to
that policy. Both Houses of Congress contained
large numbers of Southerners who favored the
existing system of repression, while President
Eisenhower's comment on Brown was that "you cannot
change people's hearts merely by law." However,
he did believe that the decisions of the Supreme
Court were the law of the land, and accordingly
sent federal troops to guarantee the admission of
nine Negro students into Central High School in
Little Rock, Arkansas after rioting had erupted
when they tried to enter that school under a Court
order.

It was not until the 1960's that the executive and legislative branches of the national
government began moving quickly in the direction
of policies that can be called stimulation of
intergroup contact. In 1964 the Johnson Administration secured the passage of a Civil Rights Act
whose Title II outlaws racial and religious discrimination in most hotels, motels, restaurants
and motion picture houses. In addition, its Title
VII bars discrimination by employers or trade
unions with more than 25 members. Its Title VI
provides that the federal government shall withhold financial aid from any state or local
political entity or private organization that engages in racial discrimination. As a result of
Title II, it is much easier for blacks travelling
from one place to another to secure a room or get
a decent meal. And, as a perhaps-unanticipated
consequence of Title VI, southern school systems,
which to avert bankruptcy must get financial support from the federal government, integrated at a
rapid pace during the decade 1965-75. In 1962
less than one-half of one percent of the black
public school pupils in the southern states that
make up the Confederacy were going to schools with
whites. By 1973-74, 46 percent of the Negro students in these 11 states attended schools in which
a majority of pupils were white, and only 9 percent attended all-Negro schools.[7] Most of this
increase was due to the fear by the south of a

loss of federal monies.

In 1965, Congress passed a Voting Rights Act, renewed in 1970 and then in 1975 for a seven-year period. This measure enabled widespread registration of southern Negroes for the first time in almost a century. In the 11 states of the old Confederacy, black voter registration increased between 1965 and 1975 from 1.5 million to 4.5 million,[8] and many blacks won elective office. The Voting Rights Act reflects a policy of tolerance while the 1968 Fair Housing Act, designed to break down the neighborhood racial segregation that prevails throughout the country, is another example of a step stimulating intergroup contact. Under this statute, supplemented by similar legislation in force in many states and cities, it is illegal to discriminate on grounds of race, color, religion or national origin in the sale or rental of most of the nation's housing stock.

Yet, despite these efforts at stimulation of intergroup contact, the United States is not an integrated society. It is difficult for blacks to move into middle-class suburbs and the nation is dotted with huge all-black ghettoes such as Harlem in New York City and Chicago's South Side. As a result of this "de facto" segregation the northern cities of the United States are currently lagging behind the south in respect to school integration. It was noted above, for example, that in 1973-74, 46 percent of the Negro students in the south attended schools in which a majority of the pupils were white: in the north and west the corresponding figure was only 28 percent.[9] In 1967, according to the U.S. Commission on Civil Rights, 90 percent of black elementary school children in Gary, Indiana were in 90-100 percent black schools; and the figures for Chicago, Cleveland, Detroit and Indianapolis were 89 percent, 82 percent, 72 percent and 71 percent, respectively.[10] There is now less, not more, integration in the schools of cities such as these.[11] The question arises: will the federal or state governments act firmly to break

179

up this segregation that has developed as the consequence of the growth of all-Negro neighborhoods?
As of now, the answer seems "no." The Fair Housing Act of 1968 and its state counterparts are on
the books, but they need more vigorous enforcement.
The suburbs have proved themselves unwilling to
allow publicly-aided housing, many of whose tenants
would be black, to be built within their boundaries; and the Burger Court upheld in 1977 a
refusal by a Chicago suburb to rezone a tract of
land to permit the building thereon of multifamily,
low income, and thus racially integrated housing.[12]
The Court also sustained a California law which
allows municipalities to block the construction of
public housing within city limits.[13]

It is true that that Court demanded an immediate end to legally-required segregation in the
public schools, even in rural Mississippi: the
time for "all deliberate speed" has ended and it is
now the duty of all school districts to immediately
convert "dual" school systems based upon a history
of legally required racial segregation into uni-
tary, non-racial school systems.[14] Furthermore, to
transform such dual systems, it may not be enough
merely to permit Negroes to attend schools with
whites: the school in some cases may have to bus
blacks to schools in white areas and whites to
schools in Negro areas. In Swann v. Charlotte-
Mecklenburg County Board of Education,[15] the Court
upheld an order of a federal district court judge
which ordered massive busing in the Charlotte-
Mecklenburg county school district in order to
achieve a ratio in every elementary school in the
area of about 70 percent white to 30 percent black,
the ratio that prevailed in the school system as a
whole. In 1979 cases arising from Dayton and
Columbus, Ohio, it cleared the way for city-wide
busing in these municipalities on the ground that
neither had exerted itself to eradicate the effects
of the intentional segregation that had been in
effect prior to Brown.[16] In 1976, it maintained
that the Civil Rights Act of 1866 bars discrimination by private schools.[17] Yet, in a major 1974

180

decision, it held that federal courts could not order blacks bused from center city (here Detroit) to white suburbs when the suburbs had their own school districts which, in turn, had not been guilty of legally requiring school segregation.[18] Also, in 1974 and 1975 Congress enacted statutory restrictions upon busing to achieve school integration.

B. Great Britain

There have been colored people in Britain since the eighteenth century. First came descendants of slaves or sailors from India or the West Indies who settled in port cities such as London or Cardiff. In 1950 there were probably fewer than 100,000 colored persons in Great Britain, but in each of the years 1955, 1956 and 1957, over 40,000 of these "New Commonwealth with Pakistan" (NCWP) immigrants entered. By 1977, there were about 1.8 million men and women of NCWP origin, or about 3.3 percent of its population. This percentage may increase a bit in the near future because of the relatively high birth rate in the NCWP communities as well as their relative youth. By 1976, this 3.3 percent was accounting for 7 percent of Britain's births and only 1 percent of its deaths.[19]

The colored people in Great Britain are hardly a homogeneous whole. Of the 924,200 living there in 1966, about 223,000 came from India, 119,700 came from Pakistan (including what is now independent Bangla Desh), and 454,000 came from the West Indies. Also, 16,000 arrived from Ceylon, 50,000 from West Africa, and 60,000 from the Far East.[20] There are some less obvious cleavages in the immigrant community, too. Some immigrants from India are Hindu; others are Sikh. Some speak Gujerati, but most of the others speak Punjabi. The Pakistanis are almost entirely Moslem, but are split into subgroups speaking Punjabi, Kashmiri and Bengali, the language of Bangla Desh. And the

newcomers from one West Indian isle may be cul-
turally very different from those from another.
Some speak regular English, some use a Creole dialect relatively close to English, still others use
a Creole dialect less closely related to English,
and some employ a Creole dialect of French.

Before 1962, citizens of countries in the
British Commonwealth of Nations and Pakistan had
an almost absolute right to immigrate to Britain.
However, legislation and administrative decrees
promulgated during the 1960's and 1970's limited
entry from these nations--especially of colored
people. For example, in 1971 the Conservative
government of Prime Minister Edward Heath successfully shepherded through Parliament a statute
under which a citizen of a Commonwealth country
who wants to enter Britain usually needs a permit
for a specific job. However, "patrials," defined
as persons born or naturalized in Great Britain or
with at least one parent or grandparent in the
country, are allowed to enter without restriction.
It takes no great imagination to see that most of
the "patrials" will be white and thus that the
immigration already reduced by the act is primarily colored immigration (down to 35,000 in
1977 and to 34,700 in 1980).[21] The statute is
in a sense a triumph for Enoch Powell, currently
an M.P. for Ulster, who, as a member of the Conservative "Shadow Cabinet" in 1968, conjured up
visions of English towns with colored populations
so huge that white women feared to go out at
night. The aim of the 1971 measure, as Home
Secretary Reginald Maudling admitted, is to assure
that there will be "no further large-scale per-
manent immigration."[22]

Towards the NCWP immigrants who have come
and who wish to stay, Britain has pursued approaches that must be labelled as, primarily,
tolerance and stimulation of intergroup contact.
In 1965, a Race Relations Act was passed banning
racial discrimination in hotels, cinemas, restaurants, and public transport. The 1968 Race

Relations Bill forbade racial discrimination in employment. It is true that when the economy is functioning smoothly, older colored people in Britain do not suffer from massive unemployment.[23] (In the United States, the black unemployment rate normally is twice that for whites.) Many London bus drivers and conductors are colored, while numerous junior hospital doctors and student nurses are immigrants. Nonetheless, the employment provision of the 1968 Bill was necessary. Racial discrimination in employment still exists in Britain; and it is difficult though certainly not impossible for a colored person, once employed, to be promoted, especially to a post in which he supervises white workers.[24] Also, in times of recession like 1980 and 1981, colored people are bedevilled by unemployment much more than are whites. Many colored (especially West Indian) youth are not getting jobs at all, or are getting positions in which they can make no use of their training; and unemployment among black youth is higher than among young whites with similar qualifications.[25]

The 1968 Bill also outlawed racial discrimination in the sale and rental of most housing, and such discrimination does in fact, exist. However, Britain still lacks huge colored ghettoes of the nature of Harlem, Bedford-Stuyvesant or Watts. In 1973, only two London boroughs were more than 7 percent non-white.[26] The center of Bradford is supposed to be almost entirely Asian; but its white population is still 22 percent. Likewise, supposedly "West Indian" Brixton in South London is only about 40 percent black.[27] English Parliamentary constituencies have about 100,000 population. According to the 1971 census, the one with the highest concentration of NCWP origin is Ealing Southall in West London with merely 20.6 percent, followed by Birmingham Ladywood with 19.9 percent and Northwest London's Brent South with 18.6 percent. London boroughs are divided into wards with an average population of 11,000. In 1971, two Ealing wards had 62.8 percent and 41.8 percent, respectively, of their population of NCWP origin; none of London's other 653 wards reached the 40 percent figure.

It is true that when one looks to percentage of live births by birthplace of mother, one finds statistics that hint at the possibility of an increase in British neighborhood ghettoization. For the Northwest London Borough of Brent in 1976, 43 percent of the women who gave birth were from NCWP ethnic groups while several other London boroughs had figures of 30 percent and London as a whole showed 21 percent. But the 1971 census indicated that in only four London wards did the concentration of NCWP children exceed 50 percent, the highest figure being 74.3 percent (attained by the first Ealing ward noted above).[28]

Moreover, not only are there no extensive ghettoes at present in Britain, but few are likely to develop despite the statistics about young people noted in the prior paragraph. Immigrants have settled disproportionately in run-down areas near the center of large towns, though these have not, it should be repeated, become little Harlems. (In the case of London, the minority concentration is in the ring of communities touching the central boroughs.) Britain is much more serious about clearing its slums than is the United States, and perhaps about one-quarter of the nation's families live in housing built by local governmental authorities.[29] Consequently, those downtown blocks with large numbers of colored people living in row or converted victorian houses will soon see these dwellings pulled down and replaced by public housing projects. These projects will contain a majority of whites, but almost surely will also have some colored people from the old accomodations as well as from other streets in the area that are being redeveloped.

The 1965 and 1968 Race Relations Bills relied mainly on conciliation. The government's Race Relations Board could neither compel

184

testimony nor make enforceable orders. To caulk
these leaky ships, the Labour government had them
supplanted by a Race Relations Act passed in 1976.
The new measure outlaws the same types of discrimination as the old. The old Board has been
replaced by a Commission for Racial Equality that
has the power to investigate patterns or individual acts of discrimination, the authority to
subpoena witnesses and documents, and the right to
issue stop-discrimination notices. In 1978, for
example, the Commission began investigations of 15
companies it suspected of employment discrimination and ordered a Birmingham restaurant to cease
refusing to serve minority group members. The Act
also makes it possible for men and women who have
suffered discrimination to take their complaint
directly to industrial tribunals in employment
cases and to the courts when the bias is not related to the workplace. Sections 37 and 38 permit
training institutions and employers to discriminate in favor of minority groups when certain
conditions are met, but few if any "affirmative
action" programs are presently underway.[30]

In the area of education, there has been a
reluctance to stimulate intergroup contact by
busing students to schools out of the neighborhood. Widespread school segregation does not
exist in Britain, though London and Birmingham
have a few schools more than 80 percent colored.
The Department of Education and Science recom-
mended in 1965 that local authorities should use
every effort to disperse colored children to
schools throughout the community; but in 1971 itself confessed that busing was not a satisfactory
educational tool. By 1978, only Bradford and the
London Borough of Ealing were using busing, and
Ealing phased out its effort in 1981.[31] (British
schools do stimulate intergroup contact by ef-
ficiently preparing immigrant youth whose native
language is not English to take classes taught in
English.)

The British government officials who most

frequently have been accused of behaving to colored people in a manner that smacks of repression are immigration officers and the police. (The reader should remind himself here that relations between police and blacks in American ghettoes are often very tense.) The immigrants, especially the West Indians, feel that the police are hostile, and some make claims of police brutality against them.[32] Violent disturbances between police and young West Indians are now common. More troubles may be in store for the future, especially as there are few colored policemen in the country.[33]

During the mid-1970's two longstanding ethnic cleavages posed an even greater problem for Great Britain than that created by massive colored immigration. "Great Britain" consists of largely Anglo-Saxon England fringed by Celtic Wales on the West and Scotland on the North. England and Wales have been legally assimilated since 1536, and England and Scotland have been bound together ever since James VI of Scotland became James I of England in 1603. Though there has always been a significant minority of Scots and Welsh that has viewed the English as colonizers, the "Celtic fringes" (excluding Ireland) have contributed more than their proportionate share of British political and cultural leadership. In recent years, however, Welsh and Scots nationalism was on the rise, leading some to believe that "Great Britain" might become three separate countries.

Wales, about the size of Massachusetts, has a population of 2.7 million. Its major industries are steel, coal mining and agriculture. In 1891 perhaps half the Welsh spoke the Welsh tongue; by 1980 only 20 percent of the Welsh knew that language (down from 20.6 percent in 1971) and it was the primary tongue of only 10 percent. This situation, together with the relatively high unemployment in the region, led to an increase in the strength of the Welsh Nationalist Party, Plaid Cymru, which demands the establishment of a Welsh

Assembly or Parliament having considerable
autonomy and which elected its first M.P. in 1966
and three M.P.'s in October, 1974. The British
Parliament has made concessions to Welsh nationalism. In 1966 the Labour government enacted a bill
declaring that Welsh had equal validity in Wales
with English, and Welsh is now taught in the
schools. The BBC offers radio and TV programs in
Welsh; road signs and drivers' licenses are now
bilingual, as are some county council proceedings;
and Welsh may now be used in the courts alongside
English. To the dismay of some of their parents,
a few students must take "O" Level exams in it.
The government also offered to create a regional
Welsh "parliament." However, this proposal was
rejected by Welsh voters in a referendum; and
Plaid Cymru won only two Parliamentary seats in
1979.[34]

In some respects, the rise of Scots nationalism was, from an English point of view, more
surprising and frightening. Only 80,000 of the
five million plus Scots know Gaelic, the ancient
language of the region. Though the Scottish
Nationalist Party is 46 years old, through the
early 1960's it could pull only 5 percent of the
vote and elect at most one Member of Parliament.
Then it captured 11 of the 71 Scottish seats in
the October, 1974, elections, pulling 30 percent
of the vote (more than the Tories). One probable
reason for this success was that Scotland has had
more than its share of emigration and unemployment, factors which lead many Scots to feel that
they are being unfairly treated by the English.
But what gave the greatest impetus to Scots
nationalism was the discovery of vast reserves
of oil revenues: some would like to see all this
money fill Scottish coffers and the region become
totally independent of England, with its increasing unemployment and rampant inflation. At
present, however, fewer than 20 percent of the
Scottish people want full independence; a proposed
Scottish Parliament did not get a large enough
majority in a referendum to permit its

establishment; and the SNP's strength in Parliament dwindled to two seats in the 1979 elections. For the moment, therefore, Welsh and Scottish nationalism are on the wane; but either or both could suddenly flare up.[35]

The British government's policies toward Wales and Scotland fall into the categories of encouragement of diversity and stimulation of intergroup contact. Policies of the former type include the teaching of Welsh in the schools, the Welsh broadcasting services, and the bilingual courts and roadsigns. However, even those Welshmen and Scotsmen whose native language is not English learn this tongue fluently at school. (As a result of past, repressive educational policies this is the mother tongue of most of them.) The natural effect of this is to produce more encounters between modern Anglo-Saxon and Celt in the political, economic and social spheres, especially as those who are adept in English can and do easily rise in public or private industry, education or government.

C. Init

India, like the United States and the Soviet Union, is characterized by ethnic heterogeneity. The previous Chapter touched upon Hindu-Moslem antagonism, and said something about caste. This section will further discuss the Indian government's treatment of caste and also analyze its reaction to the numerous linguistic and tribal differences that split the nation.

It is commonly thought that there are four castes plus a large group of outcastes labelled "untouchables." Actually, these so-called castes, the priests (Brahmins), the warriors (Kshatriyas), merchants (Vaisyas), and servants (Shudras) are really the four main divisions of Hindu society called Varnas,[36] the word used to refer to them here. Each of the four Varnas is divided into

numerous caste-groups (jatis). A caste group can
be defined as the group within which a man must
marry: "The caste-group . . . consists of a
brotherhood who observe the same rules about
pollution (i.e., rules about food, bathing,
changing clothes, and relations with other groups)
and therefore can intermarry."[37] In India at
present perhaps one-fifth of the population belongs
to the three top Varnas--Brahmins, Kshatriyas, and
Vaisyas in descending order, while slightly more
than half belongs to one or the other of the Shudra
caste groups.[38] There are also probably 85-100
million "Untouchables," persons who are Hindu but
belong to no Varna, being below even the lowest of
these four divisions. The "untouchables," also
referred to as outcastes, Harijans, and (officially)
the "Scheduled Castes," are themselves divided into
caste groups and clans.

        Though, in Hindu philosophy, one's Varna and
untouchability do not depend on skin color, there
are good reasons for treating the problem of Indian
untouchables as analogous to the race question in
America or Great Britain or to the issue of nationality groups in the U.S.S.R. First, in a given
section of the country the untouchables are on the
whole darker than the Brahmins; though, as South
Indians are generally much darker than North
Indians, in the north there are light-brown untouchables and in the south there are very dark
Brahmins. In the second place, what the Indian
government is trying to do to improve the position
of the country's untouchables is a possible model
for helping minority ethnic and racial groups in
the other countries. Third, the treatment of the
untouchables by other segments of Indian society in
the past is reminiscent of the humiliation imposed
upon the American Negro during the days of slavery
and "separate but equal." The quotation makes the
point vividly.

        The touch of (the untouchables), even their
        shadow, was pollution. They live apart.
        . . . It is pollution to take a coin from

the hand of a Harijan; it must be put on a
table. His wages must be thrown on the
ground for him to pick up . . . (T)he cow,
the peacock, the monkey, and even the
horse . . . come high about the (untouchable) sweeper. . . . (T)o be a Harijan was
worse than to be a slave in Virginia. It
is true that the Harijan could not be
sold; he was nearer to being a serf than a
slave. But the Southern house slave
cooked and mixed drinks for the masters,
nursed and suckled their babies, played
with them as children. All these human
links were sharply denied by the hammer of
the auctioneer; in the law the slave was
property. And after slavery there was
lynching. . . . Against this passionate
assertion of human rivalry but utter denial
of equality, it is hard to weigh the concept of pollution. But the man outside
caste must cross the road if he sees a
Brahmin coming; to me it seems that, of the
two, pollution was perhaps the more consistently degrading.[39]

The following stories told to Harold Isaacs by educated untouchables and taking place between 20 to
50 years ago further indicate how hard was the lot
of a Harijan in rural India--and 80 percent of
India is rural.

Our people's duty was to take away dead carcasses. They were not paid for this work and
had to eat the flesh. . . . In my childhood I
ate the food of dead carcasses and discarded
bread. . . . You couldn't touch others or go
into their houses or take water from the well.
If you wanted water, you begged for it, and
if they were kindhearted, they would draw it
and pour it into your pot. You were not
allowed to take it yourself.[40]

Even today, the life of the Harijan in rural India
is a troubled one, though his problems are the

190

product of private rather than state repression.
He works for low pay at despised jobs that have
traditionally been reserved for him--scavenging,
skinning dead animals, collecting garbage, tanning,
and disposing of human wastes. Though, perhaps because of frequent mixing on busses and railroads
the touch of outcastes is no longer considered such
a disaster, they still frequently live in segregated areas; are barred from temples, public wells,
restaurants, and barber shops; are evicted from
their land; and are not permitted to ride bicycles
and horses. At times, Harijans who demand fair
treatment are violently assaulted. Almost a dozen
were murdered one day in May, 1977; the naming of a
university after an untouchable leader led to mob
violence in 1978; and two dozen were killed in
Bihar in February, 1980. Even in large, sophisticated cities such as Bombay, untouchables suffer
from social discrimination and housing segregation.
It is true that Christianity and Islam have no
caste system, but caste practices such as untouchability carry over among converts from Hinduism to these faiths.

As seen, Article 17 of the Constitution says
that "Untouchability is abolished and its practice
in any form is forbidden," while Article 25(2)(b)
allows the government to open Hindu temples to untouchables. Furthermore, Article 14's "equal protection of the laws" guarantee, Article 15's
assertion that "the State shall not discriminate
against any citizen on grounds only of religion,
race, caste, sex or place of birth. . . .," and
Article 16(1) and 16(2)'s warranty that the State
shall not discriminate on account of caste, etc.,
in appointing people to government jobs are all
constitutional phrases the untouchable could cite
to the courts in case he is discriminated against
by any public official. Also, a 1955 law enforcing
Article 17 (and supplemented by a 1976 Untouchability (Offenses) Act) makes the practice of
untouchability illegal; and numerous cases have
been filed under this bill.[41]

India's governments have done even more to integrate the untouchables. The reader should first recall the legislation discussed in the last chapter opening Hindu temples to them. The Constitution itself (Article 330) reserves for them some seats in the lower house of the national legislature and in the state legislatures. (The untouchables are referred to in the Constitution as "Scheduled Castes"; under Article 341 the Government has published a list of the castes which are "Scheduled Castes" for constitutional purposes.) Legislation was passed permitting intercaste marriages--a major departure from orthodox Hinduism.

Both the central government and the states have adopted what an American would term the principle of the "benign quota" and reserved a certain percentage of government jobs for outcastes and other deprived groups. The national government has set aside for them 12.5 percent of its positions filled by competitive exam.[42] The purpose of this quota is to assure that the deficiencies in wealth and education which afflict most untouchables will not make it impossible for them to get decent employment. It would seem to violate Articles 16(1) and 16(2) of the Constitution prohibiting discrimination in government employment on account of caste, for it does hurt Brahmins and other Varnas. However, it is constitutional because of Article 16(4), which reads that "Nothing in this article shall prevent the State from making any provision for the reservation of appointments or posts in favour of any backward class of citizens, which, in the opinion of the State, is not adequately represented in the services under the State." Likewise the state and national governments give special financial assistance (fellowships, free books, cheap meals) to untouchable students and reserve some university places for them.[43] This would seem to violate the equal protection guarantees of Articles 14 and 15, but is in fact valid under Article 15(4) reading that "Nothing in this article or in clause (2) of

Article 29 shall prevent the state from making any special provision for the advancement of any socially and educationally backward classes of citizens or for the 'Scheduled Castes...'"

Much of this legislation for the benefit of the untouchables is classifiable as stimulation of intergroup contact, since it makes possible a situation in which they work and study with caste members. Certainly more Harijans are getting a decent education because of these measures;[44] yet the literacy rate for untouchables is still only about 12½ percent, or half the national average,[45] --and only 5 percent of the students enrolled at Indian universities are untouchables. Though the government has set aside 12½ percent of its competitive jobs for them, in practice they fill only 2.8 percent of the highest positions but 18 percent of the most menial government jobs such as messengers and sweepers.[46]

One major problem in the enforcement of the benevolent quota has been the interpretation of Articles 15(4) and 16(4). A close reading will show that they allow the government to give special help to, respectively, socially and educationally backward classes and any backward classes, not only the untouchables. The question of what is a backward (or socially and educationally backward) class is a difficult one to answer. In general, the Supreme Court of India has not shown itself too sympathetic to attempts to grant special privileges to the untouchables and other "deprived" groups in Indian society. Thus, in Venkataramana v. State of Madras,[47] Madras said it would fill vacancies in the office of District Munsif (a judicial position) as follows: 19 for untouchables, 5 for Moslems, 6 for Christians, 10 for backward Hindus, 2 for non-Brahmin Hindus and 11 for Brahmins. As a result of this formula, certain Brahmins who did well on the relevant examination could not get the position. The court held that this way of allocating the positions was not validated by Article 16(4) and thus was barred

193

by Article 16(1). Though the reservation of the seats for the untouchables and the backward Hindus was legitimated by Article 16(4), the formula also makes it possible for a Christian or Moslem to be appointed over a more-qualified Brahmin and this result Article 16(4) does not allow. In <u>Triloki Nath Tiku v. State of Jammu and Kashmir</u>,[48] the Court declared that the mere underrepresentation of groups in the service of the state does not of itself prove that they are backward classes for the purposes of Article 16(4).[49] Also, in <u>Balaji v. Mysore</u>,[50] it held that Article 15(4) did not justify reserving 68 percent of the seats in technical schools for these groups and that groups which had just slightly fewer students in high school than the state average of 6.9 high school students per thousand population could not be regarded as educationally backward groups, though groups with less than fifty percent of the state average could be.

One more excellent example is <u>T. Devadasan v. Union of India</u>,[51] where the Court confronted a situation in which the government had given 29 of 45 jobs to members of backward classes and thus had to deny positions to certain candidates who had done well on a written exam. The reason so many posts were reserved in this case was that the government carried forward from year to year any vacancies set aside for deprived groups which were left unfilled. For example, if in one year three of ten places were reserved for untouchables, etc., and none was filled, the next year the three vacancies would be carried forward so that the backward groups would get six of the positions. The court, in holding that the government had acted unconstitutionally in setting aside 29 of the 45 posts, commented that any reservation of vacancies in excess of 50 percent would be invalid and that the government must effect a reasonable balance between the rights of backward classes and those of the other citizens of the Republic. (The Court has not always opposed regulations giving special treatment to untouchables and "other

194

backward classes." In an important decision in 1961 it did hold that Article 16(4) allowed the government to give them preferential consideration when making promotions as well as initial appointments, while a 1976 case permitted Kerala to promote them without initially giving them the regular exams and to allow them an extra two years to pass them.)[52]

In connection with the problem of backward classes, it should be noted that scattered throughout India, inhabiting hills, jungles, and forests are over forty million aboriginal peoples, some of whom live in a very primitive manner. These groups differ greatly among themselves, some being extremely dark and others having Mongolian features, some speaking Dravidian languages and others Tibeto-Burman or Khmer tongues. They are referred to by the Constitution as the "Scheduled Tribes," and may receive all the special benefits granted the untouchables. Many of the tribes are being "squeezed out" of their ancestral lands by "ordinary" Indians who themselves are short of property; and there have been complaints that some states are refusing to educate the tribals in their own tongue. The Nagas in the hills of the northeastern Assam region rebelled in 1956. To please them, the government gave them their own state in 1963. This rebellion has largely but not completely died out; but guerilla warfare between neighboring Mizo tribesmen and Indian officials continues. Furthermore the Northeast was confronted in 1980 with a quarrel more serious than the Mizo and Naga affairs. In that year, tribal natives of the states of Assam and Manipur, angered by the influx of millions of Bengalis from West Bengal and Bangla Desh, turned on the immigrants. In Manipur, 1,000 were killed in June, 350 on one day. Assam produces one-third of India's output of oil, and anti-Bengali Assamese blocked the flow of Assamese oil to the rest of the country. The national government used force to end the blockade; but how it will solve the underlying problem is still unclear.[53]

However, the Northeast tribal problem in the long run is less important than the tensions between the central government and various linguistic groups. Hindi in the Devanagari script is the official language of the Republic of India though English is at present also used as an official language. Unfortunately for the country, Hindi is spoken only by about 30 percent of the populace while the closely related languages of Urdu, Punjabi, Bihari, and Rajasthani are spoken by an additional 15 percent. Other tongues employed by more than ten million people each are Telugu, Bengali, Marathi, Tamil, Gujarati, Kannada, Malayalam, and Oriya. There are numerous other tongues as well, in some cases spoken only by a few thousand people. A total of more than seven hundred languages are used in the nation, but sixteen of them account for over 90 percent of the population.

Though "very few Indians have English as their mother tongue, of the thirty million (Indians) who know two languages 'a little more than eleven million' know English while 9.36 million have Hindi as a second language."[54] Though only about 3 percent of the country has an acquaintance with English, the distribution of English speakers is much the same thoughout the country; and it remains the major language for communication between the states, business, higher education, the upper echelons of the national bureaucracy, and debates in the Union Parliament. On the state level, the regional tongue is usually used for governmental purposes. Also, more and more secondary schools and colleges have switched in recent years from English to Hindi or a regional language as a medium of instruction; and so the student population as a whole is becoming less and less proficient in English,[55] a situation which is likely to further crack India's fragmented linguistic mosaic. (A glance at a map will show that Hindi and its related languages are spoken in the north central part of the country while the Dravidian languages of Telugu, Tamil, Malayalam and Kannada are spoken in the south.[56] Thus regional suspicions are reinforced by linguistic differences.)

So the reader can visualize the scenario. On the one hand, certain elements in the northern states and the national government want to see the entire nation Hindi-speaking. On the other hand, the south fears that its culture will be destroyed and replaced by an alien culture imposed by the north, and Bengali speakers in the east and Marathi speakers in the west feel that much more of cultural and political value has been produced in their languages than in Hindi. In its first attempt to resolve the thorny language question, the government of India reorganized the states on a linguistic basis. As a result of this reorganization, there is no state with two major languages and each major linguistic group has one or more of its own states. For instance, Rajasthani speakers have Rajasthan, Bengali speakers have West Bengal, Tamil speakers have Tamil Nadu, Malayalam speakers have Kerala, Hindi speakers have Uttar Pradesh and Madhya Pradesh, and Oriya speakers have Orissa, though in almost every state there are still "minority" languages. This solution must be considered as one strongly encouraging diversity, for the natural effect of creating political subdivisions on a linguistic basis is to reserve benefits in the form of excellent jobs for those versed in the local languages and thus to provide them with a real incentive for learning these languages fluently.

English was supposed to lose its status as an official language of the Union in 1965. If this had been done, Hindi would have become the sole official language of the national government: Parliamentary debates and Supreme Court law reports would all have been in Hindi. The prospect of this made the south nervous. So, in 1963, the government said that English as well as Hindi could continue to be used in the Union and state courts, legislatures and bureaucracies. Notwithstanding this concession, 1965 saw in the south riots and

197

suicides to protest against what was viewed as
another attempt to make this region Hindi-speaking.
Frightened by this violence, the government again
compromised. In 1968, it passed the Official
Languages (Amendment) Act keeping English as a national language. As a result of this and other
decisions, English must be used for certain
official purposes of the national government until
such time as the states all agree to the employment
of Hindi for these purposes. Furthermore, examina-
tions for responsible positions with the central
government continue to test the candidates'
knowledge of English, though they are to emphasize
more and more proficiency in Hindi and perhaps in a
regional language too. The languages that are to
be taught in the secondary schools and universities
in a region are the language of the region, Hindi
(or, in Hindi areas, a regional language) and
English or another European tongue.[57] Those of
these arrangements that facilitate teaching all
Indians English and/or Hindi stimulate intergroup
contact: a south Indian is more likely to communicate with a north Indian if both have some
knowledge of Hindi or English. Those that provide
for continued teaching of or in the regional
language encourage diversity, much as does the
teaching of Welsh and Gaelic in Great Britain.

The 1968 Act has not calmed all fears. The
non-Hindi states view those who want to promote
Hindi as wanting to go beyond creating a lingua
franca, i.e., as desiring to discourage the learning and use of the regional tongues. They point to
the fact that some federal politicians are pushing
the use of Hindi on the national level (e.g., Hindi
with an English translation is used by New Delhi
when sending messages to federal offices in the
south, while some bureaucrats who pass an exam in
Hindi get a bonus); that Hindi states are soft-
pedalling the teaching of English and non-Hindi
Indian tongues; and that steps have been taken in
those states to extend the use of Hindi as their
language of government. The non-Hindi states react
by standing as firmly as possible against any use

198

of Hindi. For example, they demand the use of
English when the central government communicates
with them and are more favorable to English than
to Hindi as their second tongue. The centrifugal
effects of these tendencies and perceptions are
obvious.[58]

D. The Soviet Union

        Though many refer to the Soviet Union as
"Russia," the Russians are but one of the nationality groups in the U.S.S.R., a land which is as
heterogeneous as the United States and far more so
than Great Britain. According to the 1959 census,
there were 109 ethnic groups in the country, 22 of
which had a population of more than 900,000.[59]
The Russians are the largest group, numbering,
according to the 1980 census, 52.4 percent of a
total population of 262 million, down from 53.4
percent in 1970 and from 54.6 percent in 1955.
The second largest group in the USSR is the 41 million Ukrainians, who together with the Russians,
Byelorussians and Poles make up practically all of
the country's Slavic component. Other major Soviet
nationality groups are the Uzbeks, Kazakhs,
Georgians, Jews, Azerbaijanis, Tatars, Armenians,
Lithuanians, Latvians, Estonians and Moldavians.

        It is impossible to depict the Soviet
government's treatment of its minority nationalities in one or two sweeping sentences: the
approaches have varied from decade to decade and
from group to group. However, with a couple of exceptions, its nationality policy, unlike slavery in
the American South, Hitler's treatment of Jews and
Slavs, and South Africa's system of apartheid, cannot be classified as massive repression. In fact,
under Soviet rule, various nationalities that were
nomadic and illiterate prior to 1917 have made
rapid advances in literacy, education, and standard
of living.[60] In 1917, the literacy rate among the
little-known Yakuts of Eastern Siberia was less
than 2 percent. By 1959, it was 96.3 percent and

164 out of every thousand Yakuts had at least some secondary education. Before 1917, Yakut was almost entirely an oral language: there are now published in this tongue newspapers, journals and creative literary works.[61] The number of Yakut doctors and scientists has greatly increased. In short, in Yakutia a formerly semi-civilized people is now, under communist rule, well on the road to modernity.

The principle of equality of all Soviet peoples is recognized in Articles 34 and 36 of the Brezhnev Constitution, which outlaw racial and national discrimination "in all spheres of economic, government, cultural, and political and other public activity . . ." (Article 123 of the Stalin Constitution was analogous.) Furthermore, it is generally agreed that the government is employing people, in dispensing social services and housing, and in operating its various organizations usually does not discriminate on ethnic grounds and, moreover, that there is no one ethnic group that is consigned the unpleasant tasks (for instance, street sweeping) that every society must have performed.[62] However, the number of Jews working in the bureaucracy and studying at university is intentionally kept down.[63]

The Brezhnev Constitution allows a right of secession to the Union Republics, each of which "belongs" to a different major nationality group. (So did the Stalin Constitution.) There is, for example, a Russian Soviet Federated Socialist Republic, by far the largest in area and population, a Ukrainian Soviet Socialist Republic, and a Byelorussian Soviet Socialist Republic. However, this right to break away from the Soviet Union is verbal rather than real; and movements that are perceived as favoring secession will quickly be crushed. For example, twenty Ukrainian intellectuals who merely protested the regime's policy of "Russification" of the Ukraine and general denial of freedom to all Soviet citizens were tried and sentenced to hard labor for terms varying between six months and six years.[64]

Most of the minority nationalities are guaranteed representation in the Council of Nationalities, one co-equal House of the nation's highest legislature, the Supreme Soviet. This safeguard affords them only superficial protection. Important policy in the Soviet Union is set by the leaders of the Communist Party, not by the formal apparatus of government. And the (presently) fifteen-member Politburo, the group that heads the Communist Party, is overwhelmingly Slavic and dominated by Russians, including Leonid Brezhnev, the Secretary General of the Party. Of course, in the past, non-Slavic nationalities were more adequately represented on the Politburo: the names of the Jews Trotsky, Zinoviev, Kamenev and Kaganovich, of the Armenian Mikoyan, and of the Georgian Djugashvili--better known as Stalin-- immediately spring to mind. Another Georgian Politburo member, Lavrenti Beria, was in control of the secret police from 1938 until his arrest and execution in 1953.

In the 1920's, the Soviet state in formulating language and cultural policy encouraged diversity, taking certain steps which would motivate and enable the minority nationalities to preserve their several tongues. Thus, it tried to appoint officials for minority areas who were natives of these regions and who knew the local language and customs. In addition, the school system used the vernacular and not Russian as the major medium of instruction. Book and magazine publication in these indigenous languages was stimulated, and the speakers of the more widespread languages were urged to expand them so that they would become satisfactory vehicles of communication for a modern, technological society.[65] In fact, in the Ukraine, the large Russian and Jewish minorities were at first pressured to learn Ukrainian and to use it in governmental, party and trade union work.[66] Throughout the country the formula that was to be applied in dealing with the

201

nationality groups was "socialist in content but nationalist in form." All the peoples of the Soviet Union were to be educated in the principles of Marxism-Leninism; and customs and beliefs that were inconsistent with these principles ultimately had to disappear. But, at the same time, each people could use its language in the schools, in daily life, and in its dealings with government.

Though the formula "nationalist in form, socialist in content" has never been abandoned by the Soviet government, since the early 1930's there has been more stress on the learning of Russian by the minority groups. Russian began to be used more and more frequently in secondary and higher education. The Cyrillic alphabet, in which Russian is written, was adopted for most languages of the Soviet Union. These languages, moreover, had to employ Russian words for political, economic and technological phenomena for which they themselves had no term.[67] Though classes in primary and some high schools continued to be taught in the vernacular, the government began encouraging the publication of books and journals in the Russian language. The Russian conquests of the non-Russian areas of the Tsarist empire were deemed "objectively" a beneficial event: the Russians were denominated the "first" among all the equal peoples of the USSR, and various epics of non-Russian peoples such as the Mongols, Kirghiz, Azerbaijanis and Kazakhs were censored or modified. In one well-known instance of labelling the Russians primus inter pares (the Georgian) Stalin stated in a much-reported speech at a reception: "I drink above all to the health of the Russian people, because it is the most outstanding nation of all the nations within the Soviet Union."[68]

After the death of Stalin, the Russification policy was slowed by Khrushchev. It continues, however, until this day, though less intensively than under Stalin. Primary schools often use the native tongue as the medium of instruction, but

"the higher one goes in Soviet education, the
greater the use of Russian, and the less frequent
the use of the minority languages."[69] Russian is
almost always taught as a second language in primary schools when the language of instruction is
the vernacular, and on occasion the government
urges people to enroll their children in schools
in which the medium of instruction is Russian.[70]
Nonetheless, for the Soviet Union as a whole, the
number of students studying in minority languages
decreased less than 2 percent (from 35 percent to
33.1 percent) in the decade 1954-64; and the number of Russian children learning minority tongues
actually increased between 1959 and 1964.[71] In
the Ukraine and Byelorussia, the number of books
published in the native tongues is now exceeded by
the number published in Russian;[72] but in areas
such as Turkic Kazakhistan and Uzbekistan and the
Baltic republics the majority of books and journals
still use the vernacular.[73]

Some current language and cultural policies
of the Soviet Union stimulate intergroup contact.
The almost universal teaching of Russian falls into
this category. In some ways, the state enables and
makes it profitable for the minorities to keep
their languages alive: these are thus steps encouraging diversity. Reread, first, the example of
Yakutia. Also, as noted, in some non-Russian areas
the minority languages are used heavily in education below the university level; and are sometimes
employed in factory, shop, and farm and in local
government and Communist Party units outside the
big cities.[74] In Georgia, there are more Georgian
than Russian newspapers and road signs.[75] In
Estonia, television programs are often in Estonian
and "throughout Tallin (the capital) the Estonian
language seems to take precedence over Russian,
though many signs appear in both languages. . . .
Western and Soviet films at local theatres have
Russian soundtracks and Estonian subtitles. There
are also separate Estonian and Russian school systems."[76]

However, other Soviet language and cultural policies are still repressive. Thus, Russians are disproportionately influential in non-Russian Republic Communist parties and factories.[77] And when the state urges all parents to send their children to Russian-language schools and uses Russian in the highest units of government in certain non-Russian areas,[78] it subtly indicates to non-Russians that their native tongue is inferior and in this sense penalizes them. (Ultimately, out of motives of shame, ambition or Soviet patriotism, Soviet minorities may well speak Russian as their first tongue; but this is not yet the case. According to the 1980 Soviet census, only 16.3 million (13 percent) of the nation's approximately 125 million non-Russians claim Russian as their native language. About a quarter of the Soviet Union's citizens cannot speak Russian and many have difficulty writing it. One reason for this is that in areas such as the Baltic Republics, there are few incentives to spur its use.)[79]

Another aspect of Soviet nationality policy must be classified as "stimulation of intergroup contact." At least partly to remedy a shortage of skilled labor in the Moslem Asian and Baltic regions of the USSR, large numbers of Russians, Ukrainians and Byelorussians have been encouraged to settle in these areas. For example, in the Kazakh SSR, Kazakhs made up 57 percent of the population in 1933 and Russians and Ukrainians made up 33 percent. In 1959 the Kazakhs made up only 30 percent of the population of their Union Republic; while the Russians and Ukrainians together made up 51 percent. Between 1945 and 1970 the percentage of Russians in the Baltic Republics increased from 8 percent to 24 percent in Estonia, from 10 percent to 30 percent in Latvia, and from 2 percent to 8.5 percent in Lithuania.[80] This policy, together with the teaching of the Russian language, creates the conditions for the social and professional mixing of the Slavic groups on the one hand and the local peoples on the other. However, its "integrationist"

204

effects are more potential than actual at present. In Soviet Central Asia, for example, the Slavs do not bother learning the native tongues though most natives do acquire a little Russian.[81] More importantly, in that part of the country, "Socially, the Muslims remain aloof: although they rub shoulders with Russians in the factories, the army and the universities, their family and sex relationships, their behavior and moral standards . . . , and their leisure habits are still markedly different from those of non-Muslims. Particularly significant is the low incidence of intermarriage: Muslim men occasionally marry non-Muslim girls, but the converse is extremely rare since no respectable Muslim would allow his daughter to marry a non-Muslim."[82]

Moreover, there is taking place in Central Asia a phenomenon that counteracts the effects of the Slavic in-migration and, according to some, poses a major threat to the stability of the Soviet system. The Moslem birthrate is the highest in the country and the Moslem peoples are relatively young; while the Russian birthrate is low and the Russian people are relatively old. Thus despite the continued Slavic inflow into the Central Asian SSR's, the percentage of Slavs living there has been declining since 1959 and will continue to do so in the future unless the Moslems adopt modern methods of birth control. (Moslems could make up 25 percent of the Soviet population by the year 2000.) In fact, because of rising Moslem national sentiment and because Moslems meet no discrimination in their own Republics, more Slavs than Moslems may leave these regions.[83]

During World War II, eight national groups-- the Chechens, Ingushi, Karachai, Balkars, and Meskhetians of the Caucasus; the Kalmyks and Volga Germans of the Volga region; and the Crimean Tatars--were exiled to Siberia. In total, about 1.5 million people were deported, on the ground that these nationalities were disloyal to the Soviet Union during the war. These relocations were massively repressive: persons were punished en masse simply because they belonged to a particular ethnic group, and many of those who were uprooted died as a result of the hardships incurred in the removal. Khrushchev's famous speech to the 20th Communist Party Congress in 1956 criticized the deportations of the Balkars, Chechens, Ingushi, Kalmyks and Karachai. In 1957 these nations had their "national autonomy" restored, and by 1960, their surviving members had returned home. During the 1960's the Soviet Government admitted that the accusations against the Crimean Tatars and the Volga Germans were unfounded, as well, but has not yet ended the exile of these groups or of the Meshketians. Tatars who do try to resettle in the Crimea often will be beaten and imprisoned.[84] (There are 1.85 million ethnic Germans in the Soviet Union: two-thirds of them still regard German as their native language and many of them still attend German-language schools. About 40,000 have been permitted to emigrate to West Germany. They are the fourth or fifth largest nationality in several central Asian SSR's.)[85]

To sum up Soviet nationalities policy, one can conclude that it is rather complex. Approaches stimulating intergroup contact (e.g., the encouragement of Slav migration) and tolerance (keeping public services and facilities available to all groups) coexist with repression (the continued involuntary diaspora of the Crimean Tatars and Volga Germans.) The measures adopted with respect to minority languages are, for reasons already noted, often classifiable as stimulating intergroup contact or encouraging diversity. They are thus similar to their Indian counterparts except that the Indian government is afraid at present to vigorously push Hindi as primus inter pares.

E.   France

France is probably the most homogeneous of the five countries. The non-French ethnic groups

206

can be divided into three categories. There are,
first, peoples historically associated with a certain geographical region of the country, usually
on the periphery. There are Basques in the southwest, Bretons in the northwestern province of
Brittany, Corsicans on the Mediterranean island of
Corsica, and Alsatians in the east around the city
of Strasbourg. Secondly, there are the Jews and
gypsies, neither of which is identified with a
particular region of France. All the above groups,
though not ethnically French, have no other home-
land. Their members are French citizens and the
vast majority think of themselves as Frenchmen as
well as Jews, Corsicans, Bretons, etc. Third, the
country has seen since the 1950's the arrival of
four million immigrant workers, most of whom intended their sojourn in France to be only temporary
and who had originally planned to return to their
native lands as soon as they had earned enough
money to buy a decent home or farm there. These
immigrants, who are also to be found in other ad-
vanced Western European industrial nations, perform
the menial tasks in which French workmen are unwilling to engage, including street sweeping, rail-
road repairing, and assembly line work. Of these
workers, who now number over four million, at least
1.3 million are from the North African countries of
Algeria, Morocco and Tunisia, 882,000 are from
Portugal, 630,000 from Spain, 550,000 from Italy,
80,000 from Poland, and 94,000 from black African
nations such as Senegal.[86]

The policies of the French government toward
the non-French ethnic groups have on the whole been
ones of toleration and stimulation of intergroup
contact. With the exception of the Vichy inter-
lude, the principle of equality before the law of
all groups has by and large prevailed; and none
faces legal barriers to residence, to obtaining
public or private jobs, to property ownership, or
to schools and universities. Article 1 of the 1789
Declaration of the Rights of Man and of the Citizen,
incorporated by the 1958 Constitution, declares that
"men are born free and equal in rights," while

207

Article 2 of the 1958 Constitution proclaims that France "assures the equality before the law of all citizens, without distinction of origin, race or religion." Unlike some constitutional phraseology, Article 2 is a reasonably accurate representation of reality.

However, the French claim that "France's civilization is the highest and most universal expression of humanity. For centuries they have used this belief to justify their 'civilizing mission' in the world, and it is the one they have been most reluctant to abandon."[87] In addition, ever since the Corsican Napoleon, the French have been enamored of the highly centralized state where the local and regional units of government are subordinated to the national polity. It has, accordingly, been the policy of the French state to "Frenchify" the country's non-French ethnic groups. Some aspects of this policy have been repressive; but its primary effect has been to stimulate intergroup contact. All classes in the public schools are taught in French and, until very recently, the educational system refused to offer "local" languages such as Breton, a Gaelic tongue, and Corsican, an Italian language. (Another example of repression: fifty years ago, children were punished for speaking in Breton in the classroom.)[88] All government business is conducted in French.

In the past few years several of the ethnically non-French areas of the country have been demanding greater cultural and political autonomy and a small minority of their inhabitants desires independence. Brittany and Corsica are the two regions most affected by this quasi-separatist enthusiasm. Both are poor areas many of whose residents have to go elsewhere to find jobs. Only a minority of the people speak the "native" language. Both have, as noted in Chapter II, Section 2, seen the birth of groups (e.g., the Front for the Liberation of Brittany and Action for the Rebirth of Corsica) that have engaged in violence to attain their desired goals of autonomy or

208

independence. Banned by the government, they have nonetheless continued their activities, sometimes under another name. Both Corsica and Brittany complain that the central government has not done enough to stimulate economic development in the regions. The Corsicans, in addition, have charged that too many French foreign legionnaires are stationed on the island; that prices are much higher than on the mainland; that the major firms in the area are not dominated by Corsicans; and that not enough Corsicans are employed in, and Corsican products purchased by, the island's new tourist resorts. The French regime has responded to the stirrings in these non-French outposts of the country in some ways that can be viewed as encouraging diversity. The major public official in both departments is still a prefect appointed by and responsible to the central government and French is still the language of education and official business. (This, of course, stimulates intergroup contact.) However, Breton and Corsican may now be taught in the schools and the French radio station in Corsica now broadcasts in Corsican. Moreover, Paris has created a program of economic development for Brittany. As a result, its ports and highways have been improved and some private businesses have moved their plants there.[89]

Other ethnically based regional movements are less active. The Basque country includes both portions of Spain and France: so far, most of the efforts of Basque separatists have been directed against the regime in Madrid. Some residents of the southwest around Tolouse and Tarascon would like to see "langue d'oc", a medieval French tongue, made a second language in that area. And there is a group in Alsace that wants to preserve the traditional Germanic Alsatian dialect, which most of the younger people do not know.[90]

Of the immigrant workers those who are worst off are the North Africans, the majority of whom are Algerian, and the black Africans. Not only do these have dreary and dangerous jobs, but they are

usually paid less than native Frenchmen would be
for comparable work. Many come without their
families and perhaps half of them live in unfit
habitations. Well known are the infamous
bidonvilles (shantytowns) on the edge of large
cities: these are filled with immigrants who
work in the urban area. Other immigrants sleep
several to a room in sleazy dormitories or rooming
houses that charge an exorbitant rent. Some have
illegally been smuggled in and thus are at the
mercy of their landlords and employer. The latter
often refuses to sign them up for health and
social security benefits, while those who use an
employment agency often find that it will deduct
six months of their salary as a fee. Relationships
between the North and other Africans, especially
the Algerians, and the French working class are
not the most cordial. In 1973, after a crazed
Algerian killed a bus conductor in Marseilles, 11
Algerians were murdered by unknown assailants and
right-wing groups began demanding an end to
further immigration (suspended in 1974). On
Christmas Eve, 1980, the Communist mayor of a
working-class Paris suburb led a bulldozer attack
on a shelter built for immigrants from Mali. The
working class views the Arabs as competitors for
their jobs and prone to acts of criminal violence.
Because of differences in customs, language, religion and also because of memories of the Algerian
war, the first generation of massive North African
immigration has not assimilated.[91] The Arabs,
black Africans and other immigrant workers arrive,
as noted, with the intent of returning home as
soon as they have accumulated some savings; and if
they act in accordance with this intention there
will be no significantly large second generation
of the ethnic groups to which they belong. However, given the dreary short-term economic pros-
pects of the Mahgrebian countries and former
French black Africa, the chances are that most of
them will stay in the face of government attempts
such as that of 1977 to repatriate 100,000 of them
by paying those who left $2,000 and, furthermore,
that when the current anti-recession immigration

ban is relaxed, more will have their families with them. Thus, the odds are good that within the next twenty years there will be significant numbers of Arab and black youth in the French school system. How they will be treated by their peers, whether the French government will attempt to assimilate them, and whether, if it does so, it will be successful in this regard are all questions this book is unable to answer. At present, however, their children are rarely given special classes in the schools regardless of their knowledge of the French language.[92]

The French suspension of immigration was accompanied by a promise to improve the lot of the workers already in the country. The government says, for example, that it will dismantle the bidonvilles and provide racially integrated low-rent public housing for the immigrants. Mayors of towns with large numbers of immigrants have suggested the percentage of immigrants in their communities and in the schools in their communities be limited to 20 percent or so; and in certain areas this "quota" has been put into effect. The reasoning behind it is that if too many foreigners (especially Arabs) settle in a commune or populate a school, French families will move out of the area.[93] Similar suggestions have been made in the United States for the purpose of keeping housing projects, neighborhoods, and schools racially mixed.

The Council of State and other courts have issued more than enough decisions in respect to administrative steps taken concerning immigrants to warrant the conclusion that they are concerned to protect the newcomers' rights. In Baza[94] the Council had before it a governmental decision expelling the two wives and the children of M. Baza, an Algerian immigrant who had been deported. A Franco-Algerian treaty of December 27, 1968, provided that henceforth wives and children of Algerian immigrants had the same right to reside in France as did the head of the family. However,

211

another clause of the agreement gave all Algerians resident there prior to January 1, 1969, an automatic certificate of residence. The wives and children had received their certificates prior to 1969 and so these documents retained their validity even though the husband had lost his immigrant status. Accordingly, the decision to expel Sieur Baza's family was annulled for excess of power. Da Silva,[95] a 1975 decision of the Council, annulled provisions of certain governmental circulars relating to foreigners' conditions of stay. Though it could not rescind the act of October 9, 1974, suspending further immigration, it overturned, as unjustified by any legislation, the sections of these circulars denying foreigners permission to stay or work in the country unless they had a certificate from their employer stating that they had lodgings and unless these lodgings were clean and decent places to live. In late 1978, the Council issued four decisions overturning various anti-immigrant administrative acts, including a step denying entry to families of immigrants already in the country unless they (the wives and children) promised not to take a job themselves.[96] And in 1980, the Constitutional Council declared unconstitutional a law providing for detaining 7 days without judicial intervention foreigners who are seeking entry or whom the government wishes to expel.[97]

As of yet, the French have not experimented to any degree with the benevolent quota, perhaps feeling that it is a tool that violates the fundamental principle of equality before the law. However, in 1960, in order to win Algerian support for continued French rule, the legislature passed a measure reserving for Algerians certain higher magistracies. (Similar measures had been in force for persons of African origin.) The Constitutional Council found the law valid. There was no violation of the principle of equality, it asserted, for the act was simply trying to overcome the unequal consequences of juridical equality. Where people of different cultural backgrounds have to take the same test and do not score equally well thereon, there is no equality in fact.[98] The holding augurs well for any future laws specially designed to advance the interests of non-French ethnic groups.

Taking a cue from American and British legislation, the French on July 1, 1972 passed a law[99] that makes it a crime to discriminate in employment or in the furnishing of goods and services on the grounds of one's ethnicity, nationality, race or religion. It is still too early to see whether this French Civil Rights Act will achieve its goals. Few court decisions have applied or interpreted it and it is frequently evaded, though one case resulted in a fine imposed upon a bar owner who refused to serve Arabs, blacks or Yugoslavs and another penalized the publication of a "Europeans only" want ad.[100] In a case decided under another statute, it was held that a restaurateur who refuses to sell to a black becomes culpable even though he does so only to keep his business prosperous.[101] And the above-noted Civil Rights Act was deemed violated by a realtor who connived with a landlord to deny a black an apartment.[102]

All five nations tolerate minority ethnic and racial communites, with the Soviet Union at present being the only one to feature a significant display of repression here as well. The two countries, India and the Soviet Union, where no one tongue is the native language of the vast majority of the citizenry, are the only ones to maintain large numbers of schools and other state institutions where the language employed is not the official language of the nation. Consequently, these lands do more than the other three to encourage diversity. (The rulers of the Soviet Union are probably unhappy that this can be said about their approach to nationality problems.)

The race and ethnic relations policies of all five frequently can be labelled stimulation of intergroup contact. A heterogeneous polity that eschews the destruction or enslavement of its politically weak groups consciously or unconsciously

213

feels that its diverse elements cannot remain re-
mote from each other if national unity is to be
preserved. Even the four nations (the U.S.,
Britain, India and France) not ideologically committed to the ultimate fusion of the separate
nationalities within their borders take steps that
bring some members of these clusters closer together, at least physically. In some cases (e.g.,
ending legally required school segregation) this
is the necessary consequence of reversing past
practices of governmental repression. Other steps
of this sort, however (e.g., education in a common
language, even fair housing legislation), most
probably spring to some extent from an intuition
that no social glue can preserve a bond among
fragments that never touch.

[1]National Advisory Commission on Civil Disorders, _Report_ (New York: Bantam Books, 1968), p. x.

[2]Missouri ex rel Gaines v. Canada, 305 U.S. 337 (1938); Smith v. Allwright, 321 U.S. 649 (1944); Shelley v. Kraemer, 334 U.S. 1 (1948).

[3]347 U.S. 483 (1954).

[4]349 U.S. 294 (1955).

[5]349 U.S. at pp. 300-301.

[6]_The Strange Career of Jim Crow_, 2nd rev. ed. (New York: Oxford University Press, 1966), p. 158.

[7]_New York Times_, June 6, 1971, p. 1; April 21, 1974, Sec. 4, p. 5.

[8]_New York Times_, November 11, 1974, p. 30.

[9]_New York Times_, April 21, 1974, Sec. 4, p. 5.

[10]United States Commission on Civil Rights, _Racial Isolation in the Public Schools_ (Washington, D.C.: U.S. Government Printing Office, 1967), p. 7.

[11]See, e.g., United States Commission on Civil Rights, _Statement on Metropolitan School Desegregation_ (Washington, D.C.: U.S. Commission on Civil Rights, 1977), p. 112. In 1974, 45 percent of all black students in the midwest went to virtually all-black schools. _New York Times_, June 20, 1976, p. 21.

[12] Vill. of Arlington Heights v. Metropolitan Housing Development Corp., 429 U.S. 252 (1977).

[13] James v. Valtierra, 402 U.S. 137 (1971). However, in Hills v. Gautreaux, 425 U.S. 284 (1976), it held that federal courts may order public housing built in white suburbs.

[14] Alexander v. Holmes County Board of Education, 396 U.S. 19 (1969).

[15] 402 U.S. 1 (1971).

[16] Dayton Bd. of Ed. v. Brinkman II, 443 U.S. 526 (1979); Columbus Bd. of Ed. v. Penick, 443 U.S. 449 (1979).

[17] Runyon v. McCrary, 427 U.S. 160 (1976).

[18] Milliken v. Bradley, 418 U.S. 717 (1974).

[19] United Kingdom Office of Population Censuses and Surveys, 1977 Demographic Review: A Report on Population in Great Britain, Series DR#1 (London: HMSO, 1978).

[20] E. J. B. Rose, et al., Colour and Citizenship (London: Oxford U. Press, 1969), p. 99.

[21] The Times (London), April 7, 1978, p. 2; May 15, 1981, p. 4.

[22] A proposal as of this writing under consideration by Parliament would henceforth limit British citizenship to persons born or naturalized in the UK or born abroad of British parents. However, persons born in the UK would not be citizens if their mother were in the country illegally or temporarily. Opponents of the bill claim that it will limit the NCWP presence in Britain, since the right to live there would normally be confined to citizens. New York Times, August 8, 1980, p. A2; February 8, 1981, Sec. 1, p. 3.

[23] David J. Smith, Racial Disadvantage in Britain (Harmondsworth, Mx.: Penguin Books, 1977), pp. 67-72.

[24] Bob Hepple, Race, Jobs and the Law in Britain (London: Allen Lane, The Penguin Press, 1968), pp. 74-75; Winifred Ewing, Discrimination in Great Britain, at pp. 511, 532-33 of Willem Veenhoven (ed.), Human Rights Case Studies, Vol. 1; David J. Smith, op. cit., pp. 108-11, 138-39, 186-90.

[25] See The Times (London), August 11, 1980, p. 2; February 5, 1981, p. 1; Smith, op. cit., p. 69.

[26] Time, February 26, 1973, p. 27. American cities such as Newark and Atlanta are more than 50 percent black.

[27] Times Educational Supplement 3146:15, September 19, 1975; New York Times, March 11, 1978, p. 2. Some figures from the United States should be juxtaposed against what has been said about Britain in the text. In 1970, 77 percent of the black population of Chicago lived in census tracts 90 percent or more black. For Atlanta the figure was 75 percent; for Washington 66 percent; for Detroit 49 percent; and for Philadelphia 45 percent. In these five cities the percentage of the black population living in census tracts 50 percent or more black was 94 percent, 91 percent, 96 percent, 90 percent and 82 percent. See United States Commission on Civil Rights, Twenty Years After Brown: Equal Opportunity in Housing (Washington, D.C.: U.S. Commission on Civil Rights, 1975), pp. 128-33. The 1968 Race Relations Bill was interpreted narrowly by the courts. For example, the House of Lords refused to hold illegal the denial of public housing to an otherwise eligible Polish national, Ealing London Borough Council v. Race Rel. Board,(1972) A.C. 342.

[28]Most of the data in these two paragraphs is based on U.K. Office of Population Censuses and Surveys, Census 1971, Parliamentary Constituency Tables as Revised 1974, Parts I and II (Titch-field: Office of Population Censuses and Surveys, 1974); Commission for Racial Equality, Ethnic Minorities in Britain (London: Commission for Racial Equality, 1978), p. 32; Greater London Council, Department of Planning and Transportation, 1971 Census Data on London's Overseas Population and Their Children (London: Greater London Council, 1974), pp. 59, 62.

[29]W. W. Daniel, Racial Discrimination in England (Harmondsworth, Mx.: Penguin Books, 1968), p. 152.

[30]The information in this paragraph is based upon Commission for Racial Equality, Annual Report 1978 (London: HMSO, 1978), pp. 7, 15, 20-21 and on personal interviews with Commission officials, August, 1979.

[31]New York Times, March 28, 1972, p. 14; Times Educational Supplement 3146:15, September 19, 1975; The Times (London), June 1, 1978, p. 1; Manchester Guardian Weekly, July 30, 1978, p. 5.

[32]Rose, op. cit., p. 349; The Observer (London), November 15, 1970, p. 2.

[33]In 1976, of the 21,000 on the Metropolitan London Police Force, 39 were West Indian, New York Times, April 4, 1976, p. 7.

[34]This paragraph is based upon New York Times, November 20, 1975, p. 1; November 21, 1975, p. 2; November 28, 1975, p. 6; January 24, 1976, p. 6; March 6, 1976, p. 3; November 17, 1977, p. 1; November 6, 1979, p. A6; The Observer (London), August 31, 1976, p. 17; U.S. News and World Report, August 11, 1975, p. 55; The Times (London), March 15, 1977, Special Report on Wales, p. IV; July 26, 1977, p. 4; August 9, 1977, p. 10;

Economist, June 25, 1977, p. 26; The Telegraph (London), July 11, 1979, p. 4.

35This paragraph is based on Economist, May 18, 1974, pp. 18, 26; September 13, 1975, p. 32; New Statesman 89:167, February 17, 1975; New York Times, October 4, 1974, p. 5; August 27, 1974, p. 5; January 14, 1976, p. 2; Time, April 8, 1974, p. 30; October 28, 1974, p. 29; U.S. News and World Report, August 11, 1975, p. 55.

36Philip Mason, Patterns of Dominance (New York: Oxford, 1970), p. 138; Harold Isaacs, India's Ex-Untouchables (Bombay: Asia Publishing House, 1964), p. 26.

37Mason, op. cit., p. 143. There are about 3,000 jatis in all. J. H. Hutton, Caste in India, 4th ed. (London: Oxford University Press, 1963), p. 2.

38Isaacs, op. cit., p. 26.

39Mason, op. cit., p. 146.

40Isaacs, op. cit., p. 58.

41New York Times, November 18, 1970, p. 12. According to one source, however, only 2 percent of those accused of violating the law are punished. Current Events, February 1974, p. 65.

42Isaacs, op. cit., pp. 103, 107; New York Times, November 18, 1970, p. 12.

43Donald Smith, India as a Secular State, p. 283.

44Smith, op. cit., p. 313; Isaacs, op. cit., p. 111.

45New York Times, November 18, 1970, p. 12.

[46] *Time*, February 16, 1970, p. 20; Isaacs, op. cit., pp. 109-110.

[47] (1951) All India Rep. S. Ct. 229.

[48] (1967) All India Rep. S. Ct. 1283.

[49] In Janki Prasad v. State of Jammu and Kashmir, (1973) All India Rep. S. Ct. 930, some Kashmiri Pandits had found difficulty obtaining promotion to headmaster positions at secondary schools. The reason for this was that 42 percent of the seats had been reserved for backward classes. The case was sent back to the lower court for a redetermination of what constituted a backward class. For a class to obtain the aid of Article 15(4) it would, the Supreme Court said, have to be both socially and educationally backward. Another case declared that it would be erroneous to assume that small landowners and those persons following 62 listed traditional occupations were automatically members of backward classes. Caste and poverty may be taken into account in determining the social and educational backwardness of a group; but neither factor may be deemed conclusive for this purpose. K. K. S. Jayasree v. Kerala, (1977) 1 Sup. Ct. Rep. 194.

[50] (1963) All India Rep. S. Ct. 649.

[51] (1964) All India Rep. S. Ct. 179.

[52] The 1961 decision is General Manager, S. Rly. v. Rangachari, (1962) All India Rep. S. Ct. 36. The 1976 decision is State of Kerala v. N. M. Thomas, (1976) 2 S. Ct. Cas 310. Likewise, it is legitimate to reserve 45 percent of current and "carried forward" vacancies for backward groups, Arati Ray Choudhury v. Union of India, (1974) 1 S. Ct. Cas 87.

[53] See Christoph von Fürer-Haimendorf, The Position of the Tribal Populations in Modern India at pp. 182-206 of Philip Mason (ed.), India and

Ceylon: Unity and Diversity (London: Oxford U. Press, 1967); New York Times, February 6, 1973, p. 5; January 20, 1975, p. 8; December 1, 1975, p. 7; June 17, 1979, p. 3; June 19, 1980, p. A22; July 27, 1980, Sec. 1, p. 8; November 3, 1980, p. A8; Manchester Guardian Weekly, February 5, 1978, p. 4; The Times (London), July 4, 1980, p. 16; Statesman, September 5, 1980, p. 1.

[54] Duncan Forrester, The Madras Anti-Hindi Agitation 1965, Pacific Affairs, Vol. 39, pp. 19, 21 (1966).

[55] Philip Altbach, India's Continuing Language Problem, School and Society, Vol. 97, p. 107 (1969).

[56] Such a map can be found at p. vi of Mason (ed., 1967), op cit.

[57] What has preceded in this paragraph is based upon W. H. Morris-Jones, Language and Region within the Indian Union in Mason (ed., 1967), op. cit., pp. 51-65; Baldev Raj Nayar, National Communication and Language Policy (New York: Praeger, 1969), pp. 120-21, 136-37; Altbach, op. cit., p. 107; James J. Lynch, The Curse of Babel, Virginia Quarterly Review 46:552, 546-70 (1970); New York Times, August 7, 1978, p. 5. In 1979, 86 percent of those sitting for the All-India Civil Service exam wrote the main paper in English. Statesman, February 27, 1980, p. 9.

[58] See New York Times, August 7, 1978, p. 5; Times of India, August 3, 1977, p. 6; Times of India (Bombay ed.), May 13, 1978, p. 8; May 17, 1978, p. 4.

[59] Yaroslav Bilinsky, The Rulers and the Ruled at p. 16 of Problems of Communism, September-October, 1967.

[60] See Geoffrey Wheeler, The Muslims of Central Asia at pp. 72ff of Problems of Communism,

September-October, 1967; Violet Conolly, The
Yakuts, at pp. 81ff of Problems of Communism,
September-October, 1967.

[61]Conolly, op. cit., pp. 85, 87. In Moslem
Uzbekistan in Central Asia, "illiteracy, 98% before 1917, has been all but wiped out. . . . There
is one tractor for every 385 people. In Pakistan,
by contrast, one for 6,000. Irrigation has made
for huge cotton crops. Processing plants offer
more jobs than can be filled." New York Times,
January 14, 1980, Sec. 1, p. 14.

[62]Erich Goldhagen, Introduction, at pp. vii,
xii of Erich Goldhagen (ed.), Ethnic Minorities in
the Soviet Union (New York: Praeger, 1968); William
Korey, The Legal Position of the Jewish Community
of the Soviet Union at p. 335 of Goldhagen (ed.),
op. cit.

[63]Korey, op. cit., at pp. 336-39 of Goldhagen
(ed.), op. cit.

[64]George Luckyj, Turmoil in the Ukraine at
pp. 52-59 of Abraham Brumberg (ed.), In Quest of
Justice: Protest and Dissent in the Soviet Union
Today.

[65]Jacob Ornstein, Soviet Language Policy, p.
121 of Goldhagen (ed.), op. cit.; Merle Fainsod,
How Russia Is Ruled, p. 305; Robert Conquest (ed.),
Soviet Nationalities Policy in Practice (New York:
Praeger, 1967), pp. 50-51.

[66]Robert Sullivant, The Ukrainians, at p. 46
of Problems of Communism, September-October, 1967.

[67]Ornstein, op. cit., p. 122.

[68]Quoted in Conquest (ed.), Soviet Nationalities Policy in Practice, p. 90.

[69]Ornstein, op. cit., p. 126.

[70]Garip Sultan, Demographic and Cultural Trends Among Turkic People of the Soviet Union, at pp. 251, 261-262 of Goldhagen (ed.), op. cit.; Ornstein, op. cit., p. 127.

[71]Stanley Vardys, The Baltic Peoples, at pp. 55, 60 of Problems of Communism, September-October 1967; Harry Lipset, The Status of Minority Languages in Soviet Education, Soviet Studies 19: 181, 184, 188 (1967).

[72]Yaroslav Bilinsky, Assimilation and Ethnic Assertiveness Among Ukrainians of the Soviet Union in Goldhagen (ed.), op. cit., pp. 147, 164-65; Nicholas Vakar, The Belorussian People Between Nationhood and Extinction, pp. 218, 221-22 of Goldhagen (ed.), op. cit.; Ivan Dzyuba, Internationalism or Russification (London: Camelot, 1968), pp. 118-21. Dzyuba notes that movies shown in the Ukraine are almost always in the Russian language, Ibid., p. 125.

[73]Sultan, op. cit., p. 267; Vardys, op. cit., p. 60.

[74]See Alex Inkeles, Soviet Nationalities Policy in Perspective, at pp. 300, 315 of Abraham Brumberg (ed.), Russia Under Khrushchev (London: Methuen, 1962).

[75]Manchester Guardian Weekly, February 11, 1979, p. 12.

[76]New York Times, December 27, 1975, p. 3; Manchester Guardian Weekly, April 30, 1978, p. 11.

[77]New York Times, June 11, 1974, p. 2.

[78]Dzyuba, op. cit., pp. 156-57 asserts that in the Ukraine, Party, Young Communist, governmental, and economic institutions use Russian almost exclusively.

[79] The Times (London), November 23, 1979, p. 11; Current Digest of the Soviet Press, Vol. 32, No. 7, March 19, 1980, p. 13.

[80] Vardys, op. cit., pp. 128-48, 155; Lubomyr Hajda, Nationality and Age in Population Change, Soviet Studies 33:475, 478 (1980).

[81] Ornstein, op. cit., p. 128; New York Times, January 6, 1979, p. A3.

[82] Wheeler, op. cit., p. 75. Thus fully 94 percent of married Uzbeks are married to Uzbeks. See Wesley Fisher, Ethnic Consciousness and Intermarriage, Soviet Studies 29:395, 398 (1977).

[83] New York Times, April 17, 1971, p. 13; June 11, 1974, p. 12; February 10, 1980, p. A4; February 28, 1980, p. A9; Michael Rywkin, Central Asia and Soviet Manpower, Problems of Communism, January-February, 1979, pp. 1, 10-13; New Statesman 99:118, 119, January 25, 1980.

[84] What has preceded in this paragraph is based upon Conquest, The Nation Killers (New York: Macmillan, 1970); A Chronicle of Current Events, Nos. 28-31, p. 132; New York Times, December 27, 1977, p. 2; U.S. News and World Report, September 15, 1980, p. 33.

[85] Korey, op. cit., p. 323; New York Times, June 7, 1971, p. 1; September 12, 1974, p. 11; December 27, 1977, p. 2. About 10,000 Soviet Armenians, mostly post-World War II immigrants, were permitted to leave the USSR in 1979 and 1980. New York Times, May 25, 1980, Sec. 1, p. 6.

[86] M. Louis Pettiti, Communication, Human Rights Journal 5:217 (1972); Le Monde, June 18, 1977, p. 32; New York Times, December 30, 1980, p. A3.

[87] Edward Tannenbaum, The New France (Chicago: U. of Chicago Press, 1961), p. 206.

[88] New York Times, January 15, 1969, p. 6; August 29, 1975, p. 3.

[89] This discussion of Brittany and Corsica is based on Le Monde, March 19, 1975, p. 6; July 31, 1975, p. 20; October 30, 1975, p. 42; New York Times, January 14, 1969, p. 6; February 1, 1969, p. 3; April 24, 1974, p. 8; August 28, 1975, p. 12; August 29, 1975, p. 3; September 3, 1975, p. 10; September 15, 1975, p. 9; September 20, 1975, p. 2; November 22, 1975, p. 12; September 5, 1976, p. 10; San Francisco Chronicle, September 2, 1975, p. 9. However, Breton may be offered only in the secondary schools, only when a certain number of pupils request it, and only when the instructor is willing to offer it during his break or after school. Manchester Guardian Weekly, July 5, 1975, p. 12.

[90] New York Times, July 22, 1975, p. 10; August 29, 1975, p. 3; November 23, 1975, Sec. 4, p. 4.

[91] What has preceded in this and the previous paragraph is based on R. F. Sheehan, Europe's Hired Poor, New York Times Magazine, December 9, 1973, pp. 36ff; Newsweek, October 1, 1973, p. 54; New York Times, December 15, 1973, p. 15; May 31, 1979, p. A5; December 30, 1980, p. A3.

[92] M. Louis Pettiti, Communication, p. 223.

[93] Francine Battailler-De Michel, Éléments Sociologiques du Racisme en France, Human Rights Journal 5:99, 112 (1972).

[94] October 6, 1971, Rec. 876.

[95] January 13, 1975, Rec. 16.

[96] The four 1978 cases are summarized at Dalloz, February 28, 1979, Information Rapides, pp. 92-94.

225

[97]Forni et autres, January 9, 1980, D. May 14, 1980, p. 249.

[98]Constitutional Council, January 17, 1960, D. 1960.293 and subsequent Note.

[99]New Article 416 of the French Penal Code.

[100]Charles Markmann, Freedom à la Française, The Civil Liberties Review, Spring, 1975, pp. 73, 89. Le Monde, July 8, 1977, p. 10; November 8, 1978, p. 18.

[101]Lochard, Cour de Colmar, D. 1972.1 Somm. 83.

[102]Aguie c. M'Bengue et Diwe, Gaz. Pal. 1976. 2 Somm. 320.

CHAPTER V

CRIMINAL PROCEEDINGS IN
THE FIVE COUNTRIES

The civil liberty of concern to this Chapter is the treatment of individuals and the public by the police, courts and other agencies of social control in a way that affords them a meaningful opportunity to give their version of the relevant facts and have that version seriously considered. The police, courts, etc., can choose from among many steps in response to an implied or express claim for "fair treatment" of this sort.

To classify these steps, the following typology is useful. (Under differing circumstances, a given step, e.g., preventing the defense lawyer from attending the police interrogation, will fall into different categories. At times, reasonable people can differ on the category into which a specific action should be placed.)

A. Facilitating the punishment of persons who have not been convicted at a hearing of wrongdoing.

B. Making less likely the punishment of persons who have not been convicted at a hearing of wrongdoing.

C. Facilitating the introduction or adequate consideration

       i. of relevant pro-defendant evidence
     ii. of relevant pro-prosecution evidence

D. Impeding the introduction or adequate consideration

       i.   of relevant pro-defendant evidence
      ii.   of relevant pro-prosecution evidence

    E.   Facilitating the introduction or consideration of irrelevant evidence.

    F.   Impeding the introduction or consideration of irrelevant evidence.

    The various parts of the scheme need no detailed explanation; and thus only several preliminary points need be made.

    1.   The word "punishment," as used above includes, but is not limited to, fining, imprisonment and loss of job.

    2.   The scheme easily could be modified to fit civil proceedings, but this Chapter will discuss criminal proceedings only.

    3.   In the same criminal proceeding the state can take steps each of which fits into a different one of these categories. For example, it is possible to hold a criminal suspect <u>incommunicado</u> for several months and then give him a trial at which the relevant evidence is brought forth and seriously considered.

    4.   The word "hearing" includes both judicial and administrative sessions that determine rights and duties of particular persons and the public.

    5.   The phrase "impeding the introduction and consideration of relevant evidence" means "impeding the introduction, etc., of relevant pro-prosecution and pro-defendant evidence" unless the context makes it clear that it refers to only the one or the other type of evidence.

    There is a close connection between criminal procedure and the book's essential theme of the relationship between toleration, etc., and polarization/incumbency instability. As Lon

Fuller's classic <u>The Morality of Law</u> would agree,[1] there is a high correlation between extensive repression on the one hand, and, on the other, procedural rules that punish without hearing, impede the consideration of relevant evidence favorable to the suspect, or facilitate the introduction of irrelevant evidence. (To take just one example, the Nazi deportation of Jews and others to the gas chambers during World War II was usually not preceded by an administrative hearing, to say nothing of any trial at which there was a genuine attempt to determine whether those scheduled for deportation were really threats to the security of the German Reich.) Conversely, punishing only after a hearing, introducing all relevant evidence on the suspect's behalf, and rejecting irrelevant evidence are inextricably linked with policies of toleration, encouragement of diversity and stimulation of intergroup contact.[2] There are several reasons for this. To mention just one, a criminal justice system that is geared to protect the innocent as well as punish the guilty often is based on the assumption that every person should be treated as an end in himself and not merely as a means. Another logical demand of this philosophical position is that there should be a presumption in favor of tolerating rather than destroying those who differ from one in politics, race or religion.

Since policies featuring "due process of law" and those of toleration, etc., are geographically and temporally intertwined, the citizenry is likely to view them as Siamese twins. It is thus reasonable to assume that they would be likely under the same circumstances to polarize or generate incumbency instability. Likewise, where the one would be unlikely to have these effects, the chances are the other would not have these consequences either. The rest of this book does make these assumptions; and refers to criminal justice measures that prevent punishment without trial, that exclude irrelevant evidence, and that facilitate the introduction and adequate consideration of

229

evidence favorable to the defendant as "analogous criminal justice measures," analogous, of course, to policies of toleration, etc. (Of course, the popularity of tolerant policies that results from the nature of the group tolerated--say one favoring repeal of the income tax--tells us nothing about the acceptability of criminal justice measures.)

Also (but with some trepidation) deemed "analogous criminal justice measures" are those that impede the introduction of evidence favorable to the prosecution. The doubt arises because steps such as these may lead to an increase in the crime rate and under this circumstance, the various groups in the society will start blaming each other for the inflated level of violence, a state of affairs that will tempt the minority to introduce measures to "put the minority in its place." Nonetheless, toleration and excluding relevant pro-prosecution evidence have similar effects. Both may well protect individuals who are unpopular; and both may well shield persons who are genuinely socially dangerous. When they increase polarization or incumbency instability, they therefore often do so for the same reasons. Accordingly, a showing that a policy of rejecting good pro-prosecution testimony will in certain situations augment polarization or incumbency instability is some evidence that a policy of toleration will have a similar outcome under these circumstances (and vice versa).

A. The United States

During the 1950's and 1960's the United States Supreme Court under Chief Justice Earl Warren issued many decisions defining constitutionally-permissible methods of enforcing the criminal law. The clauses of the Constitution most frequently cited there were:

1. Amendment IV, prohibiting unreasonable searches and seizures of persons and property and

230

the issuance of warrants for such searches except by a judge or magistrate upon "probable cause."

2. Amendment V's requirement of a grand jury indictment, its prohibition of double jeopardy, and its command that no one shall be compelled in any criminal case to be a witness against himself (the self-incrimination clause).

3. The requirements of Amendment VI that in all criminal prosecutions the defendant be tried by an impartial jury; that he be informed of the charges against him and allowed to confront those who are accusing him of criminal activity; and that he have the right to a lawyer to defend him.

4. The provision of the XIV Amendment that no state shall deprive anyone of life, liberty or property without due process of law. Using this clause, the Warren Court completed a process begun in the 1930's and held that the phraseology mentioned in "1," "2" and "3" (with the exception of the grand jury requirement) was binding upon the states and their political subdivisions.

An individual arrested in the United States now gets the following benefits by virtue of Miranda v. Arizona, becoming his as soon as the police deprive him of his freedom of action in any significant way, even though they have not ex-plicitly declared him arrested or taken him down to the stationhouse for questioning.[3] Before they start interrogating him, they must first inform him that he does not have to answer any of their queries and that any statement he does make may be used as evidence against him. Second, they must allow him to have a lawyer present at the questioning if he asks for one. Third, if he makes no request for one on his own, they must inform him that he may have a lawyer on hand during the interrogation and that the state will appoint one for him beforehand in case he cannot afford to pay for one from his own resources. Fourth, once the questioning commences, it must cease if the accused indicates that he wishes to remain silent. The penalty the state will suffer for ignoring any of these rules is that any confession obtained in violation of them will not be admissible at the accused's trial.

Miranda was one of the decisions which led to accusations that the Warren Court was "coddling criminals." The likely effect of Miranda is to reduce the number of confessions the police are able to obtain from suspects and thus the number of convictions of arrested persons the state can secure; the theory is that no one will confess to the police while his lawyer is present. The rationale for the decision is that if the police interrogate a defendant in the absence of a lawyer, they will be able to use physical brutality or trickery to get him to confess. Of course, a confession obtained this way is invalid,[4] but the defendant may have a hard time proving this, which is why the Court wished to end the practice of incommunicado interrogations. Miranda is thus a decision that not only commands that certain relevant evidence be excluded at trial but that further impedes the introduction of relevant evidence by lessening the quantity of such evidence (i.e., confessions) produced. (On the other hand, those who feel that traditional police interrogations often compel innocent persons to confess will argue that Miranda's primary effect is to impede the introduction of irrelevant testimony. The evidence on whether Miranda actually makes it very difficult to obtain confessions and/or convictions is sparse and contradictory.)

Miranda is based on the Fifth Amendment's guarantee against self-incrimination, though it could have rested upon the Sixth Amendment's right to counsel clause as did Escobedo v. Illinois,[5] the case that made Miranda likely. That clause of the Sixth has on many occasions been used by the Court to aid the man accused of crime. Not only did it produce Escobedo but it also gave rise to the leading decision of Gideon v. Wainwright.[6]

232

Prior to 1963, there were many states in which an indigent criminal defendant would have to go without a lawyer unless he were a man of low intelligence or involved in a capital case or unless the U.S. Supreme Court could be convinced after the trial that the absence of a lawyer there meant that it had lacked "fundamental fairness."[7] As a result of Gideon and the follow-up decision of Argersinger v. Hamlin,[8] no one may be sent to jail, even for a petty offense, unless he is represented by counsel who, moreover, must be provided for him gratis in case he is indigent. The requirements of Gideon are in practice satisfied in one of three ways. (1) In certain areas, the court will appoint for the defendant an attorney who happens to be sitting in the courtroom. (2) In some cities and counties, there is an official known as the "public defender" whose job it is to represent indigents. (3) In New York City, the Legal Aid Society, a charitable organization which receives public funds for this purpose, employs attorneys who represent the poor in criminal cases. Gideon is a case which should, on the whole, facilitate the introduction and adequate consideration of relevant evidence and impede the introduction of irrelevant evidence: a defendant without a lawyer will often not know what should be presented as testimony on his own behalf or the techniques of cross-examining witnesses. Of course, a shrewd attorney may be able to secure the exclusion of some germane information or convince the jury that a truthful witness is not to be trusted.

One type of evidence that at present cannot be used in any criminal trial, state or federal, is testimony, however reliable, obtained through a violation of the Fourth Amendment's prohibition against unreasonable searches and seizures. Prior to 1961, it was no violation of the Federal Constitution for state courts to allow this in evidence,[9] but in Mapp v. Ohio[10] the Supreme Court said that it could not be introduced even in a state proceeding. In general, with several exceptions to be mentioned below, an "unreasonable" search and

233

seizure is one made without a warrant issued by a judge or magistrate upon "probable cause" that the property specified in the warrant is something the law makes it criminal to possess, the fruits or instrumentalities of a crime, or evidence (such as a bloody shirt) that can be used to convict a suspect. Mapp v. Ohio is a good example of a case which hinders the introduction of relevant evidence at trial. It not only commands this directly, but may well inhibit the unearthing of such evidence by deterring illegal searches and seizures.

The most common exception to the rule that searches of persons and property for "contraband" and so on must be carried out under a search warrant is that searches "incidental to a valid arrest" need not be. Even individuals taken into custody for a minor traffic offense may be subjected to a full warrantless search of their persons.[11] The second exception is that a moving car may be searched without a warrant if there is probable cause to believe that it contains articles that offend against the law.[12] The third is that where state law permits it, police officers who see an individual acting suspiciously may stop him and, where they have reason to believe that he is armed, pat down his clothing. Then if they feel something suspicious, they may search him for weapons without a warrant even where his behavior gives no justification for actually making an arrest.[13]

One thorny search and seizure problem arises when the "property" the police would like to get their hands on is not personal goods, but the suspect's voice indicating that he is a participant in a crime. To accomplish this, it is possible to "tap" his telephone wires in the hope of hearing him say something that will implicate him or "bug" him electronically for the same purpose. For example, miniscule electronic devices which a suspect cannot see but which can record his statements or transmit them to police concealed nearby can be hidden in, near or against the room in which he happens to be. The Supreme Court, in 1968, swept away a confusing group of cases and held, in Katz v. United States,[14] that warrantless wiretapping or bugging is invalid whether or not carried out on the defendant's property, if undertaken in a place where the defendant has a right to assume that his words will not reach the ears of others besides his intended listeners. (In Katz, the barred conversation was overheard via a device attached to a phone booth in which the defendant was making his calls.) However, the Court added that when "probable cause" existed, a judge or magistrate could constitutionally issue a warrant for a tap or bug. The Government took up this suggestion in Title III of the Crime Control Act of 1968, allowing the police to get warrants for bugs or taps when probable cause exists, for example, that the individual has committed certain offenses. The states and the Department of Justice used taps and bugs frequently in the years immediately after Katz but do so less now.[15]

Where the trier of fact is biased, relevant evidence will probably be ignored even if introduced. Thus, a series of court decisions seeking to insure that he is impartial facilitates the consideration of relevant evidence. Among the rules proceeding from these decisions the following may be noted. A conviction will be reversed if the judge earns more money by conviction than by acquittal.[16] If the defendant comes from a distinct minority group and that group is systematically excluded from the grand jury that indicts him or the petit jury that convicts him, he will be allowed a new trial.[17] The same is true if the original trial is conducted in an atmosphere of mob violence.[18]

American courts are overcrowded. One study notes that in recent years in large American cities, "many cases have been subject to delays of 300 to 1,000 days from arrest to trial and final disposition."[19] This is bad enough for a man who

235

can afford to make bail, but many of those arrested cannot. So court congestion forces persons not convicted of a crime to spend months in the company of hardened criminals. In terms of the classificatory scheme, it facilitates punishment without a hearing. It also leads to "machine gun" justice, in which the judges hurry through cases in order to clean up their dockets--and so exclude or ignore much relevant evidence. Even more commonly, it gives rise to the practice of plea bargaining, telling the defendant that if he pleads guilty to a relatively minor charge he will not be prosecuted for the more serious offense for which he was originally taken into custody. In many jurisdictions, a large majority of defendants are convicted through guilty pleas emanating from plea bargaining. This hurts society because it often puts a dangerous criminal out on the street in a few months or years; and also wrongs the innocent defendant. Faced with a choice of "copping a plea" of criminal trespass and possibly getting six or five years for burglary, many innocent persons will choose the former course. Plea bargaining makes unlikely the introduction of all relevant evidence and the adequate consideration of the testimony that was brought to the attention of the police, judge, prosecutor, and defense attorney; though the latter two always use the evidence favorable to their respective sides as chips in their off-the-record bargaining sessions. Speedy trial rules mandating trial within a set period (e.g., six months from arrest) are becoming much more common; but often are ignored or result simply in freeing a suspect without trial, another step that obviously prevents consideration of the relevant evidence.

B. England

England's system of criminal procedure is in most ways similar to that of the United States, and this discussion will concentrate upon the significant differences and similarities. Thus, in England, as well as the United States, the judge

236

must not only be impartial but seem so. The old case of <u>Dimes v. Grant Junction Canal Company</u> is illustrative.[20] Here a canal company sued a landowner. The equity justice known as the Vice Chancellor decided in favor of the company, and the Lord Chancellor affirmed. Unknown to the landowner, the Lord Chancellor held several thousand pounds worth of stock in the canal enterprise. The property holder then appealed to the House of Lords, which reversed the decree against him. ". . . No one can suppose that (the Lord Chancellor) could be, in the remotest degree, influenced by the interest that he had in this concern; but, my Lords, it is of the last importance that the maxim that no man is to be a judge in his own cause should be held sacred. And that is not to be confined to a cause in which he is a party, but applies to a cause in which he has an interest."[21] An English jury, too, must be unbiased so that it can adequately consider the relevant evidence.

There are some differences, though, between the American and English jury systems. Under the Criminal Justice Act of 1967, it is possible for an English criminal defendant to be convicted (or acquitted) by a vote of 10 of 11, or 10 of 12, or 9 of 10. This majority verdict system is probably unconstitutional in the United States on the federal level and is rare, though not unconstitutional, on the state level.[22] Second, the selection of the jury in England is much speedier. Unlike the United States, where the selection of a jury sometimes runs into weeks, English juries are often seated in from ten to twenty minutes. Though it is arguable that this quick structuring of a jury is likely to result in one partial to one side and that it thus hinders the adequate consideration of relevant evidence, it probably has, on balance, the opposite effect since it reduces court congestion. As for the majority verdict system, this makes it impossible for an individual to thwart a decision to which the evidence strongly points and thus, on the whole, facilitates the adequate consideration of the evidence. However, it will have a contrary result where the small minority that would be more likely to speak at length during the jury deliberations under a unanimous verdict system has some reasonable points to make.

As in the United States, "involuntary" confessions are not admissible. An involuntary confession is defined in England as one obtained either through actual torture or through threats of harm in case there is no confession or through promises of advantage in case one is made, such threats or promises being made by a person in authority. (These confessions are <u>not</u> relevant evidence, for the suspect may have <u>confessed</u> falsely to end his psychological or physical suffering. Ergo, a rule rejecting them will impede the introduction of irrelevant evidence.)

What happens when the confession is voluntary but the police, in questioning the suspect, have ignored the well-known "caution" that "you are not obliged to say anything, but, if you do, it may be used as evidence against you"? The famous "Judges' Rules" demand that

II. As soon as a police officer has evidence which would afford reasonable grounds for suspecting that a person has committed an offense, he shall caution that person . . . before putting to him any questions . . . relating to that offense.

III. When a person is charged with or informed that he may be prosecuted for an offense he shall be cautioned in the following terms (the traditional warning). . . . It is only in exceptional cases that questions relating to the offense should be put to the accused person after he has been charged or informed that he may be prosecuted.[23]

As Delmar Karlen notes, these rules are ambiguous

238

about when this caution must be forthcoming.[24] But
there is not much need to clarify their meaning,
since voluntary confessions obtained when it has
not been given are nonetheless admissible at the
discretion of the court--and courts are increas-
ingly inclined to admit them.[25] Even after the
caution, the police may in certain circumstances
refuse to let the suspect consult a solicitor; and
in practice he is often denied this privilege.[26]
In R. v. Allen,[27] a lower court held inadmissible
statements made by a defendant to police after they
refused to let him consult his lawyer; but the rule
of this case is not yet firmly entrenched in
English jurisprudence.

Another way in which the English rules concerning the rights of the criminal defendant are
more helpful than the American to the introduction
of relevant evidence is that the English declare
that evidence obtained through an illegal search
and seizure may be introduced at the trial. (Illegal searches are not a rarity in England; the
police often illegally search without a warrant the
homes of the people they arrest.)[28] In Kuruma v.
The Queen[29] the defendant was sentenced to death by
a court in Kenya, then a British colony, for unlaw-
fully possessing two rounds of ammunition. The
policemen who searched him and found the evidence
had no authority to do so: only their superiors
had this right. Lord Goddard's opinion sustaining
the sentence emphasized that the important point
was whether the evidence was relevant--not, except
for the problem of the voluntary nature of a confession, how it had been obtained. Since the
ammunition found on the defendant's person was
highly relevant, it was thus admissible.

One more respect in which the English system
of criminal justice is more conducive to the adequate consideration of relevant evidence than the
American is that an English judge can comment on
the defendant's failure to testify: in doing so,
he emphasizes what is usually a pertinent fact. In
the leading case of R. v. Rhodes,[30] the defendant

239

was convicted of stealing eggs on false pretenses. At the close of the prosecution's presentation, the defense lawyer said there were no witnesses for the defense, and both counsel then addressed the jury. In summing up, the judge commented that it was open to the defendant to testify on his own behalf. The appeals court declared that this remark by the judge was no abuse of his discretion. Had he been presiding over an American court, the self-incrimination clause of the Fifth Amendment would have necessitated reversal.[31]

When it comes to granting bail, a limited sort of "preventive detention" is legitimate in England. That is, bail can be denied if the justice of the peace thinks that the "accused will commit crimes or tamper with witnesses if he is left at liberty."[32] Many think that preventive detention even of this type is unconstitutional in the United States.[33] However, the Nixon Administration had a bill passed permitting judges in the District of Columbia to deny bail in certain circumstances where there is a possibility of the accused's committing serious crimes: no doubt, the U.S. Supreme Court will be deciding upon the constitutionality of this measure. On the whole, however, the English bail system makes less likely than does the American the punishment of those who have not been convicted at a hearing of wrongdoing. It is more common there to release the defendant "on his own recognizance" pending trial, that is, without requiring him to furnish sureties for his appearance; or to have him put up just a modest sum as bail.[34] However, bail is now refused in 20 percent of English criminal cases.[35]

In the summer of 1976, the waiting period between arrest and trial in several of the larger English cities such as Birmingham, Manchester and Leeds was only 12 weeks.[36] But in 1979, the figure was 17.2 weeks for England and Wales as a whole. In late 1978, 700 persons were being held in custody awaiting trial 3 to 6 months, compared with only 580 in 1977; and the usual wait in London

jails had reached six months. In 1976, 52 percent
of the defendants denied bail were tried within
eight weeks of committal, but in 1977, only 10 percent were.[37] In other words, the gap between
arrest and trial is increasing in England, and the
larger cities are thus no longer strangers to plea
bargaining. Nonetheless, the delays in the United
States are still somewhat larger than those in
England. Among the reasons for this are the
quicker seating of jurors in the latter country,
its much lower crime rate, and the absence of
wrangling between judge, prosecution and defense
about whether certain evidence is admissible.

C. India

        Compared to the American, the Indian Consti-
tution has relatively little to say about criminal
procedure. Articles 20 and 21 would be most
familiar to an American reader. Article 20(3) is
similar to the self-incrimination clause of the
Fifth Amendment of the United States Constitution
and declares that "No person accused of any
offense shall be compelled to be a witness against
himself." And Article 21 of the Indian Constitution reads very much like the due process clause
of the XIV Amendment to the United States
Constitution, providing that "No person shall be
deprived of his life or personal liberty except
according to procedure established by law."

        The Indian system of criminal justice, like
the American and English, starts off with a presumption that the defendant is innocent. As in
England and the United States, involuntary confessions are not admissible. And the test of whether
or not a confession or admission is voluntary is
the same as for England: it is involuntary if it
is caused by an inducement, threat or promise referring to the charge against the accused and
proceeding from a person in authority; and the
inducement is sufficient to make the suspect
reasonably believe that by confession he would

gain an advantage or avoid an evil.[38]

There is no search and seizure clause in the Indian Constitution. However, under Section 93 of the Indian Code of Criminal Procedure, searches of property must on certain occasions be carried out under a warrant issued by a magistrate. And Section 100, which has no counterpart in England or America, requires that the policemen who do the rummaging must be accompanied by at least two "respectable inhabitants of the locality."[39] Nonetheless, property obtained by searches which violate Section 100 and other "search and seizure" requirements of the Code may be introduced in evidence.[40] India thus follows England in rejecting the exclusionary rule of Mapp v. Ohio and so its policy here facilitates the introduction of relevant evidence.

The United States, as noted, has developed through court decisions and statute the general rule that incriminating statements obtained by an electronic bug or tap are admissible at a trial only when the eavesdropping was authorized by a warrant signed by a judge. The English permit the Home Secretary to allow wiretaps in cases where the offense is serious and the tap is necessary to, and likely to result in, a conviction, but these legal taps are used only to obtain leads and are not employed in court as evidence.[41] The sparse Indian law on the subject facilitates the introduction of relevant evidence. In Yusufalli Esmail Nagree v. State of Maharashtra[42] the defendant had been convicted of the attempted bribery of a public official named Shaikh. The police set up a microphone under a sofa in the outer room of Shaikh's apartment and connected the "bug" to a tape recorder in an inner room. Shaikh sat in the inner room at the request of the police. The defendant then offered a bribe to Shaikh, an offer which was duly recorded. During his trial the taped conversation between the defendant and Shaikh was offered in evidence. The defendant contended that this procedure violated Article 20(3) of the

242

Indian Constitution, its self-incrimination clause. The Court, rejecting this point of view and affirming his conviction, said that it was not a question of his having been compelled to incriminate himself; no threat had been made to him. It did add, however, that it was not approving the practices of tapping phones and hiding microphones. In Britain, on the assumption that the approval of the Home Secretary or of a magistrate is required for bugging, the bug would have been illegal. Nonetheless, following the usual English policy on searches and seizures, an illegally tapped or bugged conversation is admissible.[43] In R. v. Maqsud Ali[44] the defendant went to Bradford Town Hall to talk about a murder in which he was a suspect. He was ushered into a room with a policeman and a Pakistani liaison officer. Only the policeman knew that a microphone and a tape recorder were concealed behind a wastepaper basket: no warrant had been issued for their installation. The defendant made some incriminating statements that were picked up by the microphone; and these were admitted into evidence, the court emphasizing the advantages the new electronic devices offer for crime detection. The English rules on bugging and tapping thus also facilitate the introduction of relevant evidence.

It is probable that even in the United States the intercepted material submitted in Yusufalli Esmail Nagree and R. v. Maqsud Ali would have been admissible even though obtained without a warrant. In United States v. White,[45] the police "wired" an informer with a transmitter and the defendant's incriminating statements (made at the informer's home, in his car, and in the defendant's house) were relayed to them. Though no search warrant had been obtained they were allowed to repeat these statements in court. Since Mr. Nagree's and Mr. Ali's taped admissions also were made to parties (Mr. Shaikh and the Bradford constable, respectively) who would have been happy to report them to the judge even if the police had not relied upon the marvels of modern electronics, an American

243

court might well permit them to be introduced. It would reason, as the Supreme Court did in White, that their introduction could not prejudice the suspect because of this fact that the person to whom they were made (in White, the informer) would have testified as to their contents had there been no bug.

Because of the Indian privilege against self-incrimination, the judge cannot comment on the defendant's failure to testify.[46] This is similar to the practice in the United States but contrary to that of England. Also, to require the defendant to give fingerprints and specimens of his handwriting is, as in the United States[47] and England,[48] not a violation of the privilege.[49]

As noted previously, America now provides free legal representation to almost all indigent defendants. England's welfare state also pays the legal fees incurred by poor suspects.[50] In India, the right of a defendant to an attorney if he can afford one has been recognized since the last century.[51] Since the passage in 1973 of Section 304 of the Indian Code of Criminal Procedure, the Government must furnish an attorney gratis in certain courts; but many indigents still do not get free lawyers[52] despite a new Article 39A of the Constitution mandating the state to provide this and a Supreme Court case[53] saying that this is constitutionally necessary where the needs of justice require. In Madhav Hoskot v. State of Maharashtra[54] the Supreme Court ordered that a free lawyer be provided all poor defendants who are appealing from convictions that cost them their freedom. An appeals court has discretion to reverse a conviction if the defendant did not have counsel at trial.[55] An arrested person who can afford a lawyer may, like his counterpart in the United States, consult one as soon as he is arrested and interview him out of the hearing of the police.[56] India now adopts the rule of Escobedo v. Illinois[57] and declares[58] that a suspect being interrogated in the station house has the right to have an attorney present if he requests one. Even more so than in the United States, court calendars are crowded, some magistrates having a workload of 2,000 cases. Thus it often takes a year or two for a case to be heard while the defendant languishes in prison, even though India makes no use of juries. At the end of 1978 India's jails held 65,000 convicts and 120,000 suspects awaiting trial. As a consequence, the Supreme Court directed the states to free suspects imprisoned for more than six months unless they had been accused of murder or armed robbery.[59]

Indian criminal procedure, much more than the English or American, facilitates the punishment of persons who have not been convicted at a hearing. The reference here is to the Indian practice of preventive detention, which is broader than the English and District of Columbia policy (that the Reagan administration wants to extend) of refusing bail to some criminals pending trial on the ground that they might commit additional crimes if released. In India legislation exists that for practical purposes permits detention in jail without trial for an indefinite length of time. As seen in Chapter II, the central government originally enacted a preventive detention measure in 1950 and various states have similar statutes on the books. The federal acts have usually permitted preventive detention of individuals for reasons relating not only to defense, foreign affairs and the security of India but also for the more "domestic" purposes of the preservation of public order and the maintenance of supplies and services essential to the community. By virtue of Article 22(4) of the Constitution, a person detained under a preventive detention law cannot be kept in prison unless an Advisory Board consisting of individuals with judicial qualifications approves his detention. If it does, he can be held up to the maximum period set forth in the act. If it be thought necessary to incarcerate him longer, he can immediately be rearrested and the same procedure followed.[60]

245

Ten thousand persons were detained under the first federal act in 1950; in 1951 the number declined to 2,316 and by 1954 it was down to 325: the reason for the decrease was the abandonment by the Communist Party of its agitation for a violent revolution in the part of Hyderabad known as Telengana.[61] Between 1951 and 1970, only a few persons were held under the standard preventive detention acts. However, for most of the 1970's, they (and the federal Rules, see infra) were once again widely employed against opponents of the government. In 1974 and 1975, estimates of the number of political detainees in the country ranged from 4,000 to 35,000, with Amnesty International giving a figure of between 15,000 and 20,000 (mostly Naxalites) for West Bengal alone. As a result of the 1975 state of emergency, between 20,000 and 55,000 additional persons were incarcerated without trial. Several thousand were "politicals" and the others were suspected of "economic" crimes such as smuggling and hoarding. All the politicals were released shortly after Mrs. Gandhi's January, 1977 call for elections.

The federal preventive detention law in force between 1971 and 1978 was a hated measure known as the Maintenance of Internal Security Act. Prime Minister Desai initially repealed it; but he and the second Gandhi administration brought it back through the back door by enacting ordinances that allow detention of persons who might be engaged in smuggling or hoarding or acting prejudicially to national defense or security. Under these ordinances, now reinforced by statute, 700 had been detained by the fall of 1980.[62]

In Gopalan v. Madras,[63] the Supreme Court held that preventive detention does not violate Article 21 of the Constitution providing that no person shall be deprived of his liberty except according to procedure established by law. The Court refused to say that Article 21 subordinated the government to the idea of "natural justice" embodied in the American Due Process Clause. All

246

it means is what it literally says: that no one
shall lose his liberty except according to procedure established by law--and, under the Preventive
Detention Act, one is deprived of his liberty by a
legally-established procedure. The Court could
have come to no other conclusion about the constitutionality of the statute, for Article 22 of the
Constitution expressly permits the passage of such
a law, while granting the detainees certain
procedural guarantees. It is interesting to note,
however, that the Supreme Court in invalidating
several sections of the law setting up special
courts to try politicians accused of excesses during Mrs. Gandhi's State of Emergency did so on the
"natural justice" theory that Article 21 bans
arbitrary and oppressive procedures, including
those creating a possibility that the defendant
will be tried by a biased judge.[64] (Not only the
Indians know how to use preventive detention.
Under a now repealed Northern Irish law called the
Special Powers Act, the British Army interned
1,500 Roman Catholic Ulstermen in 1971. An anti-
terrorism act of 1976 now in force in all the
United Kingdom allows British police to detain
suspected terrorists for questioning for 48 hours
--and in some cases up to a week. The police have
already used it to detain thousands, some of whom
were merely selling Irish Republican newspapers.
Men and women accused under the act are tried in
special courts without juries.)[65]

There are certain circumstances where preventive detention is an especially high-powered
weapon for the Indian government to use. Under
the original version of Article 352 of the Constitution, the President, if he was "satisfied that a
grave emergency exists whereby the security of
India or of any part of the territory thereof is
threatened, whether by war or external aggression
or internal disturbance," could issue a Proclamation of Emergency. (The modifications introduced
by the Desai administration allow a proclamation
only in the event of war or armed rebellion and
permit legislative veto of the proclamation. See

247

Constitution 44th Amendment Act of 1978.) By
Article 359(1), when such a proclamation is in effect, he can declare that the right to move any
court for the enforcement of any of the guarantees
of the Bill of Rights is suspended during the
period for which the proclamation is in effect.
Since the Bill of Rights includes not only freedom
of speech and religion and equal protection but,
as well, the criminal procedure section of the
Constitution, including the procedural guarantees
of its Preventive Detention Article, the Indian
government can during an emergency hold anyone
incommunicado with no right to appeal to an
Article 22(4) Advisory Board or a court as long
as the emergency proclamation is in effect.

These emergency provisions of the Constitution were first employed in September, 1962. The
Chinese attacked the northern border of India and
the President issued a proclamation decreeing
that a grave emergency existed. He then promulgated an ordinance known as the Defense of India
Rules which provided that individuals who were
reasonably suspected of prejudicial activities
should be detained. These Rules were accompanied
by an order under Article 359(1) suspending for
the period of the proclamation for those detained
the right to move for the enforcement of the
rights guaranteed by Articles 21 and 22 as well
as by Article 14, the basic equal protection
clause. In 1963 over one thousand persons were
interned under these Rules (which did not expire
until 1968), while during the same year only 288
individuals were held under the "normal"
Preventive Detention Act.[66] The Supreme Court,
in Makhan Singh v. Punjab,[67] made it clear when
it refused to release certain detainees that
Article 359 means what it says: that during a
period of emergency the right of an internee or
anyone to appeal to a court for enforcement of
any of the procedural or substantive provisions
of the Bill of Rights may be suspended by
presidential order. Therefore, those detained
by the government under preventive detention

248

legislation while an emergency proclamation and suspension of rights declaration are in effect may be held without trial and without interference by any court or advisory body until such time as the regime sees fit to let them go or to let the proclamation or suspension order expire. The Makhan Singh Court emphasized that how long the proclamation should continue in effect and what rights should be suspended under it are entirely up to the discretion of the executive: abuses of this discretion are corrigible only by the people, not by the courts. Furthermore, the Gandhi regime's 1975 "state of emergency" suspension (now lifted) of a detenu's right to notice of charges and to appeal to a court against an illegal arrest also was upheld by the Supreme Court.[68] Though the President had suspended Article 21, the Indian "due process" clause, the detenus contended that the right of a person held by the administration to appeal to a court for a writ of habeas corpus is a "natural" or "common law" right and thus was not placed in limbo by the President's decree. The Court held that the right to obtain habeas corpus is an Article 21 right and nothing more.

There are several provisions of the Indian system of criminal justice that would seem to make less likely the punishment of defendants who have not been convicted, though in practice 70 percent of the prisoners in Indian jails are there awaiting trial. As is true in the United States and England, the accused must quickly be brought before a magistrate, who in turn decides whether there is sufficient reason to hold him and if there is, the amount of bail (if any) he must post.[69] One suspected of a minor offense must be granted bail. Those arrested for more serious crimes usually may be accorded bail in the court's discretion--in the exercise of which the possibility of the defendant's committing a serious crime while free may be taken into account. Finally, if there are reasonable grounds for believing that a suspect has committed an offense carrying the death penalty or life imprisonment, he usually may <u>not</u> be granted bail.[70]

D. The Soviet Union

In the 1980's, an American, Indian, English or (especially) French lawyer suddenly called upon to defend a non-political suspect in a U.S.S.R. court would find himself working in a criminal justice system with many familiar features. This is true even though during the last twenty years of Stalin's reign, especially during the great purge of 1934-38, millions of Soviet citizens were killed or sent to labor camps in farcical proceedings on phony charges that they were traitors, spies, counter-revolutionaries, saboteurs, or terrorists; and this despite the inclusion in the 1936 Stalin Constitution of the following provisions:

Article 111--"In all courts of the U.S.S.R. cases are heard in public, unless otherwise provided for by law, and the accused is guaranteed the right to defense." (Article 156 of the Brezhnev Constitution is similar.)

Article 112--"Judges are independent and subject only to the law." (Article 154 of the Brezhnev Constitution is almost identical.)

There was no general "due process of law" clause in the Stalin Constitution. Article 159 of the Brezhnev Constitution requires that no one shall be convicted of a crime other than by a verdict of a court and in conformity with the criminal law.

After Stalin's death military courts were stripped of all power over civilians except those accused of espionage; the law that allowed the secret, <u>in absentia</u> trials of political prisoners was repealed; the doctrines that in cases of counter-revolutionary crimes confessions are extremely good evidence and that the burden of proof is on the accused were rejected; and most of those

250

persons who were in forced labor camps or jail as a result of the old way of treating political suspects were released.[71]

The current Soviet system of criminal justice contains several features which facilitate the introduction and consideration of relevant evidence and which most Anglo-American, French and Indian lawyers would consider essential parts of a decent system of criminal justice. For example, it is fundamental in the jurisprudence of India, France, the United States and England that an accused be informed of the charges against him: without such knowledge, he cannot adduce the evidence that gives his defense a reasonable chance of success. Even one held under an Indian Preventive Detention Act has this right. In the Soviet Union, too, the state must let him know what he is charged with and, an analogous right that is also safeguarded in the other four lands, must allow him to become acquainted with the evidence that is being presented against him in court. Thus Article 110 of the Stalin Constitution said that "Judicial proceedings are conducted in the language of the Union Republic, Autonomous Republic, or Autonomous Region, persons not knowing this language being guaranteed the opportunity of fully acquainting themselves with the material of the case through an interpreter and likewise the right to use their own language in court." (Article 158 is the counterpart in the Brezhnev Constitution.) Nor have these constitutional provisions been ineffective in practice. For example, in the case of Schlafshtein, et al., arising from an alleged conspiracy to steal state property, the Supreme Court of the USSR in 1964 reversed the conviction of the defendants on numerous grounds.[72] Among these were that the indictments and verdicts of guilt were in Kirghiz while many of the 15 defendants were Russian and did not know Kirghiz. Another flaw in the trial necessitating reversal and showing that Soviet law, too, now demands that the accused know the charges and evidence against him was that the descriptive part of the indictment of four of the defendants

251

spoke in terms of their abusing their official position while the conclusion to the indictment charged them with the more serious crime of theft.

Another principle of the English, French, American and Indian judicial systems is that no conviction is valid unless there is substantial testimony to support it. (This doctrine facilitates the introduction and consideration of relevant evidence, since if a defendant can be convicted without evidence, there is no need to introduce or analyze it.) In fact, in all the four countries the burden is on the prosecution to prove the defendant guilty. And "the new (post-Stalin) Soviet codes place the burden of proving the guilt of the accused squarely on the prosecutor. Although the phrase 'presumption of innocence' is avoided in all the codes, all that American jurists generally mean by that phrase is spelled out in Soviet law."[73] The case of Dilanov[74] illustrates the working of the rule that a conviction must be supported by what is presented in court. Mr. Dilanov was convicted in an Azerbaijani court of taking a bribe to sell five refrigerators. He was a shop manager in the china department of a Baku department store and was jailed mainly on the basis of the testimony of one Kerimov, who had been adjudged guilty as a co-conspirator. Other witnesses for the state were the purchasers: their testimony indicated that they gave the bribe to Kerimov and that they had never met Dilanov or seen him in the store. In addition, Kerimov's statement to the investigator was that he had had business with him only once. Finally, several witnesses testified that Kerimov had had unfriendly relations with Dilanov and that the latter had once thrown the former out of the shop. The USSR Supreme Court reversed the conviction and ordered Dilanov freed: it thought that "in the materials of the case there is no objective evidence that Dilanov was guilty of taking a bribe."[75]

As mentioned earlier, it is essential to the

adequate consideration of evidence that the trier of fact be impartial. As also will be remembered, criminal trials in the USSR are heard by an elected judge, who usually has had legal training, and two "people's assessors," who are laymen. Since the assessors usually follow the lead of the judge,[76] what is imperative is that the guarantees of Article 154 of the Brezhnev Constitution that "judges are independent and subject only to the law" be followed in practice. And to some extent, this is the case in the USSR as well as in England, France, India and the United States. Witness the following decision, which calls for no comment.

Case of _Ortenberg_

Ortenberg was found guilty of stealing oil worth 143,254 rubles from the varnish and paint shop of the Odessa factory. . . .
The First Deputy Procurator General of the USSR filed a protest with the Presidium of the Odessa provincial court stating that the indictment had been approved by N. Meshkev, acting procurator of the Odessa province, and the appeal had been reviewed by his wife, serving at the time as a member of the provincial court. This violated Article 54 of the Code of Criminal Procedure of the Ukranian SSR and without question is cause for vacating the court's judgement.[77]

However, most Soviet judges are members of the Communist Party, and it is questionable whether they can remain impartial in trials having a "political" flavor where, for example, the defendant has been accused of slandering the state. Conquest asserts that the judges are subject to party pressures, including campaigns in the press demanding the eradication of a certain type of crime. Thomas Towe agrees that Soviet judges have little independence, and says that this is partly a consequence of their being under party control.[78]

An actual situation bears witness how some

judges will behave while presiding over a "political" trial. The writer-historian Andrei Amalrik was tried in 1965 for violation of an anti-parisitism law, under which it is illegal to avoid "socially useful work and . . . (lead) an anti-social parasitic way of life." His real "crime," in the eyes of the authorities, was not his lack of a regular job, but his liking for abstract art, his friendship with foreign artists and journalists, and his anti-Soviet plays. In his Involuntary Journey to Siberia,[79] Amalrik describes his interview the day before trial with the judge in his case, one Chigrinov.

> "When I read your plays," Chigrinov said to me, "I kept wondering what kind of man could write such stuff. . . ." I don't remember all the details of our conversation. He spoke not about whether I had been working, but mainly about my plays, which he referred to scathingly and described as anti-Soviet . . . (T)he judge asked me what I thought should be done with me now. I replied that I thought I should be released at once. "And what I think" Chigrinov said, "is that you should be sent to Siberia to look at things with your own eyes, not from inside somebody else's pants."[80]

Not surprisingly, Amalrik was convicted on the following day and sentenced to two and a half years' exile. The beginning of this Chapter claimed that there was a high correlation between high dosages of repression and procedural rules that punish without hearing, impede the adequate consideration of relevant pro-defendant evidence and/or facilitate the introduction of irrelevant evidence. Amalrik's Judge Chigrinov emphasized irrelevant testimony (Amalrik's plays and tastes in art) and ignored relevant evidence (the fact that Amalrik was a hard worker and anything but the "parasite" he was accused of being). Likewise Prime Minister Gandhi, instead of allowing her political opponents to go to trial during the state of emergency, simply had them preventively detained.

The Soviets, like the French, make use of a thorough study of the case by a hopefully-impartial investigator prior to the trial. The investigator interrogates the accused and the witnesses and examines all the evidence "prior to preparing the indictment, a document in which all the charges and the evidence against the accused are stated in detail."[81] The use of an investigator, if he is truly impartial, will increase the likelihood that all relevant evidence will be brought to light at trial. The suspect, unless he is a minor or is physically or mentally defective, has no right to the presence of a lawyer at his pre-trial interrogation, though the investigator must inform him of "his rights, including the right to state his side of the case during the pre-trial investigation and to examine any part of the record, including adverse evidence of which he knows nothing."[82] The absence of a lawyer will make it less likely that the defendant will withhold damaging statements and thus, more often than not, facilitate the introduction of relevant evidence. However, the lack of one will facilitate the introduction of irrelevant evidence should the investigator resort to physical or mental torture.

The privilege of self-incrimination, both before and at trial, is more limited in the Soviet Union than in the United States, and so in this respect the Soviet system is more conducive to the introduction of relevant evidence. A defendant may not be compelled to testify either at the investigation or at trial; but adverse inferences may be drawn from his silence. A witness who is not a defendant in a criminal case may be prosecuted for failing to answer questions put by a court or investigator even though the answers tend to incriminate him. Finally, at the trial, the procurator (prosecutor) must prove the charges contained in the indictment by employing the evidence produced by the preliminary investigation.[83]

There are restrictions on police search and seizure. Articles 167-177 of the Code of Criminal Procedure of the RSFSR require the investigator to get the procurator's sanction for the search unless the circumstances do not permit of delay. (Articles 55 and 56 of the Brezhnev Constitution guarantee the inviolability of the home, correspondence and telephone conversations.) In the latter situation, the procurator must be informed as soon as possible. What can be looked for is the fruit of the crime, its instruments, or other relevant evidence. Witnesses must be present at the search--and these must be either the person whose property is examined, an adult member of his family, or the representative of the management of his apartment house. In general, however, whether illegally seized (and other) evidence is admissible is within the discretion of the court,[84] and so the Soviet as well as the English and Indian rules on search and seizure facilitate the introduction of relevant evidence.

As soon as the preliminary investigation is over, the lawyer may confer with his client. At the trial, where a procurator is present, the defendant must have an attorney unless he waives the right to one. That the right to counsel here (which, as was seen, facilitates the introduction and adequate consideration of relevant evidence) is deemed important in the Soviet Union can be seen by glancing at cases such as that of <u>Filimonova</u>.[85] She was found guilty with others of abusing an official position and misappropriating state funds while working as a cashier in an office of communal enterprises and welfare services. The Supreme Court of the RSFSR reversed for a new trial because the defendants had had no legal representation though the state procurator had conducted the trial. The mere fact that they had signed statements prior to trial refusing attorneys was not a sufficient waiver of their right to counsel, because when they signed it was unknown whether a procurator would represent the state. At least some indigent defendants can get free legal advice;[86] and Article 116 of the Brezhnev Constitution declares that "in cases provided for by law, legal counsel to citizens shall be free of charge."

The deportation of the nationalities discussed in the previous chapter testifies that in times of trouble, at least, the Soviet state has no compunction about depriving one of his liberty without trial. However, in ordinary circumstances, the Soviet police must inform the procurator within 24 hours of arrest, who has an additional 24 hours to decide whether to keep the suspect in detention pending investigation, release him, or let him go on condition that third parties act as sureties or that he agree in writing not to leave his home. He can be kept in detention only if the investigator, procurator or court fears that he will engage in criminal activity while free, leave the jurisdiction to escape trial, or prevent the establishment of the truth.[87] However, this detention period can last nine months and extensions can be obtained from the Presidium of the Supreme Soviet.[88]

E. France

The French Constitution, like the Indian, contains relatively little about criminal trials. Article 66 proclaims that "No one may be arbitrarily detained. The judicial authority, guardian of individual liberty, shall insure the respect of this principle under the conditions stipulated by law." The 1789 Declaration of Rights, incorporated in the de Gaulle Constitution's Preamble, declares (Article 7) that "no man may be accused, arrested, or detained other than in the cases determined by the law and according to the forms that it has prescribed." This is a surety against arrest in situations where the legislature has not authorized this step. Article 8 of the Declaration proscribes ex post facto legislation: "No one may be punished other than in virtue of an established law promulgated before the crime and legally applied."

Many Anglo-American observers feel that the French system of criminal justice is less favorable to the defendant than its British or American analogs. One text says that "We have already noted that criminal procedure was originally intended to favor the interests of the state. Many liberal reforms have been introduced since 1806 . . . Much of the Napoleonic tradition nevertheless remains."[89] Sybille Bedford, who observed courts in several countries, says that "When the fanfares sound and his Lordship in procession passes through the streets, an Englishman's response may be some comfortable image of Magna Charta (sic), Habeas Corpus and the Common Law; French associations with the Cour d'Assises, the Palais (de Justice), or even simply justice, might be the Police State of the Ancient Regime, the Tribunal of the Revolution, the Napoleonic Code, The Commune (of 1871), the Police State of Napoleon III and the present prerogatives of the police."[90]

Similar to the Soviet investigator in function and in importance to the criminal justice system is the French examining magistrate (juge d'instruction). He is a hopefully-impartial official who is supposed to investigate a pending case thoroughly and compile a dossier that contains as much as possible of the evidence that will be introduced at trial. It is up to him to determine whether the case should be continued or the charges dropped. If after his investigation (instruction) he believes that there is considerable merit in the accusation, he is to recommend that the case be sent to the appropriate trial court, the most serious crimes (crimes) being assigned to the Assize Court (Cour d'Assise), and crimes with a maximum of 60 days to five years imprisonment (délits) to the Correctional Courts (Tribunaux Correctionels). Neither prosecutors nor police (including the investigators known as "judicial police") may give the examining magistrate orders. However, some commentators have claimed that he is too favorable to the police, especially as he relies on them for much of his information.[91]

258

In 1980 the French government passed a controversial bill entitled "Security and Liberty" that
while increasing the penalty for many offenses and
reducing judicial discretion in sentencing, to some
extent clipped the wings of the examining magistrate.
The frequently-used power of the prosecutor to by-
pass him in cases of délit was extended. Moreover,
even when the arrestee is suspected of a crime, the
prosecutor can ask the "indicting chamber" (chambre
d'accusation) of the Court of Appeal to remove him
from the case after his investigation has been under
way three--in certain cases seven--months. Even
before this reform the "indicting chamber" reviewed
the recommendation of the examining magistrate to
send the case to the Assize Court.[92] If it dis-
agrees with his suggestion, it can free the suspect
or remand the case to an inferior tribunal.

A "Flagrant Crime," defined in Article 53 of
the 1958 Code of Criminal Procedure, is one which
is being or just has been committed; or where a suspect is being pursued by "public clamor"; or where
he is found in possession of objects or evidence
leading one to believe that he has participated in
the offense. The powers of the judicial police and
the examining magistrate to some extent depend on
whether there has been a flagrant crime. If the
suspect's action falls into this category, the
judicial police can at the start of the investigation initiate a dreaded proceeding known as the
garde à vue, which has existed for a long time but
which first received legal recognition in the 1958
Code. The garde à vue is a step under which a suspect or a witness can be detained by the judicial
police for a 24-hour period. During this time, the
detainee has no right to a lawyer; nor is he told
that he has a right to remain silent. This 24-hour
period may be extended another 24 hours with the
consent of the prosecutor or the examining magistrate if grave and inculpating evidence against the
detainee has been produced.

There are certain controls over the conduct
of the garde à vue that are designed to lessen the

chances that the police will employ psychological
and physical torture during the period of detention. (Charges of brutality against the judicial
police are common and not always unfounded.) During the first 24 hours, the detenu's family may
designate a doctor to examine him. After 24 hours,
the detenu can demand such an examination but he is
not told that he has such a right. At the conclusion of the garde à vue, the police must draft a
report which notes the length of the interrogations, the reason for the garde à vue, and when it
began and ended. [93] Almost by definition, the garde
à vue facilitates the punishment of persons who
have not been convicted of wrongdoing at a hearing.
For someone against whom no formal charges have
been brought and who may have been merely a witness
to a crime, to spend 24 hours in a police station
without a lawyer and without being furnished any
information about his rights may be a terrifying
experience. It should be noted, moreover, that
there is no legal requirement that the detenu be
accorded a certain amount of rest during the garde
à vue. If the garde à vue is conducted with a
reasonable amount of humanity, it is likely, however, to facilitate the introduction of relevant
evidence. A suspect who is not informed of his
right to silence and has no counsel present during
the interrogation may well confess or provide
valuable information--and this data will be
reliable if not obtained by trickery or torture.

If the police report of the garde à vue does
not comply with the formalities required by the
law, any confession obtained during the detention
may--not must--be found invalid. [94] In the case of
Dame X., [95] a court at Douai did declare null a confession made during the garde à vue. The detenu
was interrogated far from home; and the report did
not record the length of the hours of questioning
and repose, thus placing the court in the impossible position of determining whether the damaging
statements were obtained in conditions legally and
morally acceptable. The examining magistrate
should have assured himself of the conditions under

which the confession was made and postponed his own
interrogation to give the suspect more time to
rest.

Turning to the examining magistrate's investigation, one of the first steps he must carry
out is to summon the suspect for a first appearance. At this first appearance the magistrate is
to advise him of the facts that are getting him
into trouble, of his right to silence, and of his
right to choose a lawyer or have one designated for
him. Unless the suspect wishes to talk at this
appearance he cannot be interrogated any more
there, except in situations of "urgency." Immediately after counsel is chosen for him, he has the
right to communicate freely with him at all stages
of the proceedings; and, unlike the Soviet Union,
the attorney (as well as the prosecutor) is to be
present at subsequent interrogations by the magistrate. The privilege against self-incrimination is
partially recognized. Neither at the interrogation
nor any place else may the suspect's confession or
any other statement legally be demanded from him.
However, if he doggedly remains silent, this fact
is noted on his dossier and inferences may be drawn
from it (and comments made about it) at the trial.

In the United States and England the privilege against self-incrimination is twofold: it
permits a criminal defendant to remain silent by
keeping off the stand and allows any witness in a
proceeding under oath to refuse to respond to
queries that may act as a link in a chain of evidence against him in a criminal case. In France as
well as in India and the Soviet Union mere witnesses do not have the right to withhold testimony
that may incriminate them. A witness before the
examining magistrate must take an oath to tell the
truth. If he does not take the oath, or if he refuses to testify, he may be prosecuted. The witness, unlike the suspect, is not allowed to have a
lawyer present during the interrogation. As one is
more likely to confess under these circumstances,
the magistrate will at times summon as a mere

witness the individual he really suspects of having committed the crime. This "suspect" will be heard unaccompanied by a lawyer; and the appeals court will rarely invalidate confessions obtained this way. However, if one is summoned as a suspect and not as a witness and not told of his right to counsel and right to silence, and is interrogated without a lawyer, the statements he makes may not be used against him.[96] The French rules concerning the right to silence are more likely to produce relevant testimony than are the American. Though the suspect is warned of his right to silence and has counsel present at his interrogation, he knows that it is legally permissible to draw inferences from his silence and thus is more likely to talk. More importantly, the fact that witnesses have no right to silence and no right to counsel during the magistrate's investigation means that they are more likely than their American counterparts to furnish pertinent information. As usual, the caveat is that the absence of a lawyer may lead to police brutality, which in turn will produce highly unreliable statements.

Where the crime is flagrant, the judicial police may, even prior to the appearance of the examining magistrate, search without a warrant the domicile or person of any individual suspected of having participated in the crime. (In practice, the police get away with searches of the person even where no suspicion exists.) Any relevant papers, documents, or objects may be seized as evidence. However, there are certain formalities that the police must observe: for example, they cannot begin the search before 6:00 A.M. and after 9:30 P.M. other than in exceptional cases. These seizures prior to the investigation by the examining magistrate form part of what is known as the preliminary investigation (enquête préalable). After he takes charge of the case, he can order searched all places where there might be found objects whose discovery is necessary for ascertaining the truth.[97]

There is little law on the question of
whether evidence illegally seized may be introduced
in court; and the authorities are themselves somewhat in conflict on this matter. A dossier which
refers to evidence obtained by an illegal search
will not be nullified when the sentence made it explicit that the evidence was not taken into
account.[98] However, one cannot ignore decisions
such as Acheraoui et autres.[99] Here M. Ahmed
Acheraoui and others were sentenced to jail for six
months for theft and receipt of stolen goods. The
police went into their house with the consent of
the defendants, as is required when there is no
warrant and the crime is not a flagrant one. However, this "consent" was not genuine consent, since
they were never informed by the police of the fact
that they could refuse it on the ground that the
officers did not have a warrant from an examining
magistrate. Accordingly, the search and seizure
violated the formalities required by law. The
Court of Cassation quashed their conviction on the
ground that it was exclusively based upon the objects seized illegally. Thus France's highest
court has made it clear that the exclusionary rule
does exist in France in the limited sense that convictions based entirely upon illegally seized evidence will be quashed. Moreover, the Court
recently ordered annulled the records of a search
and seizure that was illegal because the police
entered the house without a warrant from the examining magistrate, the crime not being a flagrant
one.[100] The exclusionary rule thus also prevails
in the sense that a court should require the of-
fending testimony suppressed before a verdict is
reached. However, its net is not as far flung as
the exclusionary rule of the United States, as it
is probable that a finding of guilty would be upheld though resting in part on wrongfully seized
testimony.[101] Surprising as it may seem, even the
introduction of evidence obtained by torture will
not necessarily invalidate a verdict of guilty.[102]
A decision based on such testimony may be invalidated; but in one instance all the defendant was
able to obtain was a moderation of his penalty.[103]

263

The French rules on the introduction of wiretap evidence are even more cloudy, though governmental agencies in France are notorious for conducting illegal wiretaps.[104] Despite a statute of July 17, 1970, examining magistrates (not the judicial police acting alone) may and do order both wiretaps and bugs to aid them in their investigations, a procedure approved by the Court of Cassation.[105] This statute, Penal Code Article 368, makes it a crime to record the conversations of persons in private places without the consent of the participants. Whether, even in the case of a magistrate-authorized tap or bug, it makes inadmissible the introduction of the recorded evidence at trial is still uncertain. There are some cases decided as early as the 1950's indicating that though the examining magistrates can order wiretaps to aid them in their investigation, the taps cannot be introduced at the trial. However, one writer believes that they may be admitted on the ground they are analogous to seized correspondence sent by or addressed to the defendant.[106] Since the French rules on wiretapping and on excluding illegally obtained evidence are so unclear, it is impossible to come to any firm determination whether they further or hinder the introduction of relevant evidence at a hearing.[107] As it is probable, however, that convictions based partly (but not wholly) on the use of illegally obtained evidence will be upheld, one may very tentatively assert that they, like their Indian, English and Soviet counterparts, impede the introduction of relevant evidence less than do their American analogs.

In all except the most minor cases, indigent defendants have the right to a state-paid attorney. The suspect must be informed of this right at his first appearance before the examining magistrate. Even in petty cases, a lawyer may be appointed for him; and in serious felony cases he must have an attorney whether he wants one or not.[108] Though the right to counsel is as extensive as in the United States and England, a French defense attorney has fewer prerogatives than his English or

264

American counterparts. (Moreover, charges have been made that defense counsel, paid or unpaid, is oft-times not very effective on the client's behalf.)[109] Counsel may attend the examining magistrate's interrogations but has no right of cross-examination at these sessions.[110] Even at the trial the right of cross-examination is limited. The defense lawyer can question a witness only with the consent of the presiding judge of the court-- and even then it is the judge that puts the question.[111] The major function of counsel for the defendant seems to be his speech to the jury before it retires in which he tries to prove his client's innocence or indicates why he should be treated mercifully.

It is difficult to determine definitively the effects on the introduction of evidence of the French rules on the rights and prerogatives of counsel. If one believes the assumption that cross-examination is likely, in general, to weaken the testimony of witnesses furnishing the court with erroneous, misleading, or perjured statements, then he will have to assert that the French dislike of such examination facilitates the introduction of irrelevant evidence. On the other hand, if one thinks that the main result of cross-examination is to give the trier of fact the impression that honest, careful citizens are either liars or sloppy observers, then he must view the French limitations on cross-examination as facilitating the adequate consideration of relevant evidence and hindering the introduction of irrelevant testimony. The French (and Soviet) practice of having most of the interrogation of witnesses carried out by the presiding judge rather than by the prosecutor or the defense attorney[112] on the whole facilitates the introduction of relevant evidence. The judge, supposedly impartial, is less likely to ask the persons called to the stand only those questions which benefit a particular side.

In the Assize Court the defendant is entitled to a jury trial. The jury consists of nine members, chosen from the electoral rolls. The three Assize judges and the jury retire and vote together; and for a verdict a vote of at least eight of twelve is needed. Some commentators have argued that the usual middle and lower-middle class jury of clerks and shopkeepers is not representative of all cross-sections of the French people, especially the far left and the poor.[113] Empirical research on the matter is lacking, but one observer reports that the general feeling is that the lay members of the jury often but not always follow the lead of the judges.

> The lawyers say it's all a matter of luck. The same jury sits with the same judges for a whole sessions, and the best you can hope for is for your case to come on second. The first case is hopeless, the jury'll do exactly as the judges tell them. . . . By the second case they have a change of heart. "Nous avons été trop durs, we must show independence"--<u>Acquittement</u>. By the third they feel they've gone a bit too far, a compromise--ten years. By the fourth, full reaction, after all, the professionals know best. . . . After that, one cannot tell the way they'll go, it's anybody's guess.[114]

The French rules on jury trial facilitate the adequate consideration of relevant evidence and hinder the consideration of irrelevant. The majority verdict system makes it impossible for one juror who dislikes the defendant's race, religion or politics to impede a verdict of acquittal or one who is sympathetic to him for similar reasons to prevent a verdict of guilty. Moreover, one can assume that the presence of the judges in the "deliberation" room prevents the lay jurors from relying exclusively on factors that have nothing to do with the defendant's guilt or innocence and compels them to pay attention to the most important relevent material in the record. (One study of English juries, in whose deliberations no judge participates, concludes that "the reverence judges have traditionally accorded to juries is excessive,"[115] i.e., that a jury sitting alone is far from a perfect fact-finding institution.)

The presumption of innocence prevails in France as well as in the other four nations. In felony and many misdemeanor cases the court must base its decision on proof adduced at the trial: the examining magistrate's dossier, though available to the judge, has only "informational" value. Moreover, the defendant cannot be declared guilty unless the jury has a "deep-seated conviction" that he is culpable.[116] This is not too different from the standard prevailing in the United States and Great Britain that no one shall be convicted unless the finder of fact is convinced of his guilt "beyond a reasonable doubt." To the extent the French standard of guilt is less pro-defendant than is the Anglo-American, one could argue that it facilitates more adequate consideration of the relevant evidence in that it seems to permit conviction when 95 percent of the evidence is pro-prosecution and only 5 percent is pro-defense.

In France, a suspect may well remain in jail pending trial, another aspect of the system facilitating punishment of persons who have not been convicted at a hearing of wrongdoing. It is true that a law of July 17, 1970 declares that detention awaiting trial is the exception and that freedom during this period is to be the rule; but 40 to 45 percent of the penitentiary population finds itself in this "exceptional" situation and at least half of all French defendants remain under lock and key pending trial.[117] In practice, bail is not frequently granted because only the well-to-do can afford it.[118] In case of serious offenses (crimes) it is usually up to the examining magistrate to determine whether to grant bail;[119] and he may commit the suspect to jail "provisorily" pending trial where there is reason to feel that if liberated he will commit an offense, destroy evidence, or flee the country.

However, the "indicting chamber" of the Court of
Appeal can overturn a refusal of the examining
magistrate to set the defendant at liberty. Moreover, the 1980 law on "Security and Liberty" contains provisions designed to reduce the time
between arrest and trial and keep the suspect out
of the penitentiary while his trial is on the
horizon. Previously, in cases of the misdemeanors
and felonies known as délits the prosecutor in
certain circumstances had the power to jail the
defendant until his trial. In an explit recognition of the Anglo-American concept of habeas
corpus, the 1980 Act provides that when the defendant is accused of a délit, he must be brought
before a judge within three days of his arrest.
It is then up to the judge, and not the prosecutor,
to decide whether to free him pending trial. Moreover, if he is provisorily detained and the examining magistrate has been bypassed by the prosecutor,
he must be released after two months unless he has
"appeared" before the court by that time. However,
this "appearance" is not necessarily a trial.[120]

The ability of the state to punish persons
who have not been convicted at a hearing of wrongdoing is magnified in times of emergency and between the mid-1930's and mid-1960's France was
plagued with almost continuous emergencies. The
French "provisory" detention mentioned in the preceding paragraph is a measure taken by a judicial
officer, one who is, furthermore, supposed to be
impartial in the dispute between the state and the
suspect and interested only in ferreting out the
truth. Emergency situations have led to the institution of administrative internments, which are
deprivations of liberty effectuated by employees
or officers of the executive branch such as prefects, i.e., persons who are partially dependent
for job and promotion upon the good will of the
government of the day. A decree-law of November
18, 1939, promulgated by the dying Third Republic
at the outbreak of World War II, introduced administrative internment in the country for the
first time since the 1789 revolution. It was

applied to the Communists in 1939, as this group then was following the Soviet line of "peace with Hitler's Germany," a tactic based upon the Hitler-Stalin pact of 1939. Anyone dangerous to the national defense or public safety could be detained. Vichy and then the government of the Liberation retained until the end of World War II the system of detaining politically suspect persons. Most of these seized by the latter regime were, of course, alleged or real supporters of Vichy. Some of these "Pétainist" detenus were, however, apolitical persons who were denounced as fascists by individuals having a personal grudge against them.[121] The outbreak of the Algerian revolution in the early 1950's saw the reinstitution of administrative internment. Thousands in both France and Algeria were administratively detained; and some of the detenus were tortured.[122] Most of these uses of administrative internment, of course, serve as additional examples where the punishment of persons without a hearing was correlated with the repression of critics of the government.

Neither the administrative nor judicial tribunals did much during the Algerian crisis to halt the practice of interning without trial. In fact, the Council of State took advantage of an ambiguity in the legislation to permit the creation of concentration camps during the Algerian war.[123] Persons who sued the state on the ground that their detention had been illegal found it difficult to recover.[124] The tribunals were not, however, completely prostrate before the attempt of the administration to detain persons whose politics or nationality made them suspect. For example, when a law relating to Algeria made it clear that it did not justify the creation of internment centers, the Council of State did refuse to permit their establishment under that particular act.[125]

No discussion of the French system of criminal justice or of the powers of the French government during an emergency would be complete without a reference to Article 30 of the Code of Criminal

Procedure. As will be remembered from Chapter II,
Section C, this was a law that was used to justify
the seizure on the French mainland of newspapers
and periodicals during the Algerian war and its
aftermath. Article 30 holds that when a crime
threatening the interior or exterior security of
the state may have been committed, the prefect can
take the following steps to determine whether it
has in fact taken place or to discover its authors:
interrogate suspects, hear witnesses, make searches,
seize property, and order people to appear before
him. He can commence the garde à vue, which for
crimes against the state can extend to six days in
normal times and twelve days when a state of
urgency has been declared. The upshot of all this
is that those suspected of crimes against the
state may find themselves deprived of liberty for
a few days even when (as now) there is no statute
that justifies administrative internment. Article
30 thus facilitates the punishment of individuals
without trial. Simultaneously, through expanding
the range of officials who can search, question
suspects and witnesses, and seize property, it may
result in the discovery of additional evidence and
thus facilitate the introduction of relevant evidence at the trial. However, one suspects that
lengthy interrogations begun by a politically
ambitious administrator may at times have been mis-
used to produce confessions obtained by undue
coercion and in this respect have led to the use of
worthless testimony. (The Mitterrand administration
may end the prefectorial system.)

Crimes against the security of the state not
only bring into play prefectorial powers of interrogation, search and seizure; but were also tried
by a special court, the Court of State Security,
created by a law of January 15, 1963. The members
of this court consisted of career judges and of
military officers. Its members received a special
salary and were nominated by decree. Their term
lasted for two years, but could be renewed. Their
extra salary plus the fact that they were dependent
on the government for reappointment led some to

conclude that the Court was not really impartial and independent, a conclusion accentuated by the fact that the career military personnel among its membership might have instinctively disliked persons accused of crimes against national security.[126] Thus President Mitterrand will have it abolished.

In summary, the criminal justice systems of all five countries contain many features that facilitate the introduction and adequate consideration of relevant evidence. There is little doubt that, looking to each of the systems as a whole, the English and French systems have more rules of this sort, proportionately, than the other four, despite the difficulty of appealing to a higher court in the former land. England rejects the exclusionary rules of Miranda and Mapp; allows (as do the U.S.S.R. and France) comment on a defendant's failure to testify; has an impartial judiciary; and still lacks the massive court congestion that leads to pressure on the accused to confess. The United States has Miranda, Mapp, the prohibition against comment on silence, and court crowding. India has even more court congestion and the prohibition of comments on a defendant's failure to testify; and those who preside at politically-charged trials in the Soviet Union are often biased against the suspects. Nonetheless, the fact that the Soviet Union makes use of a thorough investigation by a hopefully-impartial official prior to trial perhaps allows the conclusion that in non-political cases its judicial system is on the whole more conducive to the introduction and adequate consideration of relevant evidence than are those of the United States and India.

The French too make use of an examining magistrate who has the power to compel witnesses to appear before him and testify. Also at trial most of the questioning of defendant and witnesses is carried on by the judge. The fact that both prior to and at trial most of the interrogation of a suspect is the function of an impartial official

271

rather than of individuals who are interested in concealing important testimony or in eliciting unfounded evidence probably facilitates the introduction of relevant evidence and impedes the introduction of irrelevant. The presence of the judges in the jury's chambers is likely to improve the quality of deliberation about the evidence. The garde a vue of up to 48 hours in certain cases allows the police and examining magistrate to obtain highly valuable information. It is true that the jurisprudence relating to the use at trial of testimony obtained in violation of the rules on search and seizure and electronic eavesdropping is still quite fuzzy. If the Court of Cassation were, for example, to firmly reject Mapp and exclude evidence only when it has been obtained by physical or psychological torture, the French rules on criminal justice would be even more conducive than the English to the introduction and adequate consideration of germane evidence since England does not make use of the examining magistrate or the joint judge-lay juror voting.

The English system goes furthest in making unlikely punishment without a hearing. Though the English, Indians, Soviets and French, unlike (except in Washington, D.C.) the Americans, will refuse to grant bail to a defendant who the judge believes will commit serious crimes while free, it is easier for the poor to get bail in England than in the United States or France. Unlike the Soviet Union and India, neither England, France nor the United States will now in peacetime incarcerate without trial for a significant length of time politically suspect persons. England, like the United States, India and the Soviet Union, lacks the French garde à vue, an institution producing a short confinement that reasonably can be deemed punishment without hearing.

This summary is not to be considered a paean in praise of the English judicial system. There may well be good reasons for excluding certain relevant evidence. Thus a defender of Mapp would argue, for example, that it is better to let a few men who the evidence shows are guilty go free than to have the police breaking into private homes without the sanction of a judicial officer. One could also maintain that _Miranda's_ preclusion of police brutality is well worth the freeing of an indeterminate number of culprits and, even, that the American system of plea bargaining results in a sort of rough-and-ready justice that is often inherently fairer than a sentence imposed after a full trial at which all the testimony is thoroughly and impartially sifted by the trier of fact.

FOOTNOTES TO CHAPTER V

[1] (New Haven: Yale University Press, 1964), Ch. IV.

[2] See Hugo Adam Bedau, Human Rights and U.S. Foreign Assistance Programs, at pp. 29, 37 of Human Rights and U.S. Foreign Policy (Lexington: Lexington, 1979), ed. by Peter Brown and Douglas Maclean.

[3] See Orozco v. Texas, 394 U.S. 324, 326-27 (1969). Miranda is 384 U.S. 436 (1966).

[4] Brown v. Mississippi, 297 U.S. 278 (1936).

[5] 378 U.S. 478 (1964). In Escobedo, the defendant had been taken to the police station in handcuffs as a suspect in the slaying of his brother-in-law. His retained lawyer came to the stationhouse but was not permitted to see him. During the interrogation Escobedo admitted complicity in the murder plot and was subsequently convicted of murder.

[6] 372 U.S. 335 (1963).

[7] Powell v. Alabama, 287 U.S. 45 (1932); Betts v. Brady, 316 U.S. 455 (1942).

[8] 407 U.S. 25 (1972).

[9] Wolf v. Colorado, 338 U.S. 25 (1949).

[10] 367 U.S. 643 (1961).

[11] United States v. Robinson, 414 U.S. 218 (1973).

[12]Chambers v. Maroney, 399 U.S. 42 (1970), affirming and extending Carroll v. United States, 267 U.S. 132 (1925).

[13]Terry v. Ohio, 392 U.S. 1 (1968). In London and a few other places in England, the police may without a warrant thoroughly search anyone on the street on "reasonable suspicion." The Observer (London), April 9, 1972, p. 23.

[14]389 U.S. 347 (1967).

[15]Herman Schwartz, The Wiretap Decade, The Nation 229:161, September 8, 1979; New York Times, October 5, 1980, p. 65.

[16]Tumey v. Ohio, 273 U.S. 510 (1927).

[17]Norris v. Alabama, 294 U.S. 587 (1935) (blacks); Taylor v. Louisiana, 419 U.S. 522 (1975) (women).

[18]Moore v. Dempsey, 261 U.S. 86 (1923).

[19]National Advisory Committee on Criminal Justice Standards and Goals, A National Strategy to Reduce Crime (Washington: U.S. Department of Justice, 1973), p. 25.

[20](1852) 3 H.L.C. 759.

[21]For this quotation see pp. 300-301 of Geoffrey Wilson, Cases and Materials on Constitutional and Administrative Law.

[22]Maxwell v. Dow, 176 U.S. 581 (1900) (federal); Apodaca v. Oregon, 406 U.S. 404 (1972) (state).

[23]See pp. 364-66 of Wilson, op. cit.

[24]Anglo-American Criminal Justice, p. 123.

[25]R. v. Ovenell,(1968) 1 All E. R. 933; The Observer (London), April 28, 1974, p. 4.

[26]The Observer (London), April 28, 1974, p. 4; Street, op. cit., 4th ed., p. 29.

[27](1977) Crim. L. Rev. (Eng.) 163.

[28]Miahael Zander, The Criminal Process: A Subject Ripe for a Major Inquiry, (1977) Crim. L. Rev. (Eng.) 249, 250.

[29](1955) A.C. 197.

[30](1899) 1 Q.B. 77.

[31]Griffin v. California, 381 U.S. 957 (1965).

[32]Karlen, Anglo-American Criminal Justice, p. 138. See also The Times (London), August 5, 1978, p. 1.

[33]Karlen, op. cit., p. 138.

[34]Ibid.

[35]Economist, August 25, 1979, p. 18.

[36]The Times (London), January 31, 1977, p. 4.

[37]Manchester Guardian Weekly, January 31, 1979, p. 19; Economist, August 25, 1979, p. 18; The Times (London), June 18, 1980, p. 6.

[38]Indian Evidence Act, Art. 24. Pyare Lal v. State of Rajasthan, (1963) All India Rep. S. Ct. 1094,is one case dealing with whether a particular confession is voluntary or involuntary for the purposes of Article 24. Here the defendant had been convicted after he had confessed to the theft of a government document. While being questioned by a government official, he was told that if the whole truth did not come out, the inquiry would be handed over to the police. Thereupon, the defendant

confessed. The Supreme Court found that this confession was voluntary. Three lower courts had
come to this conclusion; and, moreover, the official's statement was not so much a threat as just
a general remark that anyone who had lost his
property would be likely to make.

[39] David Bayley, The Police and Political
Development in India, p. 173.

[40] Kochan Velayudhan v. Kerala, (1961) All
India Rep. Kerala 8; State v. Satyanarayan, (1965)
All India Rep. Orissa 136.

[41] In 1980 the British first revealed information about the number of their taps. For 1979 the
official figure was over 500 warrants. The Times
(London), April 2, 1980, p. 4. One warrant may
cover all the individuals in an organization. The
Times (London), July 28, 1980, p. 12.

[42] (1968) All India Rep. S. Ct. 147.

[43] Street, op. cit., 2d ed., p. 41 and 4th
ed., p. 47.

[44] 1966 (1) Q.B. 688.

[45] 410 U.S. 475 (1971).

[46] Baidyanath v. Bihar, (1968) All India Rep.
S. Ct. 1393. The privilege is available only to a
criminal defendant, not a mere witness. Sirdar
D. K. Sen, A Comparative Study of the Indian Constitution, Vol. 2 (New York: David McKay, 1966),
pp. 308-309.

[47] Gilbert v. Cal., 388 U.S. 263 (1967); U.S.
v. Wade, 388 U.S. 218 (1967).

[48] R. v. Voisin, (1918) 1 K.B. 531. However,
under existing English law, little can be done to
compel an unwilling suspect to furnish fingerprints,
photographs of himself, or body samples. The Times

(London), August 3, 1978, p. 1.

[49] B. P. Srivastava, Right Against Arbitrary Arrest at pp. 29, 45 of Journal of Indian Law Institute, Vol. 11 (1969).

[50] Fellman, The Defendant's Rights Under English Law, pp. 83ff. In petty cases, many magistrates reject requests for free legal aid. New York Times, August 7, 1972, p. 1.

[51] R. Prasannan, Counsel in the Criminal Process at pp. 637, 639 of Journal of the Indian Law Institute, Vol. 10 (1968).

[52] Statesman, January 28, 1980, p. 8.

[53] Hussainara Khatoon v. St. of Bihar, (1979) All India Rep. S. Ct. 1369.

[54] (1978) All India Rep. S. Ct. 1548.

[55] Prasannan, op. cit., p. 641.

[56] Srivastava, op. cit., p. 39. As seen, this right is not yet clearly embodied in English jurisprudence.

[57] 378 U.S. 478 (1964).

[58] Nandini Satpathy v. P.L. Dani, (1978) All India Rep. S. Ct. 1025.

[59] New York Times, November 12, 1970, p. 3; The Statesman, April 12, 1979, p. 8; Manchester Guardian Weekly, May 13, 1979, p. 4; India: Preventive Detention and Prison Conditions, International Commission of Jurists Rev. 1972-74, December 1974, pp. 13, 15.

[60] M.J.C. Kagzi, Judicial Control of Executive Discretion Under Preventive Detention Law: An Indian Experience, at pp. 30-33 (1965) Public Law.

[61]David Bayley, The Policy of Preventive Detention 1950-63, Indian Journal of Public Administration 10:253ff (April, 1964).

[62]This and the prior paragraph are based on Amnesty International, Report on Torture, p. 150; India, Preventive Detention and Prison Conditions, pp. 13-16; New York Times, September 10, 1974, p. 6; November 4, 1974, p. 2; June 27, 1975, p. 12; August 5, 1975, p. 10; April 27, 1976, p. 11; January 21, 1977, p. 1; March 28, 1977, p. 2; January 2, 1978, p. 6; August 18, 1980, p. A3; September 24, 1980, p. A1; December 17, 1980, p. A14; Economist, April 8, 1978, p. 16; Statesman, October 8, 1979, p. 1.

[63](1950) All India Rep. S. Ct. 27.

[64]In Re Special Courts Bill 1978, (1979) All India Rep. S. Ct. 478.

[65]Street, op. cit., 4th ed., p. 35; New York Times, December 6, 1975, p. 1; October 24, 1980, p. A3; The Times (London), February 28, 1977, p. 2; New Statesman 97:285, March 2, 1979.

[66]Bayley (1964), op. cit., p. 242.

[67](1964) All India Rep. S. Ct. 381.

[68]A.D.M., Jabalpur v. Shivakant Shukla, (1976) S. Ct. Cas. 521. It may reconsider this decision.

[69]Bayley (1964), op. cit., p. 169; Economist, January 27, 1979, p. 56. Under the Code of Criminal Procedure (Sec. 57), one must be brought before a magistrate within 24 hours. See Pradeep Kukret, New Reform in Criminal Procedure, Current Events, March, 1974, p. 67.

[70]Code of Criminal Procedure Secs. 436-437; Prasannan, op. cit., p. 650; All India Reporter, Commentaries on Code of Criminal Procedure 1973, Vol. IV, p. 221 (Nagpur: All India Rep., 1974).

Where bail is granted, it may not be too high considering all the circumstances. Times of India (Bombay ed.), August 25, 1978, p. 4.

[71] Berman, Justice in the U.S.S.R., rev. ed., pp. 58-63, 70-71.

[72] Excerpted at p. 5 of Soviet Statutes and Decisions, Vol. 1, Summer, 1965.

[73] Berman, op. cit., p. 71.

[74] Excerpted at p. 23 of Soviet Statutes and Decisions, Vol. 1, Summer, 1965.

[75] Quoted at p. 26 of Ibid.

[76] Robert Conquest (ed.), Justice and the Legal System in the U.S.S.R. (New York: Praeger, 1968), p. 31.

[77] Hazard, Shapiro and Maggs, The Soviet Legal System, rev. ed., p. 113.

[78] Conquest (ed.), Justice and the Legal System in the U.S.S.R., p. 114; Thomas Towe, Fundamental Rights in the Soviet Union: A Comparative Approach, U. Pa. L. Rev. 115:1251 (1967). The USSR Supreme Court, however, reversed the conviction of a Rostov worker dissident. The Times (London), January 18, 1980, p. 9.

[79] New York: Harcourt, Brace, Jovanovich, 1970.

[80] Ibid., pp. 100-101.

[81] Berman, op. cit., p. 302.

[82] Ibid., p. 303.

[83] Harold Berman (Intro. and Analysis), Soviet Criminal Law and Procedures: The R.S.F.S.R. Code (Cambridge: Harvard U. Press, 1966), pp. 65-66.

[84]Berman, Justice in the U.S.S.R., rev. ed., p. 73; also Berman (1966), op. cit., p. 94.

[85]Excerpted at p. 20 of Soviet Statutes and Decisions, Vol. 1, Summer, 1965.

[86]See Hazard, Shapiro and Maggs, op. cit., p. 68; E. L. Johnson, An Introduction to the Soviet Legal System (London: Methuen, 1969), p. 233. In general, fees charged by Soviet lawyers are regulated by the state and are low. Donald Barry and Harold Berman, The Soviet Legal Profession, Harv. L. Rev. 82:1, 16 (1968).

[87]Hazard, Shapiro and Maggs, op. cit., p. 98; Conquest (ed.), Justice and the Legal System in the U.S.S.R., p. 56; Berman (1966), op. cit., pp. 73-74.

[88]New York Times, January 13, 1974, p. 26.

[89]Ridley and Blondel, Public Administration in France, pp. 140-41.

[90]Sybille Bedford, The Faces of Justice (New York: Simon and Schuster, 1961), p. 278.

[91]See Ibid., pp. 141-43; Henry J. Abraham, The Judicial Process, 3rd ed., pp. 257-58; Lowell Noonan, The Politics of Continuity in Change (New York: Holt Rinehart, 1970), pp. 397-98; Jack Norton, Stanley Jennings, and Thomas Towe, Truth and Individual Rights: A Comparison of U.S. and French Pre-Trial Procedures, American Criminal Law Quarterly 2:159ff (1963-64).

[92]See Le Monde, June 8, 1980, p. 11; Manchester Guardian Weekly, July 5, 1980, p. 13.

[93]Burdeau, Les Libertés Publiques, 4th ed., pp. 149-51; Maurice Duverger, Eléments de Droit Public, 6th ed. (Paris: Presses Universitaires de France, 1970), pp. 171-73; Raymond Berg, Criminal Procedure: France, England and the United States,

DePaul L. Rev. 8:256, 287 (1958-59); Charles Markmann, *Freedom à la Francaise*, *The Civil Liberties Review*, Spring, 1975, pp. 73, 84; Jacques Verin and Mark Ancel, *The Politics of Criminal Law Reform: France*, *Am. J. Comp. L.* 21:263, 266 (1963). In 1980, the maximum length of the garde à vue was extended to 56 hours for kidnap and armed robbery suspects and to 4 days for suspected drug peddlers. *The Times* (London), December 20, 1980, p. 4.

[94]Burdeau, *op. cit.*, p. 150. In Buscia, Ct. of Cass., Vol. 169 (1973), #343 at p. 838, the Court of Cassation said in *dictum* that some of the Criminal Procedure Code's requirements about the garde à vue may be violated without making the confession null and void.

[95]D. 1963 Somm. 76.

[96]The above remarks are based on the French Code of Criminal Procedure (henceforth C.P.P.), Articles 101-18; Jean Brouchart, *Analyse et Commentaire du Code de Procédure Pénale* (Paris: Libraries Techniques, 1959), pp. 78-80; Berg, *op. cit.*, p. 291; Robert Vouin, *The Privilege Against Self-Incrimination: France*, *Journal of Criminal Law and Criminology* 51:169ff (1960).

[97]See C.P.P. Articles 54, 56, 57, 59, 76, 92, 93, 94, 99; Brouchart, *op. cit.*, pp. 50-52; Robert Daley, *The Heist of the Century*, *New York Times Magazine*, December 19, 1976, pp. 34ff.

[98]Robert Vouin, *The Exclusionary Rule: France*, *Journal of Criminal Law and Criminology* 52: 275 (1961).

[99]January 20, 1954, D.1954 J. 110.

[100]*Le Monde*, June 12, 1980, p. 14.

[101]Norton, Jennings and Towe, *op. cit.*, p. 162. In 1980 the Court of Cassation reversed a decision because of an illegal search. Gaz. Pal.

July 1, 1980, p. 11. However, the failure of the report to indicate all the relevant facts of the case makes it impossible for us to draw from it any legal conclusions.

[102]Norton, Jennings and Towe, op. cit., p. 162.

[103]The case is noted in Colliard, Libertés Publiques (3rd ed.), p. 228.

[104]New York Times, November 11, 1973, p. 12; December 17, 1973, p. 18; March 28, 1974, p. 6; February 25, 1978, p. 2; Le Monde, August 11, 1978, p. 8.

[105]Le Monde, October 11, 1980, p. 10.

[106]G. Levasseur, Les Méthodes Scientifiques de Recherche de la Vérité, Revue Internationale de Droit Pénal 43:319, 342 (1972).

[107]For a discussion of the uncertainties of the French Rules on wiretapping, see Ibid., pp. 337-44 and G. Dobry, Wiretapping and Eavesdropping: A Comparative Survey, Journal of the International Commission of Jurists 1:319ff (1957-58). See also Henri Blin, Commentaire, Protection de la Vie Privée (Art. 368 à 372), p. 4, Juris Classeur Pénal.

[108]On the right of a French defendant to a lawyer, see George Pelletier, Legal Aid in France, Notre Dame Law.42:627 (1967) and Joseph Snee and A. Kenneth Pye, Due Process in Criminal Procedure: A Comparison of Two Systems, Ohio St. L. J. 21:467, 480 (1960).

[109]Markmann, op. cit., pp. 84-85.

[110]See Ibid., p. 83.

[111]Bedford, op. cit., pp. 282-85; Snee and Pye, op. cit., p. 490. However, the prosecutor may question witnesses directly. Ridley and

Blondel, op. cit., p. 143.

[112] Ridley and Blondel, op. cit., p. 143 (France); Barry and Berman, The Soviet Legal Profession, Harv. L. Rev. 82:1, 14 (1968) (Soviet Union).

[113] Markmann, op. cit., p. 86; Le Monde, January 4, 1975, p. 3.

[114] Bedford, op. cit., p. 296.

[115] John Baldwin and Michael McConville, Trial by Jury: Some Empirical Evidence on Contested Criminal Cases in England, Law and Society Review 13:861, 886 (1979).

[116] Snee and Pye, op. cit., p. 490; Vouin, The Exclusionary Rule: France, p. 275.

[117] Le Monde, June 27, 1975, p. 1; Markmann, op. cit., p. 85; New York Times, December 19, 1980, p. A20.

[118] New York Times, December 8, 1969, p. 6.

[119] Preventive Detention: A Comparison of European and U.S. Measures, N.Y.U. Journal of Internat. Law and Politics 4:289, 293-94 (1971).

[120] See Le Monde, June 11, 1980, p. 11; Jean Varaut, Sécurité et Liberté, Gaz. Pal., May 23, 1980, pp. 7ff; Manchester Guardian Weekly, May 18, 1980, p. 1.

[121] Burdeau, op. cit., pp. 168-69; Colliard, Libertés Publiques (3rd ed.), pp. 248-49.

[122] Sources on torture of detainees during the Algerian War are numerous. For example, Richard and Joan Brace, Ordeal in Algeria (Princeton: D. Van Nostrand, 1960), Ch. 11, quotes extensively from a Red Cross report on torture of detained prisoners.

[123]Zaquin, March 7, 1958, Rec. 150

[124]Burdeau, op. cit., pp. 169-71.

[125]Ibid., p. 171. The decision is Keddar, C.E., February 3, 1965, Rec. 46.

[126]Colliard, Libertés Publiques (3rd ed.), pp. 235-37.

CHAPTER VI

POLICY CONSIDERATIONS AND
GENERAL OBSERVATIONS

A. Policy Recommendations

The testimony of the previous pages suggests
or can be used to evaluate proposals such as the
following for modifying the status quo.

1. Chapter II showed that the United States
applies a clear and present danger test to speech
that threatens localized violence. Feiner v. New
York[1] indicates one situation in which it should
not be used to determine the culpability of one
whose words endanger the public peace. The
Supreme Court dealt there with a streetcorner
radical who had irritated a Syracuse, New York,
throng by calling President Truman a "bum" and the
American Legion a "Gestapo." A spectator
threatened to push Feiner off his stand, and there
was muttering and pushing in the crowd. Feiner
was arrested by a policeman after he had ignored
two requests to stop speaking; and the Supreme
Court sustained his subsequent conviction for disorderly conduct on the grounds that his words had
created a clear and present danger of violence.
The trouble with using the clear and present danger test under circumstances such as those presented by Feiner where the violence or threat
thereof originates with an audience hostile to the
speaker's cause is that the punishment falls on
the party who is the indirect rather than the
direct cause of the disorder. Also, employing it
then will mean that speech will be tolerated when
made to the converted but repressed when made to
the antagonistic, who are those the speaker

presumably wants most to reach. A sensible way of dealing with the problem is the approach of the old English case of Beatty v. Gillbanks,[2] where the court refused to allow members of the Salvation Army to be punished for marching in violation of a police order issued because it was likely that an Army procession would be attacked by hooligans. As one judge pointed out, the Army was marching peacefully and it was the duty of the police not to stop it but, rather, to protect it from the thugs. Similar in philosophy is the French Benjamin decision,[3] where, as seen, the Council of State said that a publicist should be allowed to hold a conference because the mayor had at his disposal enough police to prevent fights between Benjamin's supporters and the leftists who were looking for a scrap with them. (Unfortunately, Beatty v. Gillbanks seems to have been forgotten by the English courts and Parliament. The rule that is now most popular in England, as we can see from Chapter II, Section A, is that one can be punished if violence is the likely consequence of his words whether or not the violence initially springs from the audience. Remember, for example, Jordan v. Burgoyne,[4] where the neo-Nazi Colin Jordan was convicted for delivering a racist speech to an infuriated London crowd. Benjamin, as noted, is still good law in France for private, indoor meetings; but it does not cover outdoor rallies or indoor conclaves open to the public.)

2. Many contend that the American political system ought to favor minority groups such as blacks and Mexican-Americans that have in the past suffered from severe discrimination. Because of this discrimination, it is argued, many members of these groups cannot compete on a level of equality with white Americans in school and on job tests. Therefore, the conclusion runs, special efforts must be made to give these persons education and employment. Treating them the same as everyone else will not improve their lot: what must be done, in addition, is to temporarily waive for them the normal requirements for jobs and school-entry,

requirements that may well have a cultural bias.
This can be done by setting a "benevolent quota,"
that is, by reserving a certain number of scholarships, seats or positions for them, even though
those chosen do not have all the paper qualifications of the passed-over whites. It can also be
accomplished by a more flexible "affirmative
action" policy in which an applicant's belonging
to a minority group is one, but only one, of
several factors deemed a "plus" in determining
whether he gets the job or the acceptance.

   In Regents of the University of California
v. Bakke,[5] a 5-4 majority of the United States
Supreme Court did hold that "affirmative action"
programs initiated by educational institutions are
both constitutional and legal under Title VI of
the 1964 Civil Rights Act. Thus one's membership
in a minority ethnic or racial group may be used
as one of the positive considerations employed in
making the admissions decision about him. At the
same time, a 5-4 majority declared benevolent
quotas invalid; and consequently held that Mr.
Alan Bakke, a white, had to be admitted to the
state-operated University of California at Davis
Medical School. The School had set aside 16 of
the 100 places in its freshman classes for black,
Chicano and Asian students: had it not been for
this reservation, Mr. Bakke would have been accepted. (Some commentators on Bakke believe that
quotas may be legitimate where the institution
itself has in the past been guilty of discrimination.)

   Chapter IV analyzed one nation's experiences
with a benevolent quota. India, on both the
national and state levels, reserves a certain percentage of seats in educational institutions and
of government jobs for untouchables, members of
primitive ethnic groups, and persons belonging to
other "backward" classes. There is nothing about
what has happened in India that provides a
conclusive argument for or against Bakke's pro-
affirmative action stance; but Indian events do

289

give us some hints about what rules and practices should be developed in the United States to implement this position.

In the first place, the Indian courts have limited the extent to which the quota legally may discriminate in favor of disadvantaged groups: for example, no more than a certain percentage of positions may be set aside for them. It might also be wise for American courts to set bounds to the protection offered by affirmative action, if only to dampen down the resentment that "reverse discrimination" now arouses among whites. United Steel Workers v. Weber[6] is in full accord with this recommendation, though not necessarily with Bakke's anti-quota stand. Here the Supreme Court upheld a voluntary agreement between Kaiser Corporation and the United Steelworkers of America setting up a program at a Louisiana factory to train workers for skilled jobs. This program was open to blacks and whites on a 50-50 basis: the agreement had been challenged under Title VII of the 1964 Civil Rights Act banning racial, etc., discrimination in employment. But in approving this plan, the majority opinion emphasized that it does not totally exclude whites, that it does not require the discharge of any white, and that it will expire as soon as the black percentage of skilled workers in the factory approximates the percentage of blacks in the local labor force. Fullilove v. Klutznick[7] is also consistent with the above suggestion. Here the Supreme Court sustained a law requiring that a certain percentage of federally-funded public works contracts be given to minority-owned businesses. The percentage in question was a relatively low 10 percent: one wonders whether the result would have been the same had it been, e.g., 30 percent.

As also mentioned, Indian courts at times have refused to classify certain groups as "backward classes" or "socially and educationally backward classes" when ascertaining whether they were entitled to preferential treatment; and American courts may soon face similar definitional problems. For example, Rutgers-Newark Law School reserves about a quarter of its seats for specified minorities and for individuals from a "disadvantaged" background. Accordingly, when an American institution sets up an affirmative action plan, it should indicate clearly who is to benefit from it. And it is, if possible, even more necessary for it to develop a persuasive set of reasons for its action when drafting such a plan than when framing other civil rights and liberties policies. Only by a well-thought-out statement can it convince the courts and the public that the classifications made by its program are equitable and socially desirable.

     3. One of the most common arguments against state aid to religious schools in the United States is that this assistance is likely to lead to state control. Some of the evidence in this book lends support to that proposition. In India, government financing of Aligarh Muslim University was followed by the appointment of a secular educator as the real head of the institution and by demands that more non-Moslems be admitted. Indian states that have funded religious elementary and secondary schools have put government representatives on their boards of trustees and secured considerable control over the employment and discharge of teachers. In England governmental benefactions to church-operated schools are conditioned upon the schools' agreeing to state appointment of most of their staff. French private schools getting public aid may not experiment radically with class size and hours; their teachers must meet certain physical as well as academic standards; and, in schools under a "contract of association," the government names and promotes the instructors and to some extent regulates pedagogical methods. State-aided Catholic schools may not fire divorced teachers who remarry except when, as in one case, the contract between them and the school assumes that they will obey Catholic religious precepts.[8] All in all, the American who favors the enactment of a massive

291

program of aid to religious schools must concede
that his opponents are not beating a straw horse
when they argue that the program will curtail the
autonomy of these institutions.

    4. The next policy recommendation is geared
to Great Britain and France rather than to the
United States and India. One can make a strong
argument that a country with the institution of
judicial review is more likely to see judicial
opinions on civil rights and liberties that explicitly grapple with the fundamental questions of
ethical, economic and/or political theory underlying the legal dispute.[9] One can compare, for
example, the American case of New York Times v.
Sullivan[10] with the British decision of Dingle v.
Associated Newspapers, Ltd.[11] Both involve libel
suits by public officials to recover damages from
persons who had said untrue and derogatory things
about them. Mr. Sullivan was not permitted to recover, but Mr. Dingle was. One can reasonably
contend that the Dingle rule that public officials
stand on a footing with other plaintiffs in libel
actions is better than the New York Times doctrine
that such officials can recover only if the untrue
and unfavorable remarks about them were made with
knowledge that they were false. However, the
opinions in New York Times are much more adequate,
for they do discuss whether lies about people in
public life significantly harm them and whether
the imposition of libel judgments upon individuals
who say untrue things about such people will deter
those who have critical but true remarks to make
about officeholders from speaking their minds.
The British Court of Appeal ignored these basic
issues, which is why its opinion is much less
satisfactory than the Supreme Court's. Likewise,
the British House of Lords in upholding a conviction for conspiring to conduct a nuclear disarmament demonstration on an airbase[12] did not concern
itself with the crucial point that such demonstrations are a form of political protest and thus
bear at least some relation to speech. The
Supreme Court in Adderley v. Florida,[13] while

292

sustaining the trespass conviction of demonstrators on a lawn outside a jail against the arrests of fellow students, at least dealt with this contention; and the majority and minority opinions taken together furnish the reader with a passably satisfactory discussion of the desirability of tolerating political demonstrations on public property normally reserved for a specific use.

One cannot blame the Court of Appeal and the House of Lords: the statute and rules they were permitted to use and could not go beyond were straightforward. The point is, rather, that the fact that an American court may invalidate governmental rules and practices that it believes violate the American Constitution, including the First Amendment, compelled the Supreme Court in New York Times and Adderley to interpret the wording of that clause. In doing so, the justices had to ask themselves questions about the broad ethical and political policies the provision is supposed to further and juxtapose these against the policies served by the state rules under challenge. And the very process of formulating such in-depth analyses not only results in more interesting and convincing opinions but also makes less likely a judge's continued acquiescence in a position reached simply on the basis of emotional reactions and instinctive prejudices. (When, analogously, a trial judge must explicitly state the particular facts on which his general verdict--e.g., guilty--is based, he may discover "that his initially contemplated decision will not jell (and be) obliged to decide otherwise.")[14]

B. Potential Trouble Spots

The experience of India, France, the USSR and (to a lesser extent) Britain indicates that where government controls the machinery, raw materials, or space that an individual requires to be able to air his views; or where its subsidies are needed to keep alive the medium of communication to which he has access, he may well tailor his political position to side with it. He may do this in response to an actual threat or simply out of a fear that the polity in the future will use against him the leverage that its economic power provides. This experience forecasts certain storms that soon could darken the American civil rights and liberties horizon. In fact, clouds heralding some of these squalls have been sighted here in the past.

Its ownership of the nation's printing presses and publishing firms is one of the most important weapons at the Soviet government's beck and call for insuring that its critics maintain silence. Almost all attacks on the regime have to be mimeographed on machines that somehow have come into the hands of the dissidents. In India, government advertisements account for a considerable percentage of the revenue of many newspapers; and some papers are cowed by the fear that this advertising will be withdrawn.[15] As for Britain, Paul O'Higgins asserts that "Although the global sums involved in state advertising in newspapers may not be enormous, they are still a not insignificant factor in helping to preserve the existence . . . of small circulation papers."[16] Though he makes no contention that these papers are afraid to criticize their political benefactors or that these have ever warned the journals to mend their ways, he is worried that this could happen. He also notes that government departments do not advertise in newspapers closely associated with the Communist Party.[17] In France the government does place its ads in journals of all political faiths, including communist;[18] but state subsidization of the purchase of newsprint is one factor setting limits to press attacks on public officials.[19] In the United States, too, a few instances already have come to light where governments have threatened to deprive newspapers of advertising revenue unless they ceased complaining about the activities of the officials responsible for inserting the advertisements.

(Governments put announcements into newspapers about, e.g., sheriff's sales and probate hearings.) For example, Robert Moses, who among his many roles was head of New York's Long Island State Park Commission, took away the Commission's legal advertising from a newspaper in Babylon, Long Island, whose publisher had opposed Moses' plan to build a highway through the beach resort of Fire Island.[20] In any event, the Indian experience, especially, should alert Americans to make sure that government censorship does not become the usual concomitant of city, town, county and state official advertising patronage.

India suffers from a chronic shortage of newsprint and thus has had to ration the supply going to the country's newspapers, journals and book publishers. In 1972 the central government promulgated a newsprint policy that limited the size of newspapers to ten pages and prevented companies that already controlled two or more papers from launching another even though they were willing to use their current newsprint quota for the new publication. Those hurt most by this policy were the large, respected English language dailies such as the Times of India and the Hindustan Times. These often printed editions of more than ten pages and in some cases were controlled by corporations owning several newspapers. Some feel it was not accidental that these journals suffered most, for Prime Minister Gandhi felt that the businessmen who own them were prejudiced against her attempt to nationalize sectors of the economy.[21] In the 1973 case of B. and C. Co. v. Union of India,[22] the Indian Supreme Court declared that this policy violated the Constitution's Article 19(1)(a) guarantee of freedom of the press, though it recognized that the government had the right to set up an equitable system for the distribution of newsprint. Notwithstanding B. and C. Co., the fear of encountering a reduction in its annual newsprint quota is one factor making the Indian press not as vigorous a critic of the government as it could be.[23] The American reader who believes that the tribulations

295

of the Times of India and Hindustan Times are
light-years removed from his existence should realize that his country may be faced with a shortage
of newsprint (or energy sources) within the next
few years. When these scarcities rear their ugly
heads, the government will have to enact a rationing scheme. And, when it does, one must be awake
to the possibility that those journals that express
their unhappiness with administration policy will
find themselves without sufficient paper, gasoline
for their delivery trucks, and heating oil and
electricity for their printing plants. (On the
other hand, given the drastic reduction in recent
years in the number of newspapers in the United
States, a loss that has transformed many communities into "one paper" towns whose residents have
only one point of view trumpeted in their press,
the French government's approach of subsidizing the
price of newsprint and giving special tax credits
to journals that purchase new machinery is attrac-
tive. Can it be adopted here without making the
press fear to roast politicians and bureaucrats?)

All governments must ration that scarce
medium known as the airwaves. Consequently, they
set up their own radio and television networks and/
or issue licenses to private parties to use certain
frequencies. Indian radio and TV is government
operated; French radio and TV is primarily a governmental responsibility; the British Broadcasting
Company is a government agency though there exist,
as well, privately-owned radio and TV stations;
while in the United States most radio and TV stations are owned by private parties who receive
licenses from the federal government every three
years. In the Soviet Union, the electronic mass
media are owned and tightly controlled by the
state. French TV's shunning of opposition politicians and news unfavorable to the administration
was discussed in Chapter II; while during Mrs.
Gandhi's first Premiership All-India Radio was
known as "All-Indira Radio."[24] Though the BBC is
on the whole not shackled politically, there have
been occasions when it has declined to show

296

programs dealing with public affairs because of
pressure from government departments.[25]   Richard
Burton was banned from BBC drama productions because he wrote an article labelling Winston
Churchill "power corrupted."[26]   Already in the
United States, the small network of public TV stations and the corporations that fund and intercon-
nect them have been involved in several censorship
episodes, including the cancellation of a show that
satirized President Richard Nixon and his foreign
affairs adviser Henry Kissinger and of a segment of
a news broadcast that exposed the use of agents-
provocateurs by the Federal Bureau of Investigation.
These events reinforce the lesson from the other
four countries that Americans must be vigilant to
prevent government's inevitable contact with the
electronic mass media from becoming a device to
muzzle the articulation of unorthodox views.

C.   The Relationship Between
Tolerance and Polarization/
Incumbency Instability

     1.   The data of social science suggest not
only concrete recommendations for change but also
the existence of relationships among people, groups,
rules and institutions.   The evidence of Chapters II
through V indicates that new or continued policies
of tolerance, encouragement of diversity, stimulation of intergroup contact, and analogous criminal
justice policies are under the following circumstances not too likely to produce or increase polarization or incumbency instability.   (For stylistic
reasons, the label "tolerant" normally will in this
section be given to policies falling into any one of
these categories; though on occasion the other head-
ings will be referred to by name.)   In fact, in some
of these circumstances policies of this stamp are
needed to keep or make the citizenry sympathetic to
the regime or the people who staff it.   These circumstances sometimes involve the reaction of interest groups and at other times the response of the
general public.   These pages will first note those

that relate to organized groups and then those that are marked by or affect the stance of the people as a whole.

a. When the interest groups that oppose toleration are highly decentralized or low in prestige. During the late 1940's and the 1950's, the Indian federal and state governments modified some traditional Hindu law. These reforms regulated Hindu temples, outlawed untouchability, legalized for Hindus inter-caste marriage and divorce, permitted them to adopt females, let persons of different faiths marry, and allowed "intrafaith" as well as "interfaith" couples to be governed by a westernized personal law.[27] One reason they were pushed through by Prime Minister Jawarhalal Nehru and his allies without adverse political consequences is that Hinduism is not a centralized religion. That is, there is lacking "a clearly defined and trained Hindu clergy subject to the discipline of superiors. . . . The Hindu 'clergy' is thus not organized for an effective political role."[28] Moreover, Hindu holy men (sadhus) and temple priests are often considered by the populace to be greedy and corrupt.[29] Thus the government had to worry about "Hindu" opinion; but since this often was inefficiently articulated and was publicized by men about whom the public was sceptical, the polity could successfully ignore it when, e.g., deciding to extend toleration to non-Hindus or allowing Harijans to mingle with caste Hindus.

b. When the groups fervently opposed to the policies of toleration have meager membership rolls and resources. And on many civil rights and liberties issues the country's most powerful interest groups, usually economic, do not take a stand. In Britain, neither the Confederation of British Industries nor the Trades Union Congress would speak out on whether, say, the recently resuscitated law of blasphemous libel should be abrogated by Parliament. (They would expect to be, and are, listened to when the government is writing legislation dealing with racial discrimination in

298

employment.)[30] The type of group that is most likely to passionately protest, e.g., the further watering down of anti-obscenity measures is poignantly described in a New York Times article informing us that sixty demonstrators from St. Sebastian's Post #870 of the Catholic War Veterans in Woodside, Queens, New York City and the Calvary Baptist Church in Manhattan paraded on an icy day along 42nd Street to demand tough laws against smut in films and books.[31] Walk along this mecca for the sexually kinky: in ten seconds one will be aware of the lack of success resulting from the efforts of groups such as these. The area around Times Square devoted to the lurid and perverted has shrunk some in area, it is true, but that is because landlords and builders have found it profitable to buy up the low-rise buildings that house most pornography establishments and replace them with skyscrapers that can be rented to respectable businessmen.

Even when a powerful interest group opposes toleration, the chances are that it is worried about just one or two particular problems. For example, certain influential clergymen might like to see the city ban a "sacrilegious" or porno-graphic film; but they would take no stand on whether a court should adopt a "clear and present danger" or "bad tendency" test for determining when speech threatening localized violence should be punished. In Britain, Mrs. Mary Whitehouse's National Viewers and Listeners Association fights to keep sexually-oriented material off radio and TV; but does not ask whether policemen should be allowed to continue their surveillance of marxist and anarchist meetings.

      c. When the governmental policy that tolerates is, viewed in another light, a cooptation of one or more important groups. That is, the measure acquires for the government this group's positive support by giving it and the people for whom it speaks material or other benefits they greatly desire.[32] Rudolph and Rudolph provide us

with the example of the Vanniyars, a caste of agri-
cultural laborers and peasants in Madras State. As
a result of the activities of the caste association, political parties representing the caste were
formed. The Congress Party in 1952 had only a plurality in the Madras legislature; but the support
of these parties gave it its majority. In return
for this help they received a couple of ministries
and the caste obtained scholarships, admission to
universities, jobs in the civil service, and nominations for membership in local executive bodies.[33]
By making it pay to declare oneself a Vanniyar the
state's political leadership shored up its position
among the membership of that group. And the 1950's
reorganization of the Indian states along linguistic lines, an encouragement of diversity like the
kindnesses to the Vanniyars, gave the leaders of
the nation's minority linguistic groups the boon
they most fervently desired. As a consequence it
damped down demands for secession and kept these
men loyal to Mr. Nehru and the Congress Party.

        d. When the norms of the country are on
the whole supportive of policies of toleration or,
at least, are moving in that direction. A switch
to a policy of toleration is one form of innovation; and sociologists have emphasized that its
compatibility with the cultural norms of the
society is a factor that will accelerate the
acceptance of an innovation.[34]

        Though there is a surprising lack of
direct evidence, it appears that in France, Great
Britain, India and the United States a majority of
the public is or is becoming generally cordial to
toleration. In France, freedom from censorship of
the mass media was defined as a "basic human right"
by 70.6 percent of the respondents in a poll; freedom to practice religion by 91 percent; and equal
rights for racial and religious minorities by 68.6
percent.[35] Sixty-five percent of the British respondents in another poll felt that American criticism of human rights violations by the Soviet Union
and other countries was a "very good" or "fairly

good" idea.[36] From this one can infer that a majority are pleased by the prevalence of freedom of
speech, press, and religion in their own country.
Furthermore, though the British public does not
favor further immigration, it does support banning
racial discrimination in housing and employment.[37]
In India, a study of university students in the
Punjab showed that 66 percent felt that "democracy"
was the best, or at least a satisfactory, system of
government.[38] Though it would be unwise to assert
firmly that this poll shows a deep commitment of
the Indian people to freedom of speech, press and
religion--the questions were not specific; it was
administered in only one section of the country;
and a majority actually favored a one-party system[39]--it is some evidence of a belief in the
desirability of a grant of these rights. Also,
despite the serious problems faced by Indian untouchables, a large and slowly increasing body of
Indian public opinion is sceptical of the religious
justification for and the social necessity of the
caste system.[40]

        As for the United States, there is
testimony that though Americans pay lip-service to
the broad freedoms embodied in their Constitution's
Bill of Rights, they are prone to reject the use of
these to benefit unpopular groups or individuals.
A poll by Samuel Stouffer noted that 60 percent of
the respondents would remove from the public library a book "against churches and religion"
written by an atheist and that 84 percent would
deny him the right to teach in college.[41] A majority would strip a communist of his citizenship
and deny him the right to teach.[42] Yet the country
is becoming more tolerant of political and religious dissent. By 1973 another poll indicated that
about 75 percent of the respondents in their 40's
and 50's and 95 percent of the respondents in their
20's would tolerate speeches against religion.
While in 1965 only 30 percent of the older and 40
percent of the younger respondents would have allowed a communist to take a position to which he
had been elected, by 1975 the figures had increased

301

to 40 percent and approximately 60 percent respectively.[43]

Moreover, the governments of nations such as the United States, Britain, France and India, whose citizens have a reasonable degree of commitment to policies of toleration, are discovering that the promulgation of such policies will have centripetal rather than centrifugal tendencies. Gabriel Almond's and Sidney Verba's The Civic Culture[44] surveys attitudes to government and political participation in five countries: the United States, the United Kingdom, Germany, Italy, and Mexico. Perceptions of government were much more favorable in the former two than in the others. The percentage of those who said that they were "proud" of their country's governmental and political institutions was 85 percent in the United States, 46 percent in the United Kingdom, 7 percent in Germany, 3 percent in Italy, and 30 percent in Mexico.[45] It could be that much of this American and U.K. pride was generated by these countries' successful economic performances--the poll was taken in 1959-60 and not in 1982--but some of it was nurtured by their relatively long traditions of tolerance. For example, some of the American respondents who admired their governmental institution cited "some feature of the American government or political tradition--the Constitution, political freedom, democracy and the like... . ."[46] A British poll showed 93 percent feeling that the country was a good or reasonable place for individual liberty; and 72 percent were satisfied with the political system.[47] In other words, in a nation where tolerant attitudes are relatively common, toleration will be a "tie that binds."

e. When the public is uninterested in the problem to which the tolerant policy relates. Here the toleration will not anger the people enough to convince them that the government is illegitimate or that the current holders of public office should be removed at the next election. And, considering that they usually intensely engage the emotions of a

302

minority, it is amazing how often the general public is uninterested in civil rights and liberties issues. Stouffer's poll noted that only one to six percent of the Americans surveyed were seriously worried about domestic communism at a time when the newspapers were replete with allegations that the Communist Party had infiltrated numerous American institutions.[48] During the 1960's many political leaders were lamenting that the United States was being swamped by a tidal wave of obscene publications. Yet, according to the Lockhart Commission on Obscenity and Pornography, only two percent of the respondents in a survey referred to the problem of "erotic materials" as a significant social issue.[49] In general, most people do not place civil rights and liberties issues high on the list of problems that are bothering them. In Stouffer's poll a full 80 percent of the persons asked "What kinds of things do you worry about most" answered solely "in terms of personal and family problems."[50] And when poll takers in India asked what the most important problems facing that country were, most mentioned economic or foreign policy concerns.[51]

f. When individuals are themselves ambivalent about the policy they want to adopt in a civil rights or liberties area. For example, the "official" (and perhaps majority) view that "smut" is sinful is supplemented by the realization on the part of many that they themselves on occasion enjoy an X-rated film or "dirty joke" session. And in all our countries except perhaps the Soviet Union, the market for both "legal" and "illegal" material about sex is huge. This Janus-faced psychological attitude to descriptions of sexual activity may well be one reason why the American, British and French governments have all significantly increased their toleration of erotic material during the past twenty-five years without suffering adverse political consequences. (Miller v. California,[52] which in 1973 tightened for the United States the rules of the Fanny Hill[53] case, did not go nearly as far as some expected in writing finis to the

303

unequivocal toleration manifest in that and related decisions.)

g. When the policy of tolerance is new but "divisible," not pushed to its physical or logical limits. Again, the adoption of a policy of toleration is an innovation; and the "divisibility" of an innovation is another factor increasing its acceptability.[54] Divisibility "is the degree to which an innovation may be tried on a limited basis."[55] There are several techniques for putting an innovation into effect upon a limited basis; and one of these is to insure that it will not be used in every situation where it is physically or logically possible to employ it. The end of theater censorship in Britain in 1968 was a "divisible" policy. It did not mean that "anything could go" on the stage. It signified, rather, that anything was permissible subject to the law of libel and the limitations of the Obscenity Act of 1959, which may be used to punish exhibitors of plays that are outrageous violations of the canons of decency. Thus it produced no public outcry: witnesses at Parliamentary hearings and correspondents to The Times of London overwhelmingly endorsed it. Even that organ of the British elite supported it, albeit lukewarmly; but did worry that under the legislation putting an end to censorship, the Attorney General's consent was needed before theater producers could be prosecuted for obscenity.[56] It is safe to infer from this trepidation that it would have opposed the measure had it freed the stage from all legal restraint.

h. When after initial antagonism to a policy of tolerance, the government imposes marginal limitations upon the policy. This strategic withdrawal may well reconcile the public to the approach. We shall see that criminal justice steps that exclude relevant pro-prosecution evidence can promote incumbency instability. Mapp v. Ohio[57] and Miranda v. Arizona[58] both proved very unpopular. Then after the anti-Miranda Richard Nixon had made four appointments to the Supreme Court, it issued

decisions limiting slightly the protection these
cases afford criminal defendants. To name just
two, United States v. Calandra[59] retreated from
Mapp by declaring that illegally seized evidence
could be used as the basis for questioning in a
grand jury hearing; while Harris v. New York[60]
modified Miranda by declaring that confessions
made in the absence of Miranda warnings could be
used on cross-examination to impeach the defendant's alibi though not as direct evidence of
guilt. Partly because of decisions such as
Calandra and Harris, the furor over Mapp and
Miranda has abated; and they have moved from a
childhood sickbed to a healthy adolescence. (Even
before Mr. Nixon became President, Mapp was made
more acceptable because circumscribed in decisions
such as Terry v. Ohio, allowing the police to "pat
down" without a warrant suspicious individuals who
they have reason to believe are armed.)[61] For example, in Ybarra v. Illinois[62] the Court held inadmissible evidence obtained from the search of a bar
patron where the warrant allowed the search of the
premises and the bartender only. And in Tague v.
Louisiana[63] it reversed a conviction based on a
damaging admission made during a police interrogation where the state could not prove that the
defendant understood his Miranda rights at the time
he waived them. It is possible that if the Supreme
Court had made the policies of Mapp and Miranda
"divisible" when it first articulated them, i.e.,
announced then that they would not be applicable to
situations such as those covered by Calandra and
Harris, they might have raised fewer hackles.

The circumstances described in this
and the previous section feature ventures upon a
path of compromise. It is elementary political
science that compromise is a valuable tool to employ when dealing with economic or "pork barrel"
legislation. One moral of these sections is that,
assuming that it will not eventuate in the bargaining away of fundamental liberties, it is also of
great help when a democratic state frames civil
rights and liberties policy.

i. When what is tolerated is a religion.
There are several reasons why letting a group of
believers alone is relatively unlikely to produce
polarization. Today most of the beneficiaries of
this type of toleration insert in their catechism,
at least, words about the brotherhood of man. They
are unlikely, therefore, to preach genocide or inquisition. Nor are they likely to clamor for armed
rebellion. The interest of most sects lies more in
salvation in the next world than in toppling
governments in this. As the Bible says: "Render
to Caesar the things that are Caesar's and to God
the things that are God's."[64] Of course, many
Roman Catholic priests in Latin America are advocates of thoroughgoing social reform and democrati-
zation and many clergy were among the bitterest
opponents of the United States involvement in Vietnam. Moreover, when a religious group feels that
it is persecuted or that the government is trampl-
ing upon its fundamental tenets it may mutiny. The
Shi'ite Moslem revolution against the Shah of Iran
in 1979 that put Ayatollah Khomeini in power was to
some extent a reaction against the government's
confiscation of land owned by Moslem priests
(mullahs) and its attempt to emancipate women in
the face of traditional Islamic doctrine.[65] Nonetheless, a tolerated religious group is likely to
make its peace with the regime of the day no matter
how unhappy it is with some of its policies. The
Roman Catholic Church, for example, concluded con-
cordats with Mussolini's Italy and Hitler's
Germany. The Orthodox Church in the Soviet Union
likewise is no hotbed of subversive activity. In
fact it (and Soviet Moslem leaders)[66] support at
home and overseas the domestic and foreign policy
positions of their nation.[67] Even Reform Baptists
and Jehovah's Witnesses, who cannot obey certain
dictates of the Soviet state and are willing to go
to jail, are unwilling to storm local party head-
quarters.

Moreover, the public is not likely to
be alienated by a governmental policy tolerating an
association of the faithful. Whatever their level

of churchgoing, there is always a significant number of people in any modern nation that has a belief in God and a hope that there will be an afterlife of eternal bliss to make up for the tribulations of this existence. Thus there is likely to be an initial feeling of sympathy for an organization that claims its purpose is the greater glory of God; though this will be dissipated if its members engage in behavior that the majority considers bizarre. The chapter on Church and State noted that the United States Supreme Court was especially careful not to uphold statutory schemes compelling a sect to violate the articles of its creed. Thus in Wisconsin v. Yoder[68] the Amish were permitted to keep their children out of high school despite the state's compulsory education laws. Yoder and similar cases can in part be explained by the popular attitude for which Justice Douglas was a spokesman in the earlier decision of Zorach v. Clauson:[69] "We are a religious people whose institutions presuppose a Supreme Being."[70] Since "we" are religious, "we" normally will not wince when Court, Congress or President grants immunity to an action done in God's name.

j. When the policy of tolerance is defended by inspiring phraseology or by careful reasoning based upon evidence. To illustrate the first point we can cite the much-praised United States Supreme Court decision of West Virginia St. Board of Education v. Barnette,[71] relieving Jehovah's Witness children of the obligation to salute the flag in violation of their religious faith. Notwithstanding the popular fondness for religion just discussed, the warmth with which Barnette was greeted was a bit of a surprise. In the first place, it overturned an 8-1 holding just three years old.[72] Secondly, it was decided in the midst of a major war, when patriotic fervor was at its height. It is quite possible that one reason for its good reception was the powerful appeal to libertarian emotions of Justice Robert Jackson's majority opinion. He proclaimed, for example, that

> Those who begin coercive elimination of dis-
> sent soon find themselves exterminating dis-
> senters. Compulsory unification of opinion
> achieves only the unamimity of the graveyard.
> . . . If there is any fixed star in our con-
> stitutional constellation, it is that no
> official, high or petty, can prescribe what
> shall be orthodox in politics, nationalism,
> religion or other matters of opinion or force
> citizens to confess by word or act their
> faith therein. If there are any circum-
> stances which permit an exception, they do
> not now occur to us.[73]

The poetry of these sentences convinces (though in-
tellect whispers that the attempt of West
Virginia's legislators to compel all to salute Old
Glory is a far cry from Hitler's concentration
camps and that Mr. Justice Jackson himself had to
take an oath to support the Constitution before
assuming his seat on the Court). Ergo _Time_, a
magazine hardly in the forefront of American liberal
opinion, quoted from "these ringing polysyllables"
in lauding the decision.[74]

In Barel[75] the Council of State
thwarted an attempt by the French government to
prevent communists from competing for seats in the
National School of Administration. The Council's
decision is dogmatic and concerns itself mainly
with a procedural problem. However, the result did
not impel the French public to call for the scalps
of the Councillors. One reason the holding was
widely accepted was that the report of the commissaire de gouvernement upon which the Council based
its decision was a cogently argued document, showing forcefully that to prevent an individual from
competing for a governmental position because of
his political opinions flies in the face of the
Council's precedents and longstanding, fundamental
principles of French law. The report of the
commissaire was published with the opinion.[76] Before this publication it had appeared elsewhere;
and the editors of Rec. Lebon in inserting it referred to it as an important document and one that

already had had a great influence (retentisse-ment).[77] Returning to the United States, another probable reason that Mapp v. Ohio[78] and Miranda v. Arizona[79] survived the initial tidal wave that threatened to engulf them is that they both are distinguished by fine argumentation. Mapp points out that Wolf v. Colorado,[80] holding the exclusion-ary rule not binding on the states, had been eroded by various subsequent Supreme Court decisions and that the adoption of that rule is in practice the only way to insure that the police respect the pro-hibition against illegal searches. Miranda empha-sizes that if no lawyer is present at the police interrogation of a suspect, the police will try to secure a confession through psychological coercion; and cites various respected manuals on police in-terrogation techniques to prove the point. The theses of both cases are hard to rebut. (Of course, the opportunity to defend a policy of tolerance intelligently is not limited to the courts; and it is quite possible for all branches of government to give cogent justifications for certain repressive policies.)

2. In the following situations, toleration may well produce or increase polarization or in-cumbency instability.

a. When a tolerant policy is seen as de-priving a major interest group or a majority of the public of various benefits it has been enjoying. A majority of the British public feels that massive immigration from the "New Commonwealth With Paki-stan" countries would threaten it economically. It believes that it would cost its members their jobs and compel them to pay more taxes to fund the extra social services that NCWP immigrants are believed to require. If a party in power allowed a large - scale influx of NCWP citizens, it surely would lose the next election. In 1970 the incumbent Labour Party was perceived as less restrictive on the immi-gration issue than were the Tories; and the votes it lost because of this helped sink it in that year's election.[81] (Of course, repression can alienate the public and create incumbency instability. Chapter

III mentioned that Indian Moslems were antagonized
by the government's takeover of Aligarh Muslim University and by the use of cow slaughter legislation
to make it more difficult to perform certain duties
incumbent on all observant Moslems. Soviet Jews
shocked by the Stalin regime's embrace of an overtly
anti-Semitic policy came to feel more Jewish and
less Soviet. As one Lyubia Bershadskaya put it,
"The Soviet government helped turn us into Jews.
They did everything to make us feel we were strangers in the country where we were born."[82]

Chapter III noted also that in turn-
of-the-century France Premier Emile Combes' government closed over 14,000 schools run by monks and
enacted legislation in 1904 that outlawed religious
orders devoted to teaching and barred their members
from following that profession. Orders that were
not "authorized" by the government found their
property taken by the state and sold for ridiculously low prices; and many monks went into exile.
Six hundred persons were convicted for violating
the 1904 legislation. Combes further angered
Catholics by having his Minister of War develop a
file listing the names of army officers whose wives
went to mass and whose children went to religious
schools. This produced such an outcry that his administration fell. Though the subsequent 1905 Law
on the Separation of Church and State did guarantee
the free exercise of religion, it further irritated
Catholics by requiring that all individual churches
be managed by "religious" associations. Another of
its clauses required the state to make a list of
the furniture and articles used by the churches for
religious purposes; and violence ensued when public
officials attempted to carry out these inventories.
Here repression led to the downfall of at least one
regime and to polarization manifested in the form
of violent resistance to state action and a situation in which the "faithful saw no other way than
the overthrow of the existing political regime to
overcome their isolation."[83] (Except vis-à-vis
Soviet Jewry, the Soviet Union of today is much
smarter than were the French anti-clericals of 1900.
When Georgian students demonstrated to demand that

the Georgian Constitution continue to define Georgian as the official language of that S.S.R., the authorities gave in.)[84])

       To return to the main theme of this subsection, the grant of special privileges to minority groups clearly is a situation where governmental tolerance appears to deny a majority some of its prerogatives. According this type of favored treatment may well provoke polarization or incumbency instability. As seen, many white Americans are opposed to the use of "quotas" for minority groups and would vote against an administration that implemented these recklessly. Even in India, where quotas have been in force many years, resentment against them led to rioting in 1978 and 1981.[85] A previous paragraph noted that toleration involving the cooptation of important groups by giving them significant benefits may reduce polarization or incumbency instability. There is no need to retract this statement; but it must be qualified by the realization that the resulting harvest of good will may be nullified by increased anger on the part of other groups who feel that these advantages are being bestowed at their expense. The moral is that a state that wants to follow policies of toleration that especially befriend one group should convince others that in the long run the measures will advance their interests as well--in essence, a point made earlier.

       b. When a court, at a time the public perceives the crime rate to be increasing, issues decisions impeding the introduction of relevant prosecution testimony; and the regime in power is identified with that court. This regime is likely to find itself in trouble at the polls. (We are not contending that it will be adversely affected by, e.g., pro-free press holdings handed down during a crime wave.) As seen in Chapter V, the United States Supreme Court during the 1960's produced decisions such as Miranda v. Arizona[86] that led to the exclusion of relevant evidence and thus perhaps made it more difficult to find guilty persons accused of crime. These

decisions coincided with a public perception that
street crime was increasing significantly. To the
question put by the Lockhart Commission about what
were the two or three most serious problems facing
the country, a full 20 percent of the respondents
mentioned the breakdown of law and order.[87]
Miranda thus proved very unpopular. Moreover, it
was issued during the Democratic administration of
President Lyndon Johnson and Vice-President Hubert
Humphrey. The administration's Attorney General,
Ramsey Clark, was its strong supporter.[88] Mr.
Humphrey, of course, was the Democratic Presidential nominee in 1968; and his Republican opponent
Richard Nixon missed no opportunity to lambaste
Miranda and Mr. Clark.[89] Mr. Humphrey, on the
other hand, refused even in the closing days of the
campaign to repudiate the Court's pro-defendant
criminal procedure opinions.[90] Mr. Nixon was thus
seen as the candidate more able to rid the nation
of "crime on the streets"; and this perception, in
turn, was an ingredient of his victory.[91]

        c. When a regime represses and then be-
comes a bit less harsh. Such a regime may well, to
its dismay, find itself confronted with political
parties that wish to destroy it. The repressive
policies may have alienated many who nonetheless
feared to act in concert with their similarly-
antagonized fellows or even to ascertain whether
they stood alone in hating the dictatorship. The
moderation of the repression might allow the disen-
chanted to organize but not simultaneously thaw
their cold fury, and thus might be midwife at the
birth of a polarizing revolutionary organization.
If the repressive regime shifted gears completely
and held free elections, the most probable outcome
would be incumbency instability. The suddenly
tolerant "ins" would be opposed at the polls by the
lately persecuted "outs," who would work diligently
to achieve an electoral majority. When Mrs. Gandhi
lifted her state of emergency in 1977 and proclaimed new elections, she was confronted and then
trounced by a Janata Party led by men who had seen
the inside of prison walls under her temporary

312

dictatorship.

    d. When toleration takes the form of al-
lowing a group advocating secession, revolution,
racism or dictatorship to obtain cabinet or high-
level judicial offices or to acquire a significant
number of seats in the legislature. In such a case
a defining characteristic of a polarized society is
met, i.e., that a party that proclaims one or more
of these viewpoints has a share of political power.
Thus in India, as noted in Chapter III, there are
various "communal" Hindu parties that demand
supremacy for Hindu culture and religion. Instead
of repressing these groups (e.g., the Jana Sangh),
they have been allowed to emerge as the major opposition parties in some state assemblies; and the
Jana Sangh was a component of the Janata Party that
ruled India for three years after Mrs. Gandhi lost
the 1977 election. Though the Jana Sangh officially disavows any desire to persecute non-Hindus,
its lower echelons often incite violence against
Moslems. In fact, M. R. Gowalkar, a leading intellectual of a paramilitary group known as the
Rashtriya Swayamsevak Sangh (RSS) that is allied
with the Hindu communal parties and that was a
caucus within the Janata Party itself, wrote that
"The Non-Hindu peoples in Hindustan must either
adopt the Hindu culture and language, must learn to
respect and hold in reverence Hindu religion, must
entertain no idea but those of glorification of the
Hindu race and culture. . . . or may stay in the
country, wholly subordinated to the Hindu nation,
claiming nothing. . . . not even citizen's
rights."[92] When persons holding attitudes similar
to Mr. Gowalkar's are welcomed into a governing
coalition, the nation becomes a polarized one.

    e. When the government tolerates for a
long period an extremist group that has not yet
grasped power but has conquered a springboard for
seizing it (by, e.g., wooing a small but significant percentage of the nation's elites or making
tangible inroads among its lower-middle or working
classes). This tolerance may eventuate in the

313

acquisition of partial or complete power by the extremist organization. To put this in another way,
such tolerance may be responsible for the transfor-
mation of a mildly polarized nation into a seriously
or totally polarized one. France provides an
appropriate case study of the "kid gloves" treatment of an extremist party that was out of power
but in a good position to obtain it. The party is
the right-wing Action Francaise.[93]

D. The French Third Republic and the Action Francaise

The Action Française and its intellectual
leader Charles Maurras have appeared earlier in
this book. Formed at the turn of the century to
defend the French army against charges that it had
unjustly convicted the Jewish army captain Alfred
Dreyfus, its activities produced a significant
amount of the French jurisprudence on indoor meetings, street rallies and freedom of association.
Why the Action Française is discussed here is not
its advocacy of monarchy but its continued denunciation of Jews, foreigners, and Protestants; its demands for the violent overthrow of the Republic;
its organization of street riots; and the attrac-
tion it held for many notable and powerful Frenchmen.

Before World War I, the Action Française not
only preached anti-Semitism and royalism but also
hoped for war with Germany to regain the provinces
of Alsace and Lorraine that had been lost during
the War of 1870. Its offshoot known as the
Camelots du Roi rioted on the streets and disrupted
lectures at the Sorbonne and plays by Jewish
dramatists. After the War, many French Catholic
intellectuals joined it or sympathized with its
aims. In December of 1926, however, the Pope condemned its leaders as men "who in their writings
are alien to our dogma and morality." He was
understandably piqued at Maurras' thesis that the

Catholic Church was a socially necessary institution but that, in the current world situation, politics was more important than religion. Though the Pope's denunciation hurt the Action Française, it began a comeback in 1931 by disrupting a pacifist meeting--in the years that had preceded and those that were to follow it became expert in breaking up meetings and plays at which it took offense. Right-wing rioting of February 6, 1934, in which it played a major role, seemed to the left to be an attempt by the reactionaries to seize Parliament. The Action Française also organized strikes and demonstrations against a law professor at the University of Paris who had been the legal adviser to Emperor Haile Selaisse of Ethiopia in the League of Nations: it had enthusiastically supported Mussolini's invasion of Ethiopia. Its hoodlums physically prevented one of the men responsible for repressing the February 6th fighting from practicing in the law courts of Paris. This and other events led to the passage of the law allowing the executive to ban associations that engage in armed fighting or preach violent overthrow and to the dissolution of the Action Française itself under this law in February, 1936--and also to a statute of January 10th of the same year "transferring certain press offenses from the indulgent juries of the Assizes to the jurisdiction of the judges in the Correctional courts."[94]

This dissolution, over thirty-five years after the founding of the group, was the first real effort by democratic France to destroy the Action Française. The only steps previously taken were police surveillance of its meetings;[95] mild punishments meted out to members who brawled and disrupted classes at the Sorbonne;[96] and several libel prosecutions against the organization's leaders. In 1923 Maurras received a four-month prison sentence for his part in Action Française violence that wrecked the offices of several opposition newspapers. However, "there is no record that Maurras ever served this sentence: amnesties always seemed to save him in time."[97] One Action

Française leader jailed in 1927 as the consequence of a slander action brought by a private party was treated handsomely while serving his five-month sentence: ". . . excellent dinners (were) brought in from outside . . . bottles of Chablis, the coffee and the newspapers fetched at breakfast time by obliging warders."[98]

The dissolution of the right-wing leagues such as the Action Française in 1936 was followed by their reconstitution under other names: by May of that year the Communist L'Humanite "was predictably revolted to see how freely royalist leaders paraded with their 'disbanded' leagues."[99] During the same month the Socialist-Communist-Radical coalition known as the Popular Front won a majority of the seats in the National Assembly; and the Socialist Léon Blum became Prime Minister in June. This led to a torrent of anti-Blum, anti-Semitic and anti-Popular Front invective on the part of the Action Française. Its journal's

. . . anti-Blum campaign was to be conducted in violently anti-Semitic terms, soon applied to the Popular Front regime as a whole: "The kike's riposte," "The Jewish ship adrift," "The Jewish revolution sings its victory. . ." Blum was subjected to a torrent of insults, frequently from the pen of Maurras. In one article only fifty lines long the royalist . . . managed to call the Premier of his country a camel sixteen times. The rest of the cabinet he described as idiots, fanatics, deserters, crooks, pederasts, traitors, prostitutes and assorted species of the animal kingdom.[100]

The Spanish Civil War then broke out; and Maurras fervently supported the authoritarian rebels of General Francisco Franco and bitterly opposed a suggestion that France give aid to the Republican side. For the most part the Spanish Republic did not get help from the French Republic, though both were headed by Popular Front regimes.

In October, 1936 Maurras went to jail for several
months for having published a list of 140 members
of Parliament who favored sanctions against Italy
for attacking Ethiopia. Following this list was
this declaration to the 140:

> In the absence of a national power capable
> of halting your treasonable enterprises, it
> is essential that supreme measures should
> be ordered. Your blood must be the first
> to flow. . . . The murders of French youth
> shall be punished by death.[101]

He was convicted of incitement to murder but his
sentence of 250 days was served in relative comfort
and he continued to publish articles in the party
paper.

In 1938, Maurras angrily denounced proposals
to aid beleaguered Czechoslovakia. It was not that
he was pro-Hitler: in fact throughout most of his
career he had equated Jews and Germans, and even in
1938 the Action Française was the only rightist
group to consistently condemn Germany and its
Fuehrer. It was, rather, that he felt that helping
the Czechs would in the long run redound to the
benefit of the communists and the Jews, who in his
eyes were even more of a danger to France than were
the hated Germans and their dictator. Once France
declared war against Germany, Maurras and his
group, though not all the extreme right, rallied to
their country's side. After its collapse, he and
his friends cheered Marshal Pétain's accession to
power. Maurras' position during the remainder of
World War II was a strange one. He remained a supporter of the Vichy regime but opposed collaboration with either the Nazis or the Free French
Movement of Charles de Gaulle. He continued his
attacks on the Jews, praising the government's
anti-Semitic laws but

> criticizing the laxity with which the anti-
> Semitic legislation was enforced. While
> noting with satisfaction that Jews had been

excluded from the Army, the Navy, the Air
Force, the universities, the public services,
and numerous professions, and that 2,000
Jewish firms in the Free Zone and about
23,000 in the North were in an administrator's
hands, Maurras called for more serious efforts
to rid the land of Jewish refugees who supposedly fed the Black Market and Gaullist
propaganda, and who continued to corrupt the
country as they had done before the war.[102]

He also demanded that captured members of the Resistance be shot and that, if necessary, the families of Gaullists should be seized as hostages.
After the war he was sent to jail and died in 1952,
aged 76.

   In terms of membership, the Action Française
never was large. Even in 1934, when its membership
rolls were at their maximum, its adherents numbered
only between 60,000 and 70,000. Moreover, it could
call upon only between 1,000 and 1,500 men for
demonstrating on the streets of Paris. However, it
exerted a significant, polarizing effect on the
course of French politics between 1900 and 1945.
Especially before his condemnation by the Church,
Maurras exercised great influence among Catholic
intellectuals. Even liberal Catholics such as the
philosopher Jacques Maritain and the writer
François Mauriac admired him. George Bernanos, who
during the 1930's became a member of the Catholic
left, began as an active member of the Action
Française and always remained under the spell of
many of the Maurrassian ideas. The author André
Malraux, who later was to become sympathetic to
communism and then Minister of Culture in the
Gaullist Fifth Republic, once referred to Maurras
as "one of the great intellectual forces of today."[103] Some contend that Charles de Gaulle drew
much of his nationalism from Maurras.[104] What is a
bit shocking about all this is that Maurras was
head of a group one of whose theme songs was as
follows. (Maurras collaborated in writing it.)

The Jew having taken all
Having robbed Paris of all she owns
Now says to France:
"You belong to us alone!
Obey! Down on your knees, all of you."

Refrain
No, No, France is astir
Her eyes flash fire
No, No
Enough of treason now

Insolent Jew, hold your tongue
Behold, your King approaches
And our race
Runs ahead of him
Back to where you belong, Jew
Our King will lead us.[105]

It is true that the careers of the intellectuals and statesmen mentioned above show no trace
of the anti-Semitism and street hooliganism that
the Action Française demanded. But many violence-
prone and hate-mongering types also heeded the
siren song of Maurras and his coterie. On July 31,
1914, at the outbreak of World War I, the great
pacifist and socialist leader Jean Jaurès was
assassinated. The right-wing crackpot who pulled
the trigger acted on his own; but it is clear that
he had imbibed the anti-Jaurès diatribes that had
been published in the newspaper Action Française
and that his reading and his personal contacts with
members of the Action Française and similar groups
had been what inspired him to commit his crime.
(Maurras' attacks on Jaurès during the month prior
to his death had denounced him as a traitor and
German agent.) Had Jaurès managed to survive the
war years he might have unified the French left and
headed a government that would have carried out the
many social and economic reforms the country needed
in the post-World War I era. The vilification
directed by Maurras and his friends against Léon
Blum when he became Prime Minister in 1936 has already been described. "These attempts to discredit

the Premier eventually stuck, even though they were
shrugged off by people with intelligence. It is
always shrewd to underestimate the intelligence of
the public, as the success of most political slander has proved, and repeated innuendos and outright
assertions that Blum was a rich, hypocritical mil-
lionaire leading a movement of expropriation were
not ignored by all who heard them."[106] Had Blum
not been attacked so viciously, his Popular Front
government might have filled the gap created by the
death of Jaurès 22 years earlier and brought about
an improvement in the miserable condition of the
French working class, a misery that even the Action
Française was willing to acknowledge. It is likewise quite possible that the Action Française's
bitter warning against French aid to the Republican
government in Spain was one of the reasons the Blum
government did not actively support the anti-Franco
forces. And the defeat of Franco could have meant
the early demise of naziism in Germany.

In September, 1937 an extreme right-wing
group popularly dubbed the "Cagoule" shocked France
by dynamiting two buildings in the heart of Paris.
During the next few months the police found in the
possession of its leaders "important caches of
arms, including machine guns, grenades, and radio
sets. . . ."[107] Though the Action Française condemned the Cagoule as irresponsible, many of its
members had until very recently been members of the
group and a few Cagoulards were still its adherents.

But the murder of Jaurès, the discrediting of
Blum, and the rise of the Cagoule do not really indicate the extent of the damage that Maurras and
his followers did to France. The following quotation brilliantly begins to make the point.

But Maurras and the shindy made on the
Boulevards and in the Latin quarter by the
jeunesse dorée never amounted to a serious
political movement. He provided a literary
high school of obscurantism, scorn and

hatred, the principal achievements of which
were in the field of lampoon, slander and
personal invective. . . . By the elegant
style in which they clothed their scurrili-
ties Maurras and his followers set the tone
for the whole of the French right. François
Mauriac summed up the experience of a life-
time of controversy when he once said " . . .
The dirt is always thrown from the extreme
right." This contumelious literature did not
fail to exercise a wider influence, however,
but without promoting the moral regeneration
which it proclaimed. Its only influence was
demoralizing. Thanks to it a whole French
social elite put on their uniforms as officers at the outbreak of the second world war
fully believing that their country was ruled
by a dishonourable pack of thieves, swindlers,
and traitors, and that it was rotten to the
core; and the collapse came to them like a
judgment of God, which they had expected, and
for which they had almost hoped. For the
theory of the corruption of the French state,
the most easily popularisable part of the
Maurras doctrine, had become familiar to a
circle far wider than the readers of the
Action Française and other, less elegantly
written, organs of corruption, and was familiar to every waiter and butcher's boy.[108]
(emphasis mine)

This belief by the French officer corps in 1939 and
1940 that it was defending a regime that was corrupt and evil played a role in Germany's easy
victory over France. Admittedly, the sad state of
French science and technology, the outmoded military theories of the French generals, the low birth
rate, and the desire to avoid the carnage of World
War I all contributed to the collapse. But, as the
writer Marc Bloch contended:

    Many men of what might still claim to be
    our ruling classes, since from them were
    drawn our leaders of industry, our senior

civil servants, the majority of our reserve
officers, set off for the war haunted by
. . . gloomy prognostications. They were
taking their orders from a political set-up
which they held to be hopelessly corrupt.
They were defending a country which they
did not seriously think could offer any
genuine resistance. The soldiers under
their command were the sons of that "people"
which they were only too glad to regard as
degenerate. . . . Our leaders not only let
themselves be beaten, but too soon decided
that it was perfectly natural that they
should be beaten.[109]

Not only was the ripple effect of Maurrassism
a factor in the collapse of France but, moreover,
many of the leaders of the authoritarian Vichy regime that governed the French south after the
armistice had at one time or another been active in
the Action Française. Though Maurras held no position in the government, Marshal Pétain was an ad-
mirer of his. "Even though actual members of the
Action Française were never very numerous at Vichy,
the place was pervaded with a strong, though
diffuse, Maurrasism."[110] For example, closely
associated with the Action Française and Maurras
was one Xavier Vallat. As the first Vichy
commissioner-general for Jewish affairs, he was
responsible for the enactment for the law of June 2,
1941 which excluded Jews from the senior civil
service, education, banking and advertising and
imposed strict quotas upon them in law, medicine,
architecture and pharmacy. It was also he who was
behind the law of July 22, 1941 under which many
Jewish businesses were requisitioned by the government. Vallat's successor as commissioner was Louis
Darquier de Pellepoix, another follower of Maurras.
It was Darquier, discovered in the late 1970's
alive and well in Spain, who was directly responsible for deporting to Germany thousands of Jews from
Vichy-controlled territory. The anti-Semitism of
Vichy generally was an Action Française legacy.
According to Weber, ". . . fed by (the) arguments

(of Action Française alumni), a pervasive anti-Semitic mood developed during the years preceding the Second World War, reaching its climax in the anti-Semitic legislation of the Vichy regime, which was inspired by and generally sponsored by friends and allies of the Action Française."111

Thus the French government's habit of tolerating the Action Française made a contribution to increasing the polarization of the nation. This beneficiary of official permissiveness addressed itself to crucial elements in the French bourgeoisie: Catholic and other intellectuals, students from wealthy homes, army officers, prominent civil servants. A minority, but not an inappreciable minority, of those belonging to these elites absorbed its ideas. When they themselves attained control of the machinery of the state, they put into effect the racist and anti-democratic components of its ideology and wrote a sorry chapter in French history.

It is not the purpose of the above paragraphs to prove that the French government should have crushed the Action Française in its infancy or young adulthood. These pages, rather have two aims. The first, already mentioned, is to demonstrate that tolerating a polarizing organization not actually holding political power could well engender a more polarized nation. The second is to reinforce the thesis that it is very difficult for a democratic society to answer the question of how best to deal with such a group.

One possible response, despite the French experience with the Action Française, is that it should be let alone until it engages in violence or makes statements that create a clear and present danger thereof. This is the position of great liberal American jurists such as Oliver Wendell Holmes and Louis D. Brandeis. Justice Holmes said in his dissent in <u>Gitlow v. New York</u>:

If in the long run the beliefs expressed in

proletarian dictatorship (for which we can
substitute interchangeably "fascist" or
"authoritarian" dictatorship) are destined
to be accepted by the dominant forces of
the community, the only meaning of free
speech is that they should be given their
chance and have their way.[112]

And as Justice Brandeis asserted concurring in
Whitney v. California:

Those who won our independence by revolution were not cowards. They did not fear
political change. They did not exalt
order at the cost of liberty. To cour-
ageous, self-reliant men, with confidence
in the power of free and fearless reasoning
applied through the process of popular
government, no danger flowing from speech
can be deemed clear and present, unless the
incidence of the evil apprehended is so
imminent that it may befall before there is
opportunity for full discussion. If there
be time to expose through discussion the
falsehoods and fallacies, to avert the evil
by the processes of education, the remedy
to be applied is more speech, not enforced
silence.[113]

With all due respect to Justices Holmes and
Brandeis, their statements are not completely adequate. First, contrary to Justice Holmes, there is
no good reason why a nation has to give a non-
democratic party a magnificent opportunity to be
accepted by the dominant forces of the community:
the consequences of being governed by the Nazis,
the Stalinist communists, or even the Vichy French
are too appalling. Second, as France's inept
handling of the Action Française indicates, the
major dangers flowing from the speech and writings
of an anti-democratic group often are not "present." These activities may sap the will of the
country to fight when attacked; and the organization may provide the personnel of a quisling,

324

authoritarian regime. However, these events may not take place until years after the initial articulation of its doctrine. Furthermore, though there is time to avert them by free discussion, free discussion may well prove impotent. The French right and military were not convinced by liberal arguments during the 1930's that, despite weaknesses, the Third French Republic was not basically rotten and there was no need to replace it by a monarchy or dictatorship. It often is not the incitements to riot that are the most baneful products of the activities of extremist groups; but their gradual conversion of some of the most powerful elements in society; their slow osmosis into the mind of a crackpot who wants to become famous and is willing to pay the price of being known in the history books as the assassin of a great democratic leader; and their transforming vigorous democratic statesmen into cowards afraid to take the steps that are necessary to relieve suffering at home and attacks from abroad. For these reasons, Justice Brandeis' theory that even extimist views should not be suppressed unless they create an imminent danger of violence or revolution is not an airtight position.

However, the experience with Maurras and the Action Française cannot reassure those who feel that a democracy should speedily and thoroughly repress polarizing groups before they obtain control of the nation. Ultimately, legal actions were taken against the Action Française and its intellectual gurus but these did not cure the disease. The association was banned but soon reconstituted itself and paraded openly under other labels. The requirement imposed in 1935 of prior authorization for outdoor meetings on the public way did not curtail the Action Française's activities. Maurras was jailed for several months but he and his disciples went on spewing forth in print their bilious theories. A 1939 decree-law outlawed inflammatory racist statements; but the Action Française's anti-Semitic propaganda continued unabated. All this time the hatred of democracy and the Jews kept flowing through the ruling classes, radiating outward from the Action Française to groups organized by its "alumni" and thence to the "respectables" in the army and civil service. Finally, French democracy collapsed; and the successor regime, in which Action Française sympathizers played a prominent role, trampled upon basic human freedoms.

There is an additional consideration beyond its possible futility that argues against taking an overly-repressive stand against polarizing organizations. In On Liberty, John Stuart Mill points out that freedom of speech and press is desirable because, inter alia, gold is often found among the dross in the same set of writings, from which it follows that suppressing these writings is likely to keep the nuggets undiscovered and thus retard the emergence of the truth.[114] Similarly, if the French government had taken steps to remove Maurras from circulation permanently, many stimulating ideas as well as much invective would never have seen the light of day. Maurras did not win election to the renowned Académie Française through being a journalistic hack. However shocking was his election to this band of "Immortals," he was a man of intellectual depth and sensitivity. The same article that denounces Jean-Jacques Rousseau (a Protestant) as entering France "fed on Jew-inspired revolt . . . like one of those false prophets . . . fixed up with an old sack, girt in camel-hide, head covered with filthy ashes, who used to trail their mournful wailings up and down the streets of Zion,"[115] also imaginatively applies the old classical-romantic dispute of literature to styles of political action. Maurras favors the classical type in both politics and literature, with its ". . . analytical approach, the confidence in reason, the passion for the continuum of thought, the clear, the intelligible"[116] to the romantic with its "violent effusions of the senses that civilization attempts to moderate: the cry of love and hate, of hope and despair, of servitude and liberty, that hysterical yearning for independence of one

326

who . . . 'flails in all directions with no other goal than his own satisfaction.'"[117] That for political behavior and philosophy the categories are too neatly drawn; that Maurras himself sounds like the romantics he despised; and that it is absurd to equate the classic spirit with Greece-Rome-Catholicism-France and the romantic spirit with Germany-Orient-Judaism, do not detract from the thesis that this romantic versus classical dichotomy may well prove helpful to the student who wishes to understand or shape politics.

Once again, this book is not contending that Maurras should or should not have been more rigorously punished than he was, that the Action Française should or should not have been more ruthlessly repressed. But the Action Française episode does indicate that any approach to a polarizing group that is marching toward political rule may well have serious weaknesses. Use of the clear and present danger or bad tendency tests, punishments amounting to slaps on the wrist, prior restraints of publications and meetings, and lengthy jail sentences all have their Achilles heel. Each may prove unhelpful to the democratic statesman in his efforts to limit the influence of the group without destroying the spirit of free inquiry. There is no way, however, that he can avoid opting for a course of conduct that closely resembles one or another of them.

However, the conclusion that there is no quick fix for a democratic society bedevilled by a polarizing movement need not mire us in depression. As seen earlier in this Chapter, the public is often uninterested in or ambivalent about civil rights and liberties issues; and the interest groups that take a stand on these matters are usually small or concerned with just a few rights and liberties problems. While these truths will not thrill the advocate of participatory democracy, they, taken together with the ability of many governments to distribute economic and honorific resources in such a way as to co-opt their

327

opponents, do indicate that the democratic polity has considerable freedom to shape civil rights and liberties policy. This autonomy can be exercised in a mindless way that will facilitate the success of anti-libertarian movements on the one hand or suppress the expression of all but the most orthodox viewpoints on the other. But there is a chance that it can be employed in a manner that will keep authoritarian parties at bay and simultaneously encourage the flowering of ideas that is so necessary to social, political and economic progress. It is the very fact of this possibility that makes it unnecessary for the supporters of political democracy to confess in despair that this political system will become extinct. However, in order to make sure that this does not happen, they must continually rethink their solutions to concrete civil rights and liberties problems and cast their recommendations in a form that will appeal both to the political elite and to public opinion. It would be presumptuous to quantify here their chances for success in these difficult endeavors.

FOOTNOTES TO CHAPTER VI

[1]340 U.S. 315 (1951).

[2](1882) 15 Cox Crim. Cas. 138.

[3]C.E. May 19, 1933, Rec. 541; D.1933.54.

[4](1961) 2 Q.B. 744.

[5]438 U.S. 265 (1978).

[6]443 U.S. 193 (1979).

[7]100 S. Ct. 2758 (1980).

[8]Roy c. Assoc. Pour l'Éducation Populaire Ste.-Marthe, Ct. Cass., Sem. Juridique, December 27, 1978, #19009.

[9]As will be remembered, a court has the power of judicial review when it has the authority to declare invalid acts of the legislature it deems to be unconstitutional.

[10]376 U.S. 254 (1964).

[11](1961) 2 Q.B. 1162 (C.A.); affirmed (1962) 2 All E.R. 737 (H.L.).

[12]Chandler v. Director of Public Prosecutions, (1964) A.C. 763 (H.L.)

[13]385 U.S. 39 (1966).

[14]Jerome Frank, Courts on Trial (New York: Atheneum, 1963), p. 183.

[15] The Observer (London), April 21, 1974, p. 91; New York Times, December 17, 1973, p. 22; January 2, 1980, p. A23.

[16] See p. 107 of his Censorship in Britain.

[17] Ibid.

[18] Markmann, Freedom à la Francaise, Civil Liberties Review, Spring, 1975, pp. 73, 91.

[19] Y. Manor, France, at pp. 234, 236 of Itzhak Galnoor (ed.), Government Secrecy in Democracies (New York: Harper and Row, 1977).

[20] Robert Caro, The Power Broker (New York: Knopf, 1974), p. 502.

[21] The Observer (London), April 21, 1974, p. 9.

[22] (1973) All India Rep. S. Ct. 106.

[23] The Observer (London), April 21, 1974, p. 9; New York Times, December 17, 1973, p. 22; October 14, 1974, p. 10; January 2, 1980, p. A23.

[24] New York Times, December 17, 1973, p. 22. The Desai administration did give the opposition an opportunity to use radio and TV. New York Times, April 5, 1977, p. 31; April 14, 1977, p. 7.

[25] Paul O'Higgins, Censorship in Britain, pp. 129-30.

[26] New York Times, November 30, 1974, p. 23.

[27] J. Duncan M. Derrett, Religion, Law and the State in India (New York: Free Press, 1968), Ch. 10; Donald Smith, India as a Secular State, Ch. 10.

[28] Smith, op. cit., p. 28.

[29] Ibid.

[30] Bob Hepple, _Race, Jobs and the Law in Britain_, pp. 4-5, 157.

[31] _New York Times_, February 21, 1972, p. 31.

[32] The idea of cooptation of elites was developed by David Selznick in _TVA and the Grassroots_ (New York: Harper and Row, 1966), pp. 14-16.

[33] Lloyd and Susan Rudolph, _The Modernity of Tradition_ (Chicago: U. of Chicago Press, 1967), pp. 49-61.

[34] Everett Rogers, _Diffusion of Innovations_ (New York: Free Press, 1962), p. 127.

[35] Stephen Szabo, _Contemporary French Orientations toward Economic and Political Dimensions of Human Rights_, _Universal Human Rights_, July-September, 1979, pp. 61, 63.

[36] Richard P. Claude, _West European Public Opinion on American Human Rights Advocacy: A Cross-National Analysis_, p. 14. Unpublished paper delivered at International Human Rights Congress, Rutgers University, 1978.

[37] Hepple, _op. cit._, p. 4.

[38] Yogrenda Malik and Jesse Marquette, _Democracy and Alienation in North India_, _Journal of Politics_, Vol. 37, pp. 35, 42 (1958).

[39] _Ibid._, pp. 43-44.

[40] Santokh Anant, _Change in Intercaste Attitudes in N. India between 1968 and 1972_, _J. Soc. Psych._ 95:275 (1975).

[41] See p. 32 of Samuel Stouffer, _Communism, Conformity and Civil Liberties_ (New York: Doubleday, 1955).

[42] _Ibid._, pp. 40, 43.

[43]M. Kent Jennings and Richard Niemi, Continuity and Change in Political Orientations: A Longitudinal Study of Two Generations, American Political Science Review 69:1316, 1334 (December, 1975).

[44]Princeton: Princeton University Press, 1963.

[45]Ibid., p. 102.

[46]Ibid.

[47]The Times (London), September 4, 1980, p. 4.

[48]Stouffer, op. cit., pp. 59, 70.

[49]Commission on Obscenity and Pornography, Report (New York: Bantam Books, 1970), p. 187.

[50]Stouffer, op. cit., p. 59.

[51]Gerald Braunthal, An Attitude Survey in India, Public Opinion Quarterly 33:69, 73 (1969).

[52]413 U.S. 15 (1973).

[53]A Book Named John Cleland's Memoirs of a Woman of Pleasure v. Attorney General of Massachusetts, 383 U.S. 413 (1966).

[54]Rogers, op. cit., p. 131.

[55]Ibid.

[56]The Times (London), February 23, 1968, p. 9.

[57]367 U.S. 643 (1961).

[58]384 U.S. 436 (1966).

[59]414 U.S. 338 (1974).

[60] 401 U.S. 222 (1971).

[61] See Fred Graham, The Self-Inflicted Wound (New York: Macmillan, 1970), pp. 196-98. Terry is 392 U.S. 1 (1968).

[62] 100 S. Ct. 338 (1979).

[63] 100 S. Ct. 652 (1980).

[64] Gospel According to St. Mark 12:17 (New American Catholic Version).

[65] Joseph Kraft, Letter from Iran, New Yorker, December 18, 1978, pp. 134, 136-37, 142-44.

[66] Sheikh Ali, The Muslim Minority in the Soviet Union, Current History, April, 1980, pp. 175-76.

[67] Walter Kolarz, Religion in the Soviet Union, pp. 62-70. See also Gerhard Simon, Church, State and Opposition in the U.S.S.R. (Berkeley: University of California Press, 1974), pp. 117-25.

[68] 406 U.S. 205 (1972).

[69] 343 U.S. 306 (1952).

[70] 343 U.S. at p. 313.

[71] 319 U.S. 624 (1943). Note, 42 Mich. L. Rev. 319-21 (1943) claims that Barnette was unanimously acclaimed.

[72] Minersville School District v. Gobitis, 310 U.S. 586 (1940).

[73] 319 U.S. at pp. 641-42.

[74] Time, June 21, 1943, p. 16.

[75] C.E., May 28, 1954, Rec. 308.

[76] At _Ibid._

[77] At _Ibid._

[78] 367 U.S. 643 (1961).

[79] 384 U.S. 436 (1966).

[80] 338 U.S. 25 (1949).

[81] Donley Studlar, _Policy Voting in Britain: The Color Immigration Issue in the 1964, 1966 and 1970 General Elections, American Political Science Review_ 72:46, 62 (March, 1978).

[82] Trudie Vocse, _Twenty Years in the Life of Lyubia Bershadskaya, New York Times Magazine,_ March 14, 1971, pp. 27, 42.

[83] Henry Ehrmann, _Politics in France_ (Boston: Little Brown, 1968), p. 49.

[84] _New York Times_, December 21, 1979, p. A2.

[85] _Times of India_ (Bombay ed.), April 1, 1978, p. 1; _New York Times_, February 2, 1981, p. A6.

[86] 384 U.S. 436 (1966).

[87] Commission on Obscenity and Pornography, _Report_, p. 188.

[88] His _Crime in America_ (New York: Pocket Books, 1971), p. 186, lauds _Miranda_.

[89] See _New York Times_, October 23, 1968, p. 28 for one of his denunciations of _Miranda_; and September 27, 1968, p. 30 for one of his attacks on Clark.

[90] _New York Times_, September 27, 1978, p. 30.

[91]A Harris poll of October, 1968 put Nixon ahead of Humphrey 38 percent to 26 percent as the candidate who could best maintain law and order. New York Times, October 23, 1968, p. 28. Time, November 15, 1968, p. 19 and U.S. News and World Report, November 18, 1968, p. 44 both think that Nixon's strong "anti-crime" stance helped him with white voters.

[92]What has preceded in this paragraph is based on Smith, India as a Secular State, Ch. 15. The quote is on p. 466 of Ibid.

[93]This discussion of Maurras and the Action Française is based upon Eugen Weber, Action Française (Stanford: Stanford Univ. Press, 1962) and Ernst Nolte, Three Faces of Fascism (New York: New American Library, 1969), pp. 51-189.

[94]Weber, op. cit., p. 362. Today, almost no violation of the 1881 Press Law is triable by a jury. Colliard, Libertés Publiques (3rd ed.), p. 487.

[95]Weber, op. cit., p. 62.

[96]Nolte, op. cit., p. 101; Weber, op. cit., p. 147, note j.

[97]Weber, op. cit., p. 147, note j.

[98]Ibid., p. 270.

[99]Ibid., p. 369.

[100]Ibid., pp. 374-75.

[101]Ibid., p. 268.

[102]Ibid., p. 462.

[103]Quoted Ibid., p. 518.

[104]Stanley Hoffman admits that some have said that de Gaulle was influenced by Maurras' conception of the state but claims that, in fact, the General-President owed very little to the monarchist journalist. See Decline or Renewal: France since the 1930's (New York: Viking, 1974), p. 265.

[105]Nolte, op. cit., p. 131.

[106]Weber, op. cit., p. 375.

[107]Ibid., p. 400.

[108]Herbert Luethy, France against Herself (Cleveland and New York: World Publishing Co., 1957), pp. 36-37.

[109]Quoted Ibid., p. 91.

[110]Weber, op. cit., p. 443.

[111]Ibid., p. 201.

[112]268 U.S. 652, 673 (1925).

[113]274 U.S. 357, 377 (1927).

[114]See p. 295 of Max Lerner (ed.), The Essential Works of John Stuart Mill (New York: Bantam, 1961).

[115]J. S. McClelland, The French Right from de Maistre to Maurras (New York: Harper and Row, 1970), p. 244.

[116]Ibid., p. 240.

[117]Ibid., p. 242.

CASES CITED

1. Explanation of Abbreviations

United States

U.S. - United States Reports - Contains decisions of the United States Supreme Court.

S.Ct. - Supreme Court Reporter. Also contains decisions of the United States Supreme Court.

F2d - Federal Reporter, 2nd Series - Contains decisions of the United States Courts of Appeal.

A2d - Atlantic Reporter, 2nd Series - Contains reports of highest courts of states in Eastern U.S.

Great Britain

A.C. - Appeals Cases. (1964) A.C. 763 means that the case is to be found in the 1964 Volume of Appeals Cases at p. 763.

All E.R. - All England Reports. (1962) 3 All E.R. means that the case is to be found in Volume 3 of All England Reports for the year 1962.

K.B. - King's Bench

Q.B. - Queen's Bench

Weekly L.R. - Weekly Law Reports

India

All India Rep. - All India Reporter. Found in the
All India Reporter for a given year are cases
of the Indian Supreme Court and the state High
Courts. Thus (1973) All India Rep. S. Ct. 106
means that the case can be found in the Supreme
Court volume of the 1973 All India Reporter at
p. 106. (1951) All India Rep. Patna 12 means
that the case can be found in the Patna volume
of the 1951 All India Reporter at p. 12.

S. Ct. Cas. - Supreme Court Cases. (1975) 1 S.
Ct. Cas. 267 means that the case can be found
in Volume 1 of Supreme Court Cases for 1975 at
p. 267.

Sup. Ct. Journ. - Supreme Court Journal

Sup. Ct. R. - Supreme Court Reporter

France

C.E. - Conseil d'État (Council of State)

D. - Recueil Dalloz. Thus D.1914.3.74 means that
the case can be found at p. 74 of Volume 3 of
Dalloz for the year 1914.

D.H. - Dalloz Hebdomadaire. For certain years,
Dalloz is divided into various sections. One
is known as "Hebdomadaire." Thus D.H. 1938.295
means p. 295 of the Hebdomadaire section of the
1938 volume of Dalloz.

D.J. - Dalloz Jurisprudence. Another section into
which Dalloz is divided in certain years. It
contains complete reports of cases. Thus
D.1944 J.66 means p. 66 of the Jurisprudence
section of the 1944 volume of Dalloz.

D. Somm. - Dalloz Sommaires. Another section into which Dalloz is divided in certain years. It contains short summaries of cases. Thus D.1975 Somm. 33 means p. 33 of the Sommaires section of the 1975 volume of Dalloz.

Gaz. Pal. - The case, etc. reporter called Gazette du Palais.

Rec. - Recueil des arrêts du Conseil d'État (Recueil Lebon). Contains decisions of the Council of State, the lower administrative tribunals, and the Tribunal des Conflits. The date of the case is always cited, thus giving the lawyer or scholar the relevant year of this series. For example, C.E. Feb. 7, 1969, Rec. 85 is a decision of the Council of State that can be found on p. 85 of Recueil Lebon for 1969.

Sem. Juridique - Semaine Juridique

Sirey - Recueil Sirey

2. Table of Cases

Ahmad v. I.L.E.A., (1977) 3 Weekly L.R. 396 - p. 167 n15

Alexander v. Holmes County Bd. of Educ., 396 U.S. 19 (1969) - p. 216 n14

Apodaca v. Oregon, 406 U.S. 404 (1972) - p. 275 n22

Arati Ray Choudhury v. Union of India, (1974) 1 S. Ct. Cas. 87 - p. 220 n52

Argersinger v. Hamlin, 407 U.S. 25 (1972) - p. 233

Assoc. Enbata, C.E. Oct. 8, 1975, Rec. 494 - p. 110 n70

Assoc. Israélite de Valenciennes, C.E. Mar. 27, 1936, Rec. 383 - p. 171 n63

Azeez Basha v. Union of India, (1968) All India Rep. S. Ct. 662 - p. 169 n32

B and C Co. v. Union of India, (1973) All India Rep. S. Ct. 106 - p. 295

Babulal Parate v. Maharashtra, (1961) All India Rep. S. Ct. 884 - p. 106 n22

Baggett v. Bullitt, 377 U.S. 360 (1964) - p. 107 n29

Baidyanath v. Bihar, (1968) All India Rep. S. Ct. 1393 - p. 277 n46

Balaji v. Mysore, (1963) All India Rep. S. Ct. 649 - p. 194

Barel, C.E. May 28, 1954, Rec. 308; D.1954.594 - pp. 63, 64, 308

Baza, C.E. Oct. 6, 1971, Rec. 876 - p. 211

Beatty v. Gillbanks, (1882) 15 Cox Crim. Cas. 138 - p. 288

Beauharnais v. Illinois, 343 U.S. 250 (1952) - p. 105 n7

Benjamin, C.E. May 19, 1933, Rec. 541; D.1933.3.54 - pp. 42, 43, 288

Betts v. Brady, 316 U.S. 455 (1942) - p. 274 n7

Beytout et Soc. Nouvelle de Cinématographie, Ct. Cass., Sem. Juridique, June 6, 1979, #19143 - p. 117 n159

Bibhuti Bhusan v. S. Kumar, (1966) All India Rep. Cal. 473 - p. 82

Board of Education v. Allen, 392 U.S. 236 (1968) - p. 154

Bowman v. Secular Society, (1917) A.C. 406 (H.L.) - p. 121

340

Brandenburg v. Ohio, 395 U.S. 444 (1969) - p. 52
Braunfeld v. Brown, 366 U.S. 599 (1961) - p. 156
Breard v. Alexandria, 341 U.S. 622 (1951) - p. 167
  n4
Brown v. Board of Educ., 347 U.S. 483 (1954) - pp.
  176, 177, 178, 180
Brown v. Board of Educ., 349 U.S. 294 (1955) - p.
  177
Brown v. Mississippi, 297 U.S. 278 (1936) - p. 274
  n4
Bucard, C.E. Dec. 23, 1936, Rec. 1151; D.1938.3.22 -
  p. 43
Bujadoux et autres, C.E. Feb. 5, 1937, Rec. 153;
  D.1938.3.19 - p. 43
Buscia, Ct. of Cass., Ch. Crim., Vol. 169, #343, p.
  838 (1973) - p. 282 n94

C. K. Kakodkar v. St. of Maharashtra, (1970) All
  India Rep. S. Ct. 1390 - p. 115 n135
Cantwell v. Conn., 310 U.S. 296 (1940) - p. 119
Carroll v. U.S., 267 U.S. 132 (1925) - p. 275 n12
Chambers v. Maroney, 399 U.S. 42 (1970) - p. 275 n12
Chandler v. Director of Public Prosecutions, (1964)
  A.C. 763 (H.L.) - p. 329 n12
Columbus Bd. of Educ. v. Penick, 443 U.S. 449
  (1979) - p. 216 n16
Committee for Public Education v. Nyquist, 413 U.S.
  756 (1973) - p. 172 n71
Commune de Saint Dezery, C.E. Mar. 1, 1912, D.1914.
  3.46 - p. 147
Consorts Weill, C.E. Jan. 19, 1944, D.1944 J.65 -
  p. 150
Constitutional Council (France) - Freedom of Asso-
  ciation Decision, L'Actualité Juridique, 27:537
  (1971) - pp. 24, 30 n30
  Race Quota Decision, D.1960.29 - pp. 212-13
  Three Judge Decision, Revue du Droit Publique et
    de la Science Politique (1975), p. 1352 - pp.
    24, 30 n30
  Vehicle Search Decision, Le Monde, Jan. 14, 1977,
    p. 12 - pp. 24, 30 n30
Coulouma, Ct. of Cass., Feb. 27, 1964, D.1964.623 -
  p. 112 n102
Cox v. La., 379 U.S. 536 (1965) - p. 106 n20

Darmon et autres, C.E. Jan. 21, 1944, D.1944 J. 65 -
    p. 150
Dartmouth College Case, 4 Wheat 518 (1819) - p. 131
Da Silva, C.E. Jan. 13, 1975, Rec. 16 - p. 212
D.A.V. College, Bhatinda v. St. of Punjab, (1971)
    All India Rep. S. Ct. 1731 - p. 173 n83
Dayton Bd. of Educ. v. Brinkman II, 443 U.S. 526
    (1979) - p. 216 n16
Dennis v. U.S., 341 U.S. 494 (1951) - pp. 50, 51, 52
Devaru v. St. of Mysore, (1958) All India Rep. S.
    Ct. 255 - p. 128
Dilanov, Soviet Statutes and Decisions, Vol. 1,
    Summer, 1965 - p. 252
Dimes v. Grand Junction Canal Co., (1852) 3 H.L.C.
    759 - p. 237
Dingle v. Associated Newspapers, (1961) 2 Q.B. 162 -
    pp. 74, 292
Duncan v. Jones, (1936) 1 K.B. 218 - pp. 45, 46

Ealing London Borough Council v. Race Rels. Bd.,
    (1972) A.C. 342 - p. 217 n27
Edwards v. South Carolina, 372 U.S. 229 (1963) -
    pp. 34, 36
Elfbrandt v. Russell, 384 U.S. 11 (1966) - p. 107
    n30
Engel v. Vitale, 370 U.S. 421 (1962) - p. 156
Époux Auerbach, C.E. Dec. 31, 1943, D.1944 J.66 -
    p. 150
Escobedo v. Ill., 378 U.S. 478 (1964) - pp. 232,
    244, 274 n5
Everson v. Bd. of Educ., 330 U.S. 1 (1947) - pp.
    152, 153, 154

F.C.C. v. Pacifica Foundation, 438 U.S. 726 (1978) -
    p. 114 n122
Feiner v. New York, 340 U.S. 315 (1951) - p. 287
Filimonova, Soviet Statutes and Decisions, Vol. 1,
    Summer, 1965 - p. 256
Films Lutetia, C.E. Dec. 18, 1959, Rec. 693;
    D.1960 J. 171
Finkelstein, Ct. of Appeals, Nancy, Gaz. Pal.
    1951.1.151 - p. 70
Forni et autres, Const. Council, Jan. 9, 1980,
    D. May 14, 1980, p. 249 - p. 226 n97

342

Jauneau et Vigne, Corr. Trib. Beauvais, Gaz. Pal.
    1951.1.200 - p. 70
John Calder v. Powell, (1965) 1 Q.B. 509 - p. 94
Jordan v. Burgoyne, (1963) 2 Q.B. 744 - pp. 37, 288
Joudoux et Riaux, C.E. June 4, 1954, Rec. 346 - p.
    149

K.A. Abbas v. Union, (1971) All India Rep. S. Ct.
    481 - p. 115 n136
K.K.S. Jayasree v. Kerala, (1977) 1 Sup. Ct. R. 194 -
    p. 220 n49
K. P. Narayanan v. Maharendrasingh, (1956) Ind. Law
    Rep. Nagpur Series 439 - p. 112 n98
Katz v. U.S., 389 U.S. 347 (1967) - p. 235
Kedar Nath v. St. of Bihar, (1962) All India Rep.
    S. Ct. 955 - pp. 40, 57
Keddar, C.E. Feb. 3, 1965, Rec. 46 - p. 285 n125
Kesavananda Bharati v. Kerala, (1973) All India Rep.
    S. Ct. 1461 - p. 29 n17
Kingsley Int. Pictures Corp. v. Regents, 360 U.S.
    684 (1959) - p. 114 n119
Kochan Velayudhan v. Kerala, (1961) All India Rep.
    Kerala 8 - p. 277 n40
Krivine et Frank, C.E. July 21, 1970, Rec. 499 - p.
    68
Kuruma v. The Queen, (1955) A.C. 197 - p. 239

Leguiader et autres - D.1974 J.242 - p. 116 n145
Lemon v. Kurtzman, 403 U.S. 602 (1971) - pp. 153,
    154
Leriche et Sacre, C.E. March 11, 1966, Rec. 206 -
    p. 174 n94
Levitt v. Comm. for Pub. Education, 413 U.S. 472
    (1973) - p. 172 n71
Librarie François Maspero, C.E. Nov. 2, 1973, Rec.
    611 - p. 110 n79
Lochard, Cour de Colmar, D.1972.1 Somm. 83 - p. 226
    n101

Madhav Hoskot v. St. of Maharashtra, (1978) All
    India Rep. S. Ct. 1548 - p. 244
Makhan Singh v. Punjab, (1964) All India Rep. S.
    Ct. 381 - pp. 248, 249

Mapp v. Ohio, 367 U.S. 643 (1961) - pp. 233, 234,
    242, 271, 272, 304, 305, 309
Marshall v. Gordon, 243 U.S. 521 (1917) - p. 111
    n87
Martin v. Struthers, 319 U.S. 141 (1943) - p. 120
Maxwell v. Dow, 176 U.S. 581 (1900) - p. 275 n22
McGowan v. Md., 366 U.S. 420 (1961) - p. 155
Meek v. Pittenger, 421 U.S. 349 (1975) - p. 154
Messières de Beaudiez, C.E. Nov. 24, 1978, Rec.
    839 - p. 174 n95
Miller v. Calif., 413 U.S. 15 (1973) - pp. 90, 91,
    303
Milliken v. Bradley, 418 U.S. 717 (1974) - p. 216
    n18
Mills v. Ala., 384 U.S. 214 (1966) - p. 111 n80
Min. de L'Éduc. Nat. c. Centre Ménager et Technique
    "La Providence à Valence," C.E. Nov. 27, 1968,
    Rec. 598 - p. 174 n93
Min. de L'Éduc. Nat. c. Moulignier, C.E. Oct. 2,
    1968, Rec. 469 - p. 174 n92
Min. de l'Éduc. Nat. c. Syndicat de la Métallurgie
    Auboise, C.E. March 8, 1968, Rec. 171 - p. 174
    n91
Min. de l'Intérieur c. Girodias, C.E. Dec. 17, 1958,
    Rec. 968 - p. 102
Min. Publ. c. Malliavin, Ct. of Appeals, Paris,
    D.1959 J.552 - p. 69
Min. Publ. c. Pauvert, Jan. 10, 1957, D.1957.259 -
    p. 69
Minersville School Dist. v. Gobitis - 310 U.S. 586
    (1940) - p. 333 n72
Miranda v. Arizona, 384 U.S. 436 (1966) - pp. 231,
    232, 271, 272, 273, 274 n3, 304, 305, 309, 311,
    312, 334 n88, n89
Missouri ex rel Gaines v. Canada, 305 U.S. 337
    (1938) - p. 215 n2
Moh'd Ali Khan v. Lucknow, (1978) All India Rep.
    All. 281 - p. 132
Monus, C.E. July 13, 1973, Rec. 527 - p. 110 n78
Moore v. Dempsey, 261 U.S. 86 (1923) - p. 275 n18
Moreux, Lionel, Corr. Trib. Seine, Gaz. Pal. 1966.
    1.349 - p. 86

Nandini Satpathy v. P.L. Dani, (1978) All India Rep.
S. Ct. 1025 - p. 278 n58
Near v. Minn., 283 U.S. 697 (1931) - p. 46
New York Times v. Sullivan, 376 U.S. 254 (1964) -
pp. 72, 73, 74, 76, 81, 292, 293
New York Times Co. v. U.S., 403 U.S. 713 (1971) -
pp. 46, 47
Norris v. Alabama, 294 U.S. 587 (1935) - p. 275 n17

Orozco v. Texas, 394 U.S. 324 (1969) - p. 274 n3

Parti National Populaire, C.E. Nov. 29, 1936, D.
1937.3.14 - p. 67
Pasteau, C.E. Dec. 8, 1948, Rec. 464 - p. 148
Pennekamp v. Fla., 328 U.S. 331 (1946) - p. 78
Pinkus v. U.S. 436 U.S. 293 (1978) - p. 114 n126
Plenel, C.E. March 8, 1968, Rec. 168 - p. 110 n63
Powell v. Alabama, 287 U.S. 45 (1932) - p. 274 n7
Proc. Gen c. B et S, Gaz. Pal. March 18, 1979, p.
8 - p. 113 n105
Pujo, C.E. April 4, 1936, D.1938.3.38 - p. 66
Pyare Lal v. St. of Rajasthan, (1963) All India
Rep. S. Ct. 1094 - p. 276 n38

Quareshi v. Bihar, 21 Sup. Ct. Jour. 975 (1958) -
p. 130

"R . . .," Gaz. Pal. 1974.1.353 - p. 113 n103
R. v. Aldred, 22 Cox Crim. Cas. 1 (1909) - pp. 53,
54
R. v. Allen, (1977) Crim. L. Rev. (Eng.) 163 - p.
239
R. v. Calder and Boyars, (1969) 1 Q.B. 151 - p. 93
R. v. Editor of New Statesman, (1928) 44 T.L.R.
301 - pp. 77, 78
R. v. Hicklin, (1868) L.R. 3 Q.B. 360 - pp. 91, 92,
96
R. v. Lemon, (1978) 3 All. E.R. 175; aff'd. (1979)
1 All. E.R. 898 (H.L.) - p. 122
R. v. Malik, (1968) 1 All E.R. 582 - p. 105 n6
R. v. Maqsud Ali, 1966 (1) Q.B. 688 - p. 243
R. v. Metropolitan Police Comm'r. ex parte Black-
burn, (1968) 2 All E.R. 319 - p. 111 n90
R. v. Ovenell, (1968) 1 All E.R. 933 - p. 276 n25

Société les Éditions du Fleuve Noir, C.E. Jan. 3,
    1958, Rec. 4 - p. 102
Soeurs de la Visitation Ste. Marie de Troyes et
    autres, C.E. April 3, 1908, D.1909.3.89 - p. 146
State of Kerala v. N.M. Thomas, (1976) 2 S. Ct. Cas.
    310 - p. 220 n52
State of Maryland v. West, 9 Md. App. 270, 263
    A.2d 602 (1970) - p. 121
State v. Satyanarayan, (1965) All India Rep. Orissa
    136 - p. 277 n40
Swann v. Charlotte-Mecklenburg County Bd. of Educ.,
    402 U.S. 1 (1974) - p. 180
Syndicat de la Magistrature, Sem. Juridique, 1978
    Tab. Juris., p. 168 - p. 113 n105

T. Devadasan v. Union of India, (1964) All India
    Rep. S. Ct. 179 - p. 194
Tague v. Louisiana, 100 S. Ct. 652 (1980) - p. 305
Taylor v. Louisiana, 419 U.S. 522 (1975) - p. 275
    n17
Teff et Bec Marceau, Corr. Trib. Montpellier, Gaz.
    Pal. 1950.1.370 - p. 110 n75
Teissier, C.E. March 13, 1953, Rec. 133; D.1953
    J.735 - p. 65
Terminiello v. Chicago, 337 U.S. 1 (1949) - pp. 35,
    105 n2
Terry v. Ohio, 392 U.S. 1 (1968) - pp. 275 n13, 305
Tilton v. Richardson, 403 U.S. 672 (1971) - p. 154
Torcaso v. Watkins, 367 U.S. 488 (1961) - p. 167 n1
Triloki Nath Tiku v. St. of Jammu and Kashmir, (1967)
    All India Rep. S. Ct. 1283 - p. 194
Tumey v. Ohio, 273 U.S. 510 (1927) - p. 275 n16

Udeshi v. Maharashtra, (1965) All India Rep. S. Ct.
    881 - pp. 96, 115 n136
Union des Syndicats Ouvriers de la Région Parisienne
    CGT, C.E. Feb. 19, 1954, Rec. 113 - p. 45
United States v. Calandra, 414 U.S. 338 (1974) - p.
    305
United States v. Robinson, 414 U.S. 218 (1973) p.
    274 n11
United States v. Wade, 388 U.S. 218 (1967) - p. 277
    n47

INDEX

351

352

355

France (Cont'd.)
    Constitutional Worth - pp. 24-25
    Chambre d'Accusation (Indicting Chamber) - pp.
        259, 268
    Civil Rights (Anti-Discrimination) Law of 1972 -
        p. 213
    Code of Criminal Procedure
        Article 30 - pp. 88-89, 269-70
        Article 53 - p. 259
        Articles 54, 56, 57, 59, 76, 92-94, 99 - p.
            282 n97
        Articles 101-18 - p. 282 n96
    Commission for the Control of Films - pp. 99-100,
        103-04
    Constitution of 1946 - See Preamble, 1946 Consti-
        tution
    Constitution of 1958 - pp. 20, 23, 24, 25, 69,
        86, 143, 162, 207-08, 257
    Constitutional Council - pp. 20-21, 24, 30 n30,
        68, 165, 212
    Council of State - pp. 21-22, 42, 43, 44, 45, 47,
        63, 64, 65, 66, 67, 68, 71, 100, 101, 102,
        146, 147, 148, 149, 150, 151, 164, 211-12,
        269, 288, 308
    Court of Cassation - pp. 19, 20, 85, 112 n102,
        263, 264, 272, 282 n94, n101
    Court of State Security - pp. 270-71
    Criminal Proceedings in - pp. 251, 252, 253,
        257-71, 272, 282 n93, n94, n101, 283 n111,
        n112, 315, 335 n94
    Criticism of Government and Public Officials in -
        pp. 72, 84-89, 112 n102, 113 n104, 116 n148,
        268-70, 294, 296
    Declaration of Rights of Man of 1789 - pp. 23, 24,
        41-42, 63, 207, 257
    Decree Law of Oct. 23, 1935 - pp. 44, 45, 148,
        325
    Decree Law of Nov. 18, 1939 - pp. 268-69
    Duty of Reserve for Civil Servants - pp. 64-65
    Emergency Power of President - p. 20
    Equality Before the Law, Doctrine of - pp. 23,
        24, 63, 207-08
    European Commission and Court of Human Rights
        and - pp. 25-26

France (Cont'd.)

361

India (Cont'd.)

Mill, John Stuart - p. 326
Miller, Henry - p. 90
Minority Languages, Status of - pp. 141, 186, 187, 188, 196-99, 200, 201-04, 208, 209, 213, 223 n72, 225 n89, 310-11
Miranda Rules (U.S.) - pp. 231-32, 271, 273, 304-05, 309, 311-12
Mitterrand, François - pp. 87, 88, 271
Mizos, pp. 57, 195
Mob Violence, Trials under Threat of - p. 235
Moldavians - p. 199
Mongols - p. 202
Monnet, Georges - p. 66
Mormons - pp. 120, 123
Morris-Jones, W. H. - pp. 112 n97, 221 n57
Moses, Robert - p. 295
Moslems - pp. 57, 108 n41, 122, 124, 125, 128, 130-33, 142, 144, 169 n33, 181, 188, 191, 193-94, 204-05, 222 n61, 224 n82, 291, 306, 310, 313
Murphy, Walter - p. 28 n1
Muslims (See Moslems)

Nabokov, Vladimir - p. 102
Nagas - pp. 57, 129, 195
Napoleon - pp. 208, 258
Napoleon III - p. 258
National Advisory Commission on Criminal Justice Standards and Goals - p. 275 n19
National Front (Great Britain) - p. 46
Natural Consequences Test - pp. 36, 48, 54
Natural Justice - pp. 246, 247
Natural Rights - p. 249
Naxalites (India) - pp. 56, 57, 246
Nayar, Baldev Raj - p. 221 n57
Nehru, Jawaharlal - pp. 78, 125, 298, 300
Newth, J.A. - p. 171 n49
Nicholas, Barry - p. 30 n30
Niemi, Richard - p. 332 n43
Nixon, Richard M. - pp. 55, 240, 297, 304, 305, 312, 335 n91
Nolte, Ernest - pp. 335 n93, n96, 336 n105
Noonan, Lowell, p. 281 n91
Northern Ireland - See Ireland, Northern
Notice of Charges, Right to - pp. 231, 251, 261

379